The
1100s

HEADLINES IN HISTORY

Books in the Headlines in History series:

The 1100s

HEADLINES IN HISTORY

Helen Cothran, *Book Editor*
Laura K. Egendorf, *Assistant Editor*

Bonnie Szumski, *Editorial Director*
Scott Barbour, *Managing Editor*

Greenhaven Press, Inc., San Diego, California

Every effort has been made to trace the owners of copyrighted material. The articles in this volume may have been edited for content, length, and/or reading level. The titles have been changed to enhance the editorial purpose.

Library of Congress Cataloging-in-Publication Data

The 1100s / Helen Cothran, book editor, Laura K. Egendorf, assistant editor.
    p. cm. — (Headlines in history)
    Includes bibliographical references and index.
    ISBN 0-7377-0529-9 (pbk.)—ISBN 0-7377-0530-2 (lib.)
    1. Twelfth century. 2. Civilization, Medieval—Twelfth century. 3. Europe—Church history—500–1500. 4. Europe—Social conditions—To 1492. 5. Chivalry—Europe—History—To 1500. 6. Indians—History. 7. China—Civilization—960–1644. I. Title: Eleven hundreds. II. Cothran, Helen. III. Series.

CB354.6 .A200   2001
909.07—dc21
                                                                00-064035

Cover photos: (left) St. Bernard, © Archivo Iconografico, S.A./Corbis; (top, left to right) Ghengis Khan, AKG London; Confucius, © Archivo Iconografico, S.A./Corbis; (bottom right) Japanese samurai warriors, © North Wind Picture Archives
Digital Stock: 150
Dover: 34
Library of Congress: 54
North Wind Picture Archives: 118, 244

Copyright © 2001 by Greenhaven Press, Inc.
P.O. Box 289009, San Diego, CA 92198-9009

Printed in the USA

CONTENTS

Chapter 4: The Twelfth-Century Renaissance

human intelligence. The human mind has a limited ability to perceive because of arrogance, ignorance, training, and the complexity of the subjects studied.

9. Vertical Cathedrals: The Rise of Gothic Architecture

Gothic architecture developed out of earlier Romanesque designs, which were characterized by rounded arches, heavy columns, and dark interiors. By contrast, Gothic cathedrals are characterized by pointed arches, stained glass windows, and soaring heights.

Chapter 5: Asia

1. The Rise of China as a Sea Power

A variety of geographic, economic, and social factors led to the rise of China as a sea power in the twelfth century. As people began to migrate from impoverished northern regions to the coast in search of opportunity, coastal economies grew and sea trade expanded. The expansion of China's sea trade provided opportunities for people to travel to new lands and explore new ideas.

2. Confucianism in Twelfth-Century China

Three Confucian schools developed in China during the Sung dynasty. Neo-Confucianism aimed to reform traditional Confucian views of government and society. New Policy sought fundamental improvements, and the School of Mind de-emphasized the role of conduct and morality in Confucianism.

3. Chinese Rituals in the Twelfth Century

Chu Hsi was a prominent Chinese philosopher during the twelfth century. In this excerpt from his book *Family Rituals*, he explains how sacrificial rites should be performed.

4. The Samurai Code of Honor

During the eleventh and twelfth centuries in Japan, the samurai became a distinct social group who valued honor, military professionalism, and courage. Although the samurai often violated the rules of warfare, people nevertheless admired them as men of principle.

FOREWORD

Chronological time lines of history are mysteriously fascinating. To learn that within a single century Christopher Columbus sailed to the New World, the Aztec, Maya, and Inca cultures were flourishing, Joan of Arc was burned to death, and the invention of the printing press was radically changing access to written materials allows a reader a different type of view of history: a bird's-eye view of the entire globe and its events. Such a global picture allows for cross-cultural comparisons as well as a valuable overview of chronological history that studying one particular area simply cannot provide.

Taking an expansive look at world history in each century, therefore, can be surprisingly informative. In Headlines in History, Greenhaven Press attempts to imitate this time-line approach using primary and secondary sources that span each century. Each volume gives readers the opportunity to view history as though they were reading the headlines of a global newspaper: Editors of each volume have attempted to glean and include the most important and influential events of the century, as well as quirky trends and cultural oddities. Headlines in History, then, attempts to give readers a glimpse of both the mundane and the earth-shattering. Articles on the French Revolution, for example, are juxtaposed with the then-current fashion concerns of the French nobility. This creates a higher interest level by allowing students a glimpse of people's everyday lives throughout history.

By using both primary and secondary sources, students also have the opportunity to view the historical events both as eyewitnesses have experienced them and as historians have interpreted them. Thus, students can place such historical events in a larger context as well as receive background information on important world events.

Headlines in History allows readers the unique opportunity to learn more about events that may only be mentioned in their history textbooks, or may be ignored entirely. The series presents students with a variety of interesting topics that span cultural, historical, and political arenas. Such a broad span of material will allow students to wander wherever their curiosity will take them.

L evels of development and living standards varied widely throughout the world during the 1100s. Farmers in Europe were using water mills to irrigate fields they had planted according to a complex three-crop rotation schedule. In contrast, the Toltec Indians, who lived in the arid region of central Mexico, were watering corn crops by diverting rainwater into crude ditches that ran to the fields. Although Europe, Asia, and the Americas were all developing at different rates, technological and agricultural advancements improved the lives of all people across the globe during this century. Art and architecture also flourished throughout Europe, Asia, and the Americas. Another commonality among regions was the existence of a hierarchical class system that accorded the affluent greater benefits from new developments and burgeoning economies. Landed sons in Europe lived in castles, for example, and peasants tended the land for them, while the vast majority of Europeans lived outside castle walls and subsistence-farmed.

European Improvements in Sanitation

Twelfth-century Europe was a time of economic and intellectual vitality. The population expanded, new towns were built at an unprecedented rate, and trade flourished. This new prosperity provided money to sponsor the Crusades, build schools, and create a new, merchant middle class. Most people, however, still eked out a living from the land and lived as peasants. Historian Sidney R. Packard estimates that more than 90 percent of Europe's population lived close to the soil and was engaged in agricultural activities. And though daily standards of living improved generally, these land-working peasants often were treated brutally by aristocratic overseers, who enjoyed many more of the latest technological developments than the peasants did.

One such fundamental development was in sanitation, in particular, the latrine. The more affluent were able to afford an outhouse removed from the main house by several feet. Royal castles commonly featured a special latrine tower that could be accessed from within the castle. The common people who lived in town, by contrast, usually dug a pit in the floor of the home into which fecal waste was deposited. This pit led to a shaft, which emptied into the basement. The waste was collected in a refuse barrel under the house and was emptied by hand. Improvements in sanitation helped prevent outbreaks of disease, so it is likely that the rich enjoyed better health during the twelfth century than did the poor.

In the cities, refuse removal was a constant problem. Most streets in London and Paris, for example, were sloped so that rainwater—and the waste that was carried with it—would flow down the center of the street. Refuse was simply dumped in the streets from the windows of houses that lined them. Those who walked beneath the windows were constantly at risk of being soiled by human wastes and garbage that was tossed from the houses. A tradition thus developed whereby the gentleman would walk to the outside toward the street and the lady closer to the wall, out of harm's way. Unfortunately, the center-ditch disposal system often did not work as desired. According to Urban Tigner Holmes Jr., "Drainage must have been remarkably bad . . . a ditch that was dug remained open to the air. Filth found its way constantly into the muddy streets." People who could afford them bought thick-soled shoes that protected their feet from filth. Many people of means preferred to ride horses in town despite the crowded streets because the horses kept them safely above the sewage. Raw sewage polluted waterways such as the Langourn in London, which dumped filth into the Thames River, then out to sea. This contamination was a constant source of disease, but most common people at the time did not question sanitation methods. As Holmes explains, "The majority [of Europeans] accepted smells and 'sights' as part of the daily scene."

Serfs and Technology

The matter of sanitation clearly indicates the advantages that money could bring in twelfth-century Europe. During the economic revival of the 1100s, however, inflation helped improve even the peasants' standard of living. Many of the poorest peasants—called serfs—owed their landlords fixed annual fees. As prices rose with inflation, these peasants were able to collect more money from their farms, yet the fee to their lords remained unchanged. As a result, some serfs were gradually able to earn more money than they owed, and were, in time, able to save enough money to purchase their own land. Other peasants escaped from their lords into the new towns, where they became free peasants—called villeins—and enjoyed more freedom and affluence. Packard argues that peasants "undoubtedly improved their standard of living a good deal. They certainly ate better in 1200 than in 1100."

Improvements in agricultural techniques also helped improve the lives of common people who depended on the land for subsistence. With the development of the horseshoe, horses were utilized to plow the fields. Before the horseshoe, the soggy soils of northern Europe quickly eroded the hooves of the horses, rendering them useless for pulling ploughs. Oxen were used to pull the increasingly heavy ploughs, but oxen are much slower than horses; as a consequence, cultivation took much longer. When a peasant was able to afford a horse to pull his plow, he could work more land in less time and make more profit.

In addition to agricultural advances, technological devices made manual tasks easier and changed European society forever. According to Packard, these devices included

water mills . . . notably in the fulling process in the manufacture of woolen cloth, thus displacing the use of human feet; the skillful and imaginative use of waterworks designed to employ fully the entire force of an adjacent river . . . the windmill, late in the century; and the more extensive use of sails to replace oars and the building of larger ships better able to utilize wind power.

Packard adds:

The willingness of twelfth-century men to use the forces of nature (water, wind, and animal) and their developed skills in actually doing so have greatly impressed the historians of engineering. Some of them see what they call a revolution in the use of power in this period as one of the most important facts of all European history.

In addition to these labor-saving devices, many technological advances boosted production in the trades. Craftsmen developed better methods for making glass and improving the quality of metalwork. Lead was used more widely from England to Germany, and silver mines began producing unheard-of volumes of ores, aided by new mechanical devices such as the crank and the cam. The magnetic compass was developed late in the period, making travel and trade easier. Historian Lynn Townsend White has pointed out that

the technological history of the twelfth century accentuates the basic nature of European history in this period. It was not a civilization built on slave labor but one in which many individual men deliberately made progress in harnessing the forces of nature, recognized the dignity of human labor, and probably unconsciously, accelerated the secularization of Europe.

Advances in Medicine and Law

Unfortunately, progress in medicine was slow. Indeed, medical practices in Europe were less advanced than they were in the Middle East. The Muslim historian Usama gives an account of a European remedy for broken bones. Bernard, treasurer to the king of Jerusalem, sustained a compound fracture of his leg in fourteen places. The European physician who was called in washed the injured limb repetitively in strong vinegar alcohol—but did not set the bones. Holmes reports that doctors in Europe commonly believed

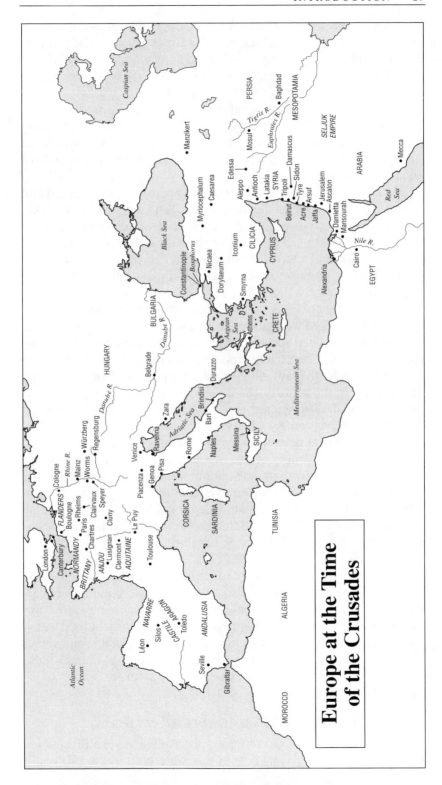

Europe at the Time of the Crusades

that "hard foods were not good for the kidneys. People were advised to let blood on general principles four times a year." The primary tenet of European medicine was that the body was composed of four essential humors—phlegm, blood, bile, and black bile—that had to be kept in balance or the person would fall ill.

Such theories helped few patients, but in spite of many wrong-headed ideas, twelfth-century doctors were successful in treating many illnesses and injuries. For example, they knew that mineral springs could be salubrious, and they effectively used silk sutures and drains for wounds.

The practice of law was also a mixed bag of the enlightened and the ignorant. People from the lower classes and women, in particular, suffered under early-twelfth-century law codes. Holmes explains that "a serf who was accused was usually given the ordeal of water. A huge cask was filled and a wooden board was set across the top. The victim undergoing the test was bound with rope and lowered into the cask. If innocent he was supposed to sink; if guilty, he would float." He adds: "Women of higher rank preferred the ordeal with the hot bar of iron. They walked with this in the bare hand before many witnesses. If the burn healed in a specific length of time, the defendant was adjudged innocent." Landed lords and other people of means fared somewhat better under the law. Although inequity plagued the application of law early in the century, the concept of legal authority began to evolve during the later half of the 1100s. In fact, Packard argues that "the idea of the supremacy of laws in human affairs is . . . [a] fundamental achievement in twelfth-century Europe."

Three different kinds of law were practiced in Europe of the 1100s: customary, Roman, and canonical. Customary law was the law of the land as it had evolved over centuries. Roman law took its precepts from ancient texts that set legal guidelines for the Roman Empire. Canonical law considered the opinions and procedures of the church. In the twelfth century, scholars—including those studying to be lawyers—developed a new method of learning to replace the encyclopedic method of rote memorization. This new method was called disputation. Students were required to build rational arguments by establishing a conclusion, and then systematically supporting and defending it. This new method of study helped transform twelfth-century legal practices from the inequitable and sometimes cruel system that employed hot rods and drowning as measurements of innocence to one that employed sound principles of argumentation to prove guilt.

Developments in Art and Architecture

A transformation in architecture also occurred in the twelfth century. Many of the cathedrals and castles that were built in the 1100s still stand today as testaments to twelfth-century wealth, ingenuity, and engineering skills. Castles were built as homes to feudal lords and kings, but they served primarily a military function. Packard explains that castles "were the work of men of strength and imagination: they constituted an almost perfect defense against the weapons and the tactics of the preceding century. The castle was itself undoubtedly the most powerful single weapon of the twelfth century." Philip Warner notes that "the principal stabilizing factor in the Middle Ages was the castle" because these structures were so successful in protecting secular rulers from enemies. The castles of the twelfth century were significant aesthetic as well as military achievements. Transformed from the motte and bailey castle—essentially a mound of earth with a ditch at the bottom and a palisade, or row of strong stakes, around the top—castles became enormous and elaborate edifices built by skilled craftsmen. They were situated in strategic locations to make them easier to defend, and were built of impenetrable stone and masonry. Many had turrets and towers, and some had moats and drawbridges.

Many art historians consider castles and cathedrals the primary art of the twelfth century. The enormous stained glass panels found in cathedrals were made possible by the change from Romanesque to Gothic architecture. Builders following Romanesque design principles were forced to erect heavy columns to support the weight of the cathedral roof. These columns were so large they filled the church and made the inclusion of windows impossible. Gothic design, however, employed pointed arches and exterior flying buttresses, which provided support for the roof without heavy columns. Gothic architecture made it possible for architects to include many windows in their designs, and stained glass panels gradually became the standard decoration of church windows, intended to glorify God. Thus a very practical development—the pointed arch—led to a primarily aesthetic one—stained glass.

Despite the social and technological progress of the 1100s, most Europeans led relatively poor, rural lives. The benefits of developments in sanitation, trade, law, and architecture went mainly to the few born into the aristocracy. As Packard argues, "Europe in the twelfth century was still a land of fires, floods, drought, the pest, and local famines, despite much progress in many places. Europe in this period never got very far away from the subsistence level."

Medieval Achievements in Japan

Technological developments, improved standard of living, and artistic achievements in Europe had many parallels in Japan and China. Feudalism, for example, remained the dominant economic model in Japan as it was in Europe. Although feudalism in Japan tended to benefit landed people while leaving the vast majority of the population at the subsistence level, poorer people did enjoy a better standard of living than they had in the past. As in Europe, also, there was a great blossoming of artistic and intellectual pursuits in Japan and China during the twelfth century.

During the Fujiwara period—named after the dynastic succession of emperors—Japanese society began to develop an interest in art and architecture. One example of Japanese blending of architecture and art was the Amida Halls, temples to the god Amida. Amida was believed to have descended from Paradise to gather the souls of believers at the moment of death and transport them in lotus blossoms to Paradise. Amida Halls melded the secular with the religious: they housed numerous Buddha images within a structure that resembled the mansions of the nobility.

One of the high points of Japanese painting during this period was the proliferation of images illustrating the *Tale of Genji*. The paintings were based on the writings of Muraskaki Shikibu, a lady-in-waiting to the empress Akiko, about the life and loves of Prince Genji. Artists painted scenes from the tale in an attempt to convey the characters' emotions. Later paintings of the period began to emphasize active motion achieved by quick brush strokes and vibrant colors. Art and architecture flourished during the 1100s in Japan, and as in Europe, the artistic endeavors of the people were a blending of the secular and the religious.

Chinese Art and Architecture

Like Japan, China enjoyed a great artistic awakening during the twelfth century. René Grousset calls the Sung dynasty "the flower of Chinese culture." The century is traditionally divided into two artistic periods, the Kaifeng period (960–1127) and the Hangchow period (1127–1276). During the Kaifeng period, artists began to create realistic landscapes suggesting that the artists were close observers of nature. Typical landscapes included distant mountains shrouded in mists. Later, during the Hangchow period, the landscapes became more deeply imbued with meaning. Grousset explains that for the Hangchow masters the material elements of nature, which they depicted so painstakingly, "served merely as a vehicle for transporting the thoughts to a purely spiritual plane." As with Japanese and European art, Chinese aesthetic pursuits were very much concerned with religious matters.

The Chinese also built elegant temples for their god, Buddha. Pagodas continued to be the major type of religious structure. Sung architecture tended, like Gothic architecture, to prefer height to breadth. Engineers designed special support systems made of crossbeams that could support increasingly heavy roofs. Like Gothic cathedrals, Chinese buildings at this time emphasized the sensation of open space and light. Curved roofs, a characteristic long associated with Chinese architecture, reached their apex during the Sung period.

Halfway across the world from Asia, people in the Americas were also developing new architectural designs and innovative art forms. The Chimú Indians in Peru, the Toltec Indians in Mexico, and the Anasazi Indians in the southwestern United States all established remarkably rich cultures prefiguring greater civilizations to come. The Chimú Indians were eventually supplanted by the Incas, the Toltec Indians gave way to the Aztecs, and the Anasazi were the first of the Pueblo Indians which include the Zuni and Hopi Indians who still live today in the southwestern United States. Although the Indians living in the twelfth century were not as technologically advanced and did not enjoy as high a standard of living as did people in Europe, they left a significant legacy to the people who came after them.

Chimú Art and Religion

As in Europe, the Chimú lived under a rigid class system. The privileged higher classes cultivated their crops on the slopes of the Andes, where more rain fell. The poor were relegated to the lower slopes, which were arid and unforgiving. Archaeologist Michael E. Moseley argues that "hydrology distinguished and generated tension between uplanders living where rain fell and lowlanders receiving only runoff."

As did European cathedrals and Chinese pagodas, many of the buildings in the kingdom of Chimor, as the Chimú homeland was called, served a religious function. The pyramidal mound was the dominant feature in Chimú settlements. Usually U-shaped, these mounds, called huacas, were usually built of stone and functioned as temples. Mountainlike, the huaca seemed to transfer power from the great Andes, which rose up behind it, to the temple itself. Not surprising given the proximity of the Andes and their role in determining the amount of annual rainfall, the Chimú were mountain worshipers.

The Chimú were extraordinarily artistic and are perhaps best known for their pottery. This pottery was designed to be of practical use, but artists took great care to shape and paint the clay to portray in realistic detail the daily lives of the people. The Indians also produced sculpture, which portrayed deities or huacas, and made realistic models of temples and houses. They also made colorful textiles and tapestries that depict scenes from Chimú life. Chimú pottery has best survived the passage of time, however. Because it communicates so clearly knowledge of life in the kingdom of Chimor, some modern archaeologists call the pottery the Chimú's language.

Toltec Ingenuity

The Toltec Indians who occupied the city of Tula—the ruins of which have been unearthed outside modern-day Mexico City—were also able artisans. They sculpted massive heads, which depicted their rulers. Toltec relief carvings can be found on their religious buildings and depict gods or warriors in battle. Enormous columns were erected to support the roofs of buildings and many of these columns were carved into figures of warriors.

In addition to temples, the houses of the common people provide insight into the daily lives of the Toltecs. The houses were never built as detached residences but were attached to other houses, forming a complex of as many as five houses. Each house faced an interior courtyard. Most of the domestic dwellings were relatively unadorned, but occasional houses contained friezes and other valuable items such as sculptures or goblets. Richard A. Diehl surmises that these houses must have been the homes of more affluent people, suggesting that there were clear class divisions in Tula. In general, the domestic architecture in Tula was practical and comfortable; it utilized locally abundant building materials, and the thick adobe and stone walls insulated inhabitants from heat and cold.

Tula, located in central Mexico, is a land of extremes. At a high elevation, Tula experienced extremely wet summers and long dry winters. Hydrology served a crucial function in Toltec civilization, and although their irrigation technology was rudimentary, the Toltecs were able to grow some crops successfully. Corn was their primary crop, and the corn tortillas that women made were the mainstay of their diet. The Toltecs also planted squash and beans. These crops were made possible by irrigation and water-storing techniques.

Anasazi Architecture

The Anasazi Indians of the four-corners region of the United States, like the Toltecs, also grew corn, squash, and beans in an arid climate characterized by seasonal extremes. Their ancestors—called the Basketmakers—were primarily a nomadic people who gathered edible plants and hunted as they moved around the arid landscape. Not until the Anasazi obtained a drought-resistant corn from Mexico, probably from the Toltecs, were they able to settle down in one place and grow crops. They eventually added squash, then beans, to their diet, which provided them ample nutrition.

Although the Anazasi eventually settled throughout the four-corners region, some settlements are better known to modern observers than others. One such famous site is at Mesa Verde in Colorado. There, the Anasazi built their dwellings under limestone outcroppings in the south-facing cliffs. These cliff dwellings, renowned for their beautiful architecture, are constructed of carefully shaped sandstone blocks joined with mortar. Kivas, key-shaped ceremonial chambers, were added within rooms. Multistoried towers were common at Mesa Verde, as well. The Anasazi who lived in the cliff dwellings of Mesa Verde planted their fields on the flat mesas above the cliffs. Some archaeologists speculate that the Anasazi began to build in cliff walls for protection from enemies, but others believe that they built cliff dwellings in order to leave the mesa tops available for planting crops.

The Anasazi and the other Indians living in the Americas survived a time of great prosperity and incredible hardship. Like the people of Europe and Asia, they produced new art forms, built aesthetically pleasing buildings, and developed innovative technology. Although the technologies that Europeans developed were superior to those developed in Asia and the Americas, the advances achieved by people around the world were driven by the same desire: to manipulate the natural world for human benefit. From harnessing water and energy, to protecting themselves from the elements, to creating symbols out of the living world as representation of the gods, Europeans, Asians, and Americans alike sought order, safety, and transcendence.

The Rise of
the Papacy

PREFACE

In A.D. 395, the mighty Roman Empire fell. Too large to rule effectively, the great Roman church was divided into the Western Church, based in Rome, and the Eastern Church, based in Constantinople. With the fall of the Roman Empire, Europe was plunged into a prolonged period of poverty and famine, invasions from without and instability within. This period ended at the conclusion of the eleventh century. As the twelfth century dawned in Europe, Europeans began to enjoy a prosperous and dynamic era. New towns were built, goods and ideas were traded with others outside Europe, enormous cathedrals were erected, and new technology like the windmill was developed. The economy expanded rapidly, and the Western Roman Church capitalized on the increased affluence of the region.

As invasions by outsiders subsided, Europeans were able to own and remain on land long enough to establish flourishing estates. Abundant food allowed the population to expand rapidly, which necessitated the building of new towns. Each new town required a new church and clergy and monks to run it. The new churches were then able to extract money—church dues called tithes—from the townspeople, much of which landed in the popes' coffers.

The medieval institution that most benefited the church was the feudal system, which was widespread throughout Europe during the 1100s. Although feudalism took different forms in different places, most areas in Europe operated under some form of feudal system. This economic and political institution originated in the tumultuous times after the fall of the Roman Empire, in response to the absence of central governments that could provide military protection for landowners. Under feudalism, landed lords granted aspiring vassals, including knights, land in exchange for homage and services during wars. The system helped aristocratic young men, who had few options other than becoming knights, earn a living, and also helped lords maintain control over their estates. But the feudal contracts, which outlined the rules governing the relationship between knights and lords, did not apply to the social and political relationships between other people. Thus no effective centralized government could make laws and control the populace. Under these conditions, the popes stood as the central authority on secular and religious matters.

The healthy economy and the stability it produced also made the Crusades possible. The Crusades were Christian expeditions that traveled to the areas around Jerusalem in order to wrest the Holy Land from the Muslims. The papacy—with its newfound affluence—sponsored these wars with the stated intent of protecting the holy places so that pilgrims from Europe could continue to travel there safely. However, the papacy's unspoken purpose was to increase its own wealth and authority. One way the popes used the Crusades to gain power was by granting immunity from paying tithes to those who would participate in them. With the incentive of saving money and obtaining divine grace, thousands of men and women—who cooked and gathered supplies for the men—joined knights and monks in the holy wars. Thus the church was assured of a vast and ready army to defend its interests, at little cost to itself. With the success of the First Crusade, religious fervor deepened, and people began to give their money, lands, and lives to the church without question.

As a result of the church's increased wealth and power, the popes enjoyed influence in all areas of public life. Enormous Gothic cathedrals dominated many towns, and the rituals of the church dominated people's lives. Ecclesiastical schools were established to train new clergymen to manage the new churches, and the rejuvenation of learning helped set off a twelfth-century renaissance. Monasteries became enormously popular with aristocratic young men who, as second or third sons not eligible to inherit land, viewed service to the church as an attractive alternative to knighthood. Austere orders such as the Cistercian could boast of astonishing numbers of young adherents willing to undergo enormous personal hardship for the church. Even some orders of knights, such as the Knights Templar, sought and obtained the church's blessing so that their members could attain the highest level of respect.

The church's rise to power did not follow a linear trajectory—it endured many conflicts, for example, over papal succession and increasing abuses of power within the church by rogue clergymen. In addition, toward the close of the century, kings began to establish centralized political control over their territories, and, as a result, began to contain the church's authority. Finally, as later Crusades failed to wrest the Holy Land from the Muslims, support for continued warfare, and by extension for the church, began to wane. But for the majority of the twelfth century, the popes enjoyed great esteem, enormous affluence, and far-ranging power.

The Rise of the Papacy: An Overview

Bernhard Schimmelpfennig

Bernhard Schimmelpfennig is a medieval historian at the University at Ausburg, Germany. According to Schimmelpfennig, the power of the papacy increased during the twelfth century due to the growth in the number and size of towns. As new territories were settled, the church was called upon to deliver services to the increasing population. Monasteries enjoyed enhanced power as they played a dominant role in developing new settlements, Schimmelpfennig argues. These growing settlements also required more churches and clergy, which enlarged the range of papal power. As pilgrims became more numerous, the power and wealth of the church grew as well; pilgrims traveling to holy places were largely able to do so because the church exempted them from obligations such as tithes owed to the church in exchange for holy relics brought back upon their return. Although secular rulers also enjoyed increased power at this time, the church remained sovereign. Anyone who excoriated the church or called for reform was branded as a heretic by the papacy, according to Schimmelpfennig, which effectively silenced all criticism. As a result of this lack of accountability, abuses within the church grew.

In contrast to such predecessors as Leo IX, Gregory VII, Urban II, and Callistus II, the pontiffs of the twelfth century, apart from a few exceptions like Adrian IV, are often portrayed as having weak char-acters. Nevertheless, they were able to expand the foundation that had been laid in the eleventh century and to increase the real influence of the papacy to such an extent that Innocent III (1198–1216) could rule as *arbiter mundi* (arbiter of the world). This can only be understood if important changes of this period are taken into consideration.

Settlements Empower the Papacy

The twelfth century is the period within the Middle Ages in which the greatest horizontal and vertical mobility can be observed in a broad spectrum of social classes. Without going into great detail, it should be emphasized that areas that had already been settled for a long time were now made more accessible, and previously uncultivated areas were opened up. This helped to improve the legal and social status of settlers. Freedoms were also expanded for those persons living in the growing or newly founded cities. This new mobility also included the aristocracy, as the ascendency of the ministerials [ministers of reli-gion] with their new-found freedom shows. These same ministerials were the most important force in the new age of chivalry that was shaped by Christian values. The consequences for the church and the papacy were many. At times, new monastic orders such as the Cister-cians played a decisive role in developing the new settlements. The intensification of settlements in the countryside as well as the expan-sion and increase of the cities required a further development in the caring of souls and in the organization of the parish. Another conse-quence was the growing stream of pilgrims, which benefited, in par-ticular, wellknown sites such as Jerusalem, Rome, and Santiago de Compostela. To handle these pilgrims, new bridges were constructed, roads improved, and hospitals built, mostly under the direction of canons regular. The pilgrims in Rome brought increased wealth and prestige to the papacy, though the papacy gained even more promi-nence by granting charters to hospitals, particularly the bigger ones, by granting dispensations, and by regulating, in its capacity as law-maker, the life of the pilgrim and the pilgrim's family back home. The attitude of the papacy toward autonomy movements in the cities, how-ever, was ambivalent. At times, the papacy exploited the cities, as in Northern Italy during the conflict with Frederick I Barbarossa,[1] while at other times it aided them. If in doing so, however, their own control or that of the obsequious episcopal rulers was jeopardized, then such autonomy movements were deemed heretical. Since this trend of de-claring autonomy movements heretical was dominant after the Peace of Venice in 1177, it would leave its mark on ecclesiastical law, with effects that were to continue into modern times.

---

1. King of Germany who wanted Italy to become part of his empire.

The intensification of settlements also contributed to the concentration of secular power. And since the hypothetical basis for this power had been removed as a result of the preceding conflicts, the actual extent and theoretical foundation of this power now changed. The new rulers, who were put in place to guarantee peace and the justice of God (*pax et iustitia*), intensified feudal law, cited Justinian law and often tried to subject the clergy to their legal authority. As we shall see later, this new way of doing things also provoked conflicts with the papacy. These differences were heightened when, in this same period, the clergy, as a unified class and the highest one in Christendom, was consolidated with its own ecclesiastical privileges (*privilegium ordinis*) and its own judicial administration (*privilegium fori*), which prohibited any intervention by secular courts. This meant that, in the eyes of clerical protagonists, the legal situation of late antiquity to which secular rulers made reference had become obsolete.

The theoretical basis for the legitimization of power was deepened on both the secular and clerical side. This process was made easier by the heavier emphasis on and idealization of phenomena of late antiquity as a result of the so-called twelfth–century renaissance, which was also marked by new developments in the schools of that time, leading to a new flowering in the spiritual as well as secular sciences. Though the rediscovery of Roman law may have benefited both sides, it was the clergy, all the way up to the papacy, who profited from the new scholasticism in theology and in church law.

Reformers Are Branded Heretics

It should also be noted that, by the middle of the twelfth century at the latest, reform fever had pretty much subsided, even though offenses such as simony and marriage of clergymen continued to be dealt with by synods. Popes were no longer at the front lines in implementing ecclesiastical reforms; rather, they were concerned with maintaining and expanding their own position. In so doing, they approved practices which would have been condemned earlier, and not just by radical reformers like Humbert of Silva Candida or Gregory VII. Consequently, criticism of the papacy and the church was on the upswing just at the time when understanding for criticism and interest in doing something about the sad state of affairs in the church were waning among those in power. It was Pope Clement II who, in the end, formulated a decretal (X 5.26.1) stating that criticism of the papacy constituted a serious crime. But, since the religious impetus that had been unleashed, chiefly by Gregory VII, could not even restrain the laity any longer, the vacuity of the "official church" led in the twelfth century to the establishing of religious movements which, except for Catharism, initially demanded reforms. They were soon accused of heresy, however, approving practices that no longer coincided with official doctrine or liturgy. And it was after Pope Lucius III met with Barbarossa in Verona in 1184 that the papacy strove to fight and wipe out, with the help of the "secular arms," all heresies. The lack of interest on the part of the pontiffs in meaningful reforms and a better religious instruction for the laity was one of the main reasons that from the twelfth century Latin Christendom was divided once again. At the same time, this meant that the basis for the historical legitinilzation of the papal position, namely, the implementation of ecclesiastical reform, could no longer be used. For this reason, it is understandable that henceforth opponents of the papacy used historical arguments, while the popes and their supporters preferred maxims of dogma and church law that were not bound to history.

St. Bernard and the Rise of Cistercian Monasticism

Louis J. Lekai

Louis J. Lekai argues that men joined monasteries in unprecedented numbers during the 1100s. This mass movement is difficult to explain, especially since the majority of men joined the most austere monasteries run by the Cistercian order. One explanation for Cistercian popularity, Lekai maintains, is the powerful personality of the Cistercian monk, Bernard of Clairvaux, who was widely admired for his eloquence and holiness. Bernard became a powerful figure in Church politics during a time of great upheaval and was even called upon to select the Pope between two men who were vying for the appointment. Bernard had a difficult time convincing other church leaders to back his choice, but eventually he succeeded. According to Lekai, Bernard enjoyed many victories: he successfully preached the second Crusade to reclaim the Holy Land from the Moslems, he held down a violent revolt against German heretics, and his former pupil, Eugenius III was elected Pope. With the help of St. Bernard, the Cistercian order became the first international monastic order. Lekai has written several books on monastic orders including *Hungarian Cistercians in America.*

That religion vocations were plentiful in the "age of faith" is a matter of common understanding. The first half of the twelfth century stands out, even in the Middle Ages, as a unique era of de-

votional enthusiasm, when monasticism turned into a mass movement of unparalleled proportions. As in the case of similar other phenomena, such as the Crusades,[1] no rational explanation can fully account for the countless thousands who were willing to leave the
"world" and seek God behind the walls of institutions where everything was geared to giving ample opportunity to practice a life of
heroic austerities.

Contemporaries, too, were well aware of what was happening, although, searching for reasons, they were just as baffled as we are.
As the often quoted Ordericus Vitalis observed: "Though evil
abounds in the world the devotion of the faithful in cloisters grows
more abundant and bears fruit a hundredfold in the Lord's field.
Monasteries are founded everywhere in mountain valleys and plains,
observing new rites and wearing different habits; the swarm of
cowled monks spreads all over the world." A source of equal amaze-
ment to the same author was the fact that it was the most austere order, the Cistercian, which fared best; the White Monks' appeal
seemed to break through all social and intellectual barriers: "Many
noble warriors and profound philosophers have flocked to them on
account of the novelty of their practices, and have willingly embraced the unaccustomed rigor of their life, gladly singing hymns of
joy to Christ as they journey along the right road." A somewhat older
contemporary, Bishop Otto of Bamberg (d. 1139), who watched and
promoted monastic growth, tried to rationalize it by a strangely familiar, though somewhat premature, argument: "At the beginning of
the world, when there were few men, the propagation of men was
necessary, and therefore they were not chaste. . . . Now, however, at
the end of the world, when men have multiplied beyond measure, is
the time of chastity; this was my reason, my intention in multiply-
ing monasteries."

There is no doubt that in the circumstances [the monastery at]
Cîteaux was bound to succeed. Its ascetic program was the epitome
of everything contemporaries were looking for; it was organized under an inspiring and capable leadership and its constitution insured
the cohesion of the movement in the event that it spread beyond the
confines of Burgundy. Grandmont, Savigny, Grand Chartreuse and
many similar reforms prospered with fewer potential assets than
those of Cîteaux. The amazing fact that the Cistercian Order virtually exploded and by the middle of the twelfth century possessed
nearly 350 houses in every country of Europe, can be explained,
however, only by the dynamic character and activity of the "man of
the century," Saint Bernard of Clairvaux. The often voiced notion
that he was the true founder of the Order is a pardonable exaggera-

1. The military expeditions undertaken by European Christians to recover the Holy Land from the
Moslems.

tion, but the fact that for centuries Cistercians were widely known as "Bernardines" was not without justification.

St. Bernard

Bernard was born in 1090, of noble Burgundian stock at Fontaines, near Dijon. After his education in the midst of his deeply religious family he was sent to Châtillon for formal studies at the school of the canons of Saint Vorles. Returning home, he lived the life of contemporary youth with his older brothers, but the silent and reserved boy soon decided that his place was at Cîteaux, already well known in the neighborhood. As soon as he became certain of his own vocation, he set about convincing all his brothers, his closest relatives and his friends to join him in his holy endeavor. This was the first occasion which proved him to be a born leader with an unwavering will and irresistible personal appeal. In the spring of 1113 he, together with his companions, asked for admission at Cîteaux. The austere reli-

gious training in the abbey did not change his character; on the contrary, Bernard found in Cîteaux the most congenial surrounding for his own spiritual temperament, and in turn, Bernard proved to be the most effective and eloquent interpreter of Cîteaux's message to the world. Abbot Stephen recognized in him a God-sent genius, and in 1115 the young man of twenty-five became the founder and abbot of Clairvaux. The trials and hardships of the founders of Cîteaux were relived during the first years of Clairvaux, but Bernard's faith and determination remained unbroken. The heroic spirit of the Abbot

In 1115, at age twenty-five, Bernard became the founder and abbot of Clairvaux.

attracted so many recruits that in only three years Clairvaux was able to found her first daughter house at Trois-Fontaines.

On the wings of his early writings the fame of Bernard's holiness and wisdom soon spread all over France, and, although he never cared for publicity, he soon found himself in the spotlight of an era desperately searching for able and competent leadership. It was a time of political turmoil throughout Western and Central Europe. In Germany, the powerful Emperor Henry V, the last member of the

Salian house, died without heir (1125) and the country was torn between the partisans of the two contesting families, the Welfs (Guelphs) and Ghibellines. Similar disturbances broke out in England after the reign of King Henry I, while the boy king of France, Louis VII, was still too young and inexperienced to take over his father's role. Meanwhile in Italy, the powerful cities and the most influential families, utilizing the impotency of their northern neighbors, started anew their bloody rivalries. When, in Rome, the papacy again fell victim to the fighting parties, a perilous schism in the Church resulted. After the death of Pope Honorius II in 1130, two opposing parties elected on the same day two popes, Innocent II and Anacletus II. The befuddled Christian world was at that moment utterly incapable of dealing with the problem; the only power able to restore order in Rome would have been the Emperor Roger II of Sicily, who was, however, using the occasion to extend the territory of his new kingdom.

A convention of French clergy and nobility at Etampes committed the decision of this crucial question to Saint Bernard, who declared in favor of Innocent II. Much more difficult to solve were the political ramifications of the dual election; namely, the task of convincing the contending powers to acknowledge Innocent unanimously and driving the usurper out of his Roman stronghold. It took eight years of tedious travelings, conferences, personal meetings, and hundreds of letters to achieve the goal. During these years Saint Bernard stood literally in the center of European politics, yet he never acted merely as a diplomat. He never yielded nor used threat of force, nor did he compromise. The secret of his success was his moral superiority, his unselfish good will, and the magic of his personality. On the other hand, the fact that the whole European world obeyed the poor and humble Abbot of Clairvaux indicates an era when moral ideals still prevailed over brutal violence.

Preaching the Crusades

The zenith of Saint Bernard's earthly career was reached the moment when his pupil, a former monk of Clairvaux, was elected pope as Eugenius III (1145–1153). On this Pope's order, the Saint launched the Second Crusade in 1147. By his preaching, he moved hundreds of thousands of people even when they could not understand his language. His powerful words and irresistible personality worked wonders in another field of his activity, among the Manichean heretics of Germany and France. The South of France was at the edge of an open revolt against the Church; nevertheless, Saint Bernard, in his strong belief that "faith is a matter of persuasion, not of compulsion," refused to advocate violent measures against them. Though his mission had only temporary effects, his sermons and miracles left a deep impression. Not so much by his eloquence as by his penetrating mind and deep erudition, he fought victoriously against doctrinal aberrations, most notably those of Abelard, and later, Gilbert de la Porrée [twelfth century intellectuals].

Saint Bernard's public activity was not limited to these issues of political and ecclesiastical importance. For about thirty years, he and his letters, written in a masterful Latin, were present every time peace, justice, or the interest of the Church demanded his intervention. The Cistercian Order grew and expanded with his own expanding fame and popularity. His biographers remarked that the power of his eloquence was such that "mothers hid their sons and wives their husbands" in order to keep them safe from the Saint's recruiting efforts, which brought a constantly overflowing population to his beloved Clairvaux. This abbey alone established sixty–five daughter houses during the lifetime of Bernard. Several other abbeys were almost as successful as Clairvaux, and France was soon dotted with some two hundred Cistercian establishments. Not all of these abbeys, however, were entirely new foundations. The seemingly irresistible trend drove many already existing monasteries into the Cistercian camp. Thus, for example, In 1147, of fifty–one new houses recorded, twenty–nine had belonged to the reform congregation of Savigny, while some others had been members of smaller organizations under the monasteries of Obazine and Cadouin. By this time the White Monks were well on their way in stepping across the borders of France and establishing themselves permanently in other countries of Christian Europe. Former monastic reforms, including Cluny, had largely been restricted to the countries of their origin, either because their programs were lacking universal appeal, or they were unable to control effectively a great number of distant, affiliated houses. Cîteaux, for the first time, broke through these barriers successfully, becoming the first truly international religious order in Church history.

Bernard's Sermon on Humility

Bernard of Clairvaux

Bernard of Clairvaux was a French monastic reformer who helped
found the austere Cistercian monastic order in 1115. He also preached
the Second Crusade and helped elect Pope Innocent II. In his sermons
based on the Bible's "Song of Songs," Bernard refuted the ideas pro-
pounded by men of his day whom he and other traditional church leaders considered heretics. His sermons appeared in book form but were
also delivered as talks. In Sermon thirty–four excerpted here, the Abbot of Clairvaux argues that members of the Church should be humble
before Christ. True humility, he maintains, is necessary in order to attain divine Grace. People must embrace humiliation given to them by
others; however, only those who voluntarily humiliate themselves will
be exalted, he argues.

"If you do not know, O fairest among women, go forth and follow
the flocks of your companions and pasture your kids beside the
shepherds' tents."[1] Of old, taking advantage of the familiar friendship that had developed between him and God, that holy man Moses
so longed for the great favor of seeing him that he said to God: "If I
have found favor in your sight, show yourself to me."[2] Instead of that
he received a vision of an inferior kind, but one which nevertheless
would help him to attain eventually to the one for which he longed.
Following the guileless urging of their hearts, the sons of Zebedee
also dared to ask for a great favor, but they too were directed back

1. Song 1:7   2. Ex 33:13

Excerpted from "Sermons on the Song of Songs," by Bernard of Clairvaux, translated by Kilian
Walsh in *The Works of Bernard of Clairvaux* (Kalamazoo, MI: Cistercian Publications, 1976).

to the way by which they must ascend to higher things.[3] In similar fashion now, when the bride[4] seems to demand a very special concession, she is rebuffed with an answer that, though harsh, is meant to be helpful and trustworthy. Anyone who strives forward toward the spiritual heights must have a lowly opinion of himself; because when he is raised above himself he may lose his grip on himself, unless through true humility, he has a firm hold on himself. It is only when humility warrants it that great graces can be obtained, hence the one to be enriched by them is first humbled by correction that by his humility he may merit them. And so when you perceive that you are being humiliated, look on it as the sign of a sure guarantee that grace is on the way.[5] Just as the heart is puffed up with pride before its destruction, so it is humiliated before being honored.[6] You read in Scripture of these two modes of acting, how the Lord resists the proud and gives his grace to the humble.[7] Did he not decide to reward his servant Job with generous blessings after the outstanding victory in which his great patience was put to the severest test? He was prepared for blessings by the many searching trials that humbled him.[8]

Accept Humiliation from Others

II. 2. But it matters little if we willingly accept the humiliation which comes from God himself, if we do not maintain a similar attitude when he humiliates us by means of another. And I want you to take note of a wonderful instance of this in St David, that time when he was cursed by a servant and paid no heed to the repeated insults, so sensitive was he to the influence of grace. He merely said: "What has this to do with me and you, O sons of Zeruiah?"[9] Truly a man after God's own heart,[10] who decided to be angry with the one who would avenge him rather than with the one who reviled him. Hence he could say with an easy conscience: "If I have repaid with evils those who offended me, let me rightly fall helpless before my enemies."[11] He would not allow them to silence this evil-spoken scoundrel; to him the curses were gain. He even added: "The Lord has sent him to curse David."[12] A man altogether after God's own heart, since the judgment he passed was from the heart of God. While the wicked tongue raged against him, his mind was intent on discovering the hidden purpose of God. The voice of the reviler sounded in his ears, but in his heart he disposed himself for blessings. Was God in the mouth of the blasphemer? God forbid! But he made use of it to humiliate David. And this was not hidden from the

---

3. Mt 20:21
4. Members of the Church.
5. Ps: 85:17
6. Prov 16:18
7. Jas 4:6
8. Job 1:8, 2:3
9. 2 Sam 16:10
10. Acts 13:22
11. Ps 7:5
12. 2 Sam 16:10

Prophet, to whom God had manifested the unpredictable secrets of his wisdom.[13] Hence he says: "It was good for me that you humiliated me, that I might learn your statutes."[14]

3. Do you see that humility makes us righteous? I say humility and not humiliation. How many are humiliated who are not humble! There are some who meet humiliation with rancor, some with patience, some again with cheerfulness. The first kind are culpable, the second are innocent, the last just. Innocence is indeed a part of justice, but only the humble possess it perfectly. He who can say: "It was good for me that you humiliated me," is truly humble. The man who endures it unwillingly cannot say this; still less the man who murmurs. To neither of these do I promise grace on the grounds of being humiliated, although the two are vastly different from each other, since the one possesses his own soul in his patience,[15] while the other perishes in his murmuring. For even if only one of them does merit anger, neither of them merits grace, because it is not to the humiliated but to the humble that God gives grace.[16] But he is humble who turns humiliation into humility, and he is the one who says to God: "It was good for me that you humiliated me." What is merely endured with patience is good for nobody, it is an obvious embarrassment. On the other hand we know that "God loves a cheerful giver."[17] Hence even when we fast we are told to anoint our head with oil and wash our face,[18] that our good work might be seasoned with spiritual joy and our holocaust[19] made fat.[20] For it is the possession of a joyful and genuine humility that alone enables us to receive grace. But the humility that is due to necessity or constraint, that we find in the patient man who keeps his self possession,[21] cannot win God's favor because of the accompanying sadness, although it will preserve his life because of patience. Since he does not accept humiliation spontaneously or willingly, one cannot apply to such a person the scriptural commendation that the humble man may glory in his exaltation.[22]

One Must Humble Oneself

III. 4. If you wish for an example of a humble man glorying with all due propriety, and truly worthy of glory, take Paul when he says that gladly will he glory in his weaknesses that the power of Christ may dwell within him.[23] He does not say that he will bear his weaknesses patiently, but he will even glory in them, and that willingly, thus proving that to him it is good that he is humiliated,[24] and that it is not

13. Ps 50:8
14. Ps 118:71
15. Lk 21:19
16. Jas 4:6
17. 2 Cor 9:7

18. Mt 6:17
19. A sacrificial offering that is consumed by flames.
20. Ps 19:4
21. Lk 21:19

22. Jas 1:9
23. 2 Cor 12:9
24. Ps 118:71

sufficient that one keep his self-possession by patience when he is humbled; to receive grace one must embrace humiliation willingly. You may take as a general rule that everyone who humbles himself will be exalted.[25] It is significant that not every kind of humility is to be exalted, but that which the will embraces; it must be free of compulsion or sadness.[26] Nor on the contrary must everyone who is exalted be humiliated, but only he who exalts himself, who pursues a course of vain display. Therefore it is not the one who is humiliated who will be exalted, but he who voluntarily humiliates himself; it is merited by this attitude of will. Even suppose that the occasion of humiliation is supplied by another, by means of insults, damages or sufferings, the victim who determines to accept all these for God's sake with a quiet, joyful conscience, cannot properly be said to be humiliated by anyone but himself.

5. But where does this take me? I feel that your endurance of this protracted discussion on humility and patience is an exercise in patience; but let us return to the place from which we digressed. All that I have said developed from the answer in which the Bridegroom[27] decided that the bride's aspiration toward lofty experiences should be restrained, not in order to confound her, but to provide an occasion for more solid, more deep humility, by which her capacity and worthiness for the sublimer experiences she desired would be increased. However, we are but at the beginning of this present verse, so with your permission, I shall postpone discussion of it to another sermon, lest the Bridegroom's words be recounted or heard with weariness. May our Lord Jesus Christ, who is blessed for ever,[28] avert this from his servants. Amen.

25. Lk 14:11
26. 2 Cor 9:7

27. Jesus Christ.
28. Rom 1:25

Frederick I Barbarossa: Power over the Papacy

Marcel Pacaut

Marcel Pacaut is a professor in the Letters and Human Sciences department at the University of Lyons, France. Pacaut argues that Frederick I Barbarossa is the most renowned leader of medieval Germany. Under Barbarossa's reign from 1152 to 1190, the monarchy in Germany grew stronger, Germany's imperial power over Italy increased, and the authority of the church decreased. An intelligent, well-respected leader, Barbarossa was also a realist—he confined his imperialist ambitions to regions he could control. Barbarossa was not a perfect leader, however. Because Barbarossa relied so heavily upon the aristocracy to support him, he eventually had to give up his ambitions of building a vast empire in order to deal with increasing feuds in Germany between aristocratic families who supported the monarchy and other princely families loyal to the church.

For a real assessment of the life of Frederick Barbarossa we must leave the realms of legend and myth, and return to history.

At Barbarossa's coronation in 1152, his empire was weak, his princes divided, and Germany under the thumb of the Holy See. In Italy, the authority of the empire was fast vanishing and the imperial principle had ceased to govern the political organization of society. But by the time Frederick had done, the power of the monarchy was fully restored in Germany, the Welfs[1] were on the run and most princes anxious to show their loyalty to the crown. In Italy, cities and nobles alike had come to accept the authority of Frederick's agents and officials; the Pope's sphere of influence and authority had been greatly reduced and his property rights circumscribed, and Sicily was ruled by Frederick's son Henry VI.

In short, within less than forty years, the empire had recovered "all its splendour"; never before had its "honour" shone so brightly; never before had it been so venerated and feared. No emperor, since Charlemagne and Otto the Great, had been so brilliantly successful, none so admired and revered. For although Otto had consolidated the power of the crown and of his own House in Germany, he had been quite unable to make his presence felt in Italy. Charlemagne's achievements, too, although on a grander scale, had proved far more transitory than Barbarossa's—his sons, unlike Frederick's, were unfit to step into their father's shoes.

But then Barbarossa, unlike his glorious predecessor, did not seek control of the entire West. Thus, on the highest level, Charlemagne may, perhaps, be said to have been the greater of the two, one who by spreading and deepening the Christian faith, by lending new vigour to the concept of the state, and by resurrecting the Roman Empire, had helped to found those very institutions which, although changed by time, still form the basis of Western civilization. For all that, his work was dwarfed by the very size of the stage on which it was set—Charlemagne lacked a clear "geographical perspective" of the great area over which he ruled.

Barbarossa the Realist

Barbarossa, by contrast, had a clear vision of his empire. His realism was the fundamental trait of his genius, though at times, in Lombardy for example, he was slow to face up to the facts. Realism explains his increasing caution towards Southern Italy, the relinquishment of all direct designs on the Kingdom of Sicily, his disinterest in the east, and his early tolerance of, and later sternness to, King Henry the Lion [of England]. The area to which he restricted his activities was one he knew well—it extended in the north to just beyond the Lahn; in the east to Lusatia and Austria; in the west it took in the Moselle valley, modern Lorraine, Alsace and Franche-Comté, and in the south it ran as far as the southern borders of the Duchy of Spoleto and the March, that is to the confines of Rome. He was able to leave his mark on all these parts, and to bind them closely to the empire. And it is precisely because Charlemagne overstepped these narrow limits that Barbarossa must be considered the most illustrious ruler to have come out of medieval Germany.

1. A German princely family opposed to Frederick.

But despite all his successes and the glory that attached to his name, Barbarossa's reign fell far short of perfection. Thus more than any other German he fostered the feudalization of social and political life, by greatly increasing the power of the princes. Possibly he could see no alternative, perhaps none even existed. But maintaining the authority of the crown by relying on the support of increasingly powerful princes called for enormous personal exertion, indefatigable energy, and, above all, for peace, both at home and abroad. Only by renouncing his major ambitions in Italy could Frederick have hoped to prevent abuses at home. As it was, the nobility raised ever-new territorial demands, and insisted that Barbarossa apply his own principle of obligatory reinfeoffment; nor had the breach between the Welfs and the Hohenstaufen [feuding princely families] ever been completely healed. And, in the game of feudal power politics, local interests tended quite naturally to take precedence over the good of the nation.

In Italy, though Barbarossa, after more than twenty years of fighting, eventually came to terms with the urban phenomenon, the Lombard cities continued to oppose his plans of empire. Moreover, he realized that if he pursued his "conservative" policy in Central Italy, the Tuscans, at least, would rise up against him just as the Lombards had done in 1167.[2] And so Frederick was increasingly forced to reduce his sovereign claims, to refrain from running every city and county with the help of his own men or of loyal supporters—from 1183 onwards, he readily granted rights and privileges to anyone who would help him. From Head of State, the emperor had shrunk to the head of a party: the leader of the Ghibellines, who opposed the Guelphs out of personal conviction no less than for private advantage.[3] German might thus introduced a deep and lasting split into Italy.

Successes and Failures

When all is said and done, therefore, we are left with Barbarossa's glory and undeniable qualities, with the unflinching resolve with which he tackled his life's work, but also with his profound failure to grasp certain essentials, and a number of decisions that, however skilful and realistic they may have appeared to be at the time, in the long run helped to blight his dreams of empire. On balance, Frederick's was no mean achievement; a memorial great enough for any man—in the rough and tumble of human history there is no one who is entirely without flaw, no one who is without error. This truism,

2. The Tuscans and Lombards are people who come from Tuscany and Lombard, regions in Italy.
3. Ghibellines were members of the aristocratic political faction who fought for German imperial control of Italy against the Guelphs, who favored Papal control.

which helps us to set limits upon the actions of all individuals, is no mere platitude in Barbarossa's case. For here we find an intelligent, energetic and respected leader grappling with overpowering political, social and psychological situations—among them the urban phenomenon in Italy and the feudal phenomenon in Germany. His very greatness was that he tried to come to terms with them, perhaps against his will; that he tried not to swim against the stream, while yet making resolutely for the shore he had set out to reach.

Frederick Barbarossa was a great man in his day, but one whose ambitions were strictly circumscribed by the limitations of his age.

The Becket Controversy

Roger of Hoveden

Roger of Hoveden was a twelfth-century historian whose career spanned much of King Henry II's reign in England. The majority of people in the historian's day were loyal to the church, and most would side with the clergy in conflicts between church and king. Roger of Hoveden was no exception; his account of the Becket controversy shows sympathy to the archbishop rather than to the king because he believed that Becket was a victim of Henry's grab for power over the church. Roger reports that in 1162, King Henry II of England and Thomas Becket, archbishop of Canterbury, collided over the division of secular and ecclesiastical power in England. Henry attempted to force the church to submit to his authority by ordering clergymen who were accused of crimes to be tried in secular courts. Becket, however, wanted to enforce the sovereignty of the church, so he argued that accused clergymen should be tried in ecclesiastical courts. King Henry was furious with the archbishop and tried to force him to comply with his laws. Several times Becket would accede, but in the end, the archbishop refused to confirm the king's law. Becket spent seven years in exile as a result of the conflict, but he eventually returned to his Canterbury church and resumed his ascetic and devoted life. There, in 1170, Becket was assassinated by men loyal to the king. Immediately after the assassination, clergymen reported a number of Becket miracles: the clergymen claimed that the archbishop arose from the dead and gave them the benediction, and that later he was seen sixty miles from the place where his body rested.

Excerpted from *The Annuals* (London: H.G. Bohn, 1853) by Roger of Hoveden, translated by Henry T. Riley.

In 1162, a great dissension arose between the king of England [Henry II] and Thomas [Becket], archbishop of Canterbury, relative to the ecclesiastical dignities, which the said king of the English was attempting to disturb and lower in estimation, whereas the archbishop endeavoured by every possible means to keep the ecclesiastical power and dignities intact. For it was the king's wish that if priests, deacons, subdeacons, and other rulers of the church should be apprehended on the commission of theft, or murder, or felony, or arson, or the like crimes, they should be taken before secular judges, and punished like the laity. Against this the archbishop of Canterbury urged, that if a clerk in holy orders, or any other ruler of the Church, should be charged upon any matter, he ought to be tried by ecclesiastics and in the ecclesiastical courts; and if he should be convicted, that then he ought to be deprived of his orders, and that, when thus stripped of his office and his ecclesiastical preferment, if he should offend again, he ought to be tried at the pleasure of the king and of his deputies.

Concessions and Compromise

In the year of grace 1164, being the tenth year of the reign of king Henry, son of the empress Matilda, the said Henry gave to Henry, duke of Saxony, his daughter Matilda in marriage. In the same year, having called together a great council, and all the archbishops and bishops of England being assembled in his presence, he requested them, out of their love for and obedience to him, and for the establishment of the kingdom, to receive the laws of King Henry, his grandfather, and faithfully to observe them: on which Thomas, archbishop of Canterbury made answer for himself and the others, that they would receive those laws which the king said were made by his grandfather, and with good faith would observe the same; saving their orders and the honour of God and of the Holy Church in all respects. But this reservation greatly displeased the king, and he used every possible method to make the bishops promise that they would, without any exception whatever, observe those laws; to this, however, the archbishop of Canterbury would on no account agree.

A considerable time after this, Ernulph, bishop of Lisieux, came over to England, and anxiously endeavoured, day and night, to make peace between the king and the archbishop, but was unable to ensure complete success. Upon this, by the advice of the bishop of Lisieux, the king separated Roger, archbishop of York, Robert Melun, bishop of Hereford, Robert, bishop of Lincoln, and some other prelates of the church, from the society and counsel of the archbishop of Canterbury, in order that through them he might more easily induce the archbishop to yield to his own attempts. After this, there came to England a certain man belonging to the religious orders, named Philip de Elcemosyna, being sent as legate "a latere," by Alexander the Supreme Pontiff, and all the cardinals, for the purpose of making peace between the king and archbishop of Canterbury; by whom the pope and all the cardinals sent word to the archbishop of Canterbury, that he must make peace with the king of England his master, and promise, without any exception, to obey his laws. Assenting therefore to this and other advice on the part of these great men, the archbishop of Canterbury came to the king at Woodstock, and there made a promise to the king and agreed that he would in good faith, and without any bad intent observe his laws.

Shortly after this, the clergy and people of the kingdom being convened at Clarendon, the archbishop repented that he had made this concession to the king, and, wishing to recede from his agreement, said that in making the concession he had greatly sinned, but would sin no longer in so doing. In consequence of this, the king's anger was greatly aroused against him, and he threatened him and his people with exile and death; upon which, the bishops of Salisbury and Norwich came to the archbishop, together with Robert, earl of Leicester, Reginald, earl of Cornwall, and the two Templars, Richard de Hastings and Tostes de Saint Omer, and in tears threw themselves at the feet of the archbishop, and begged that he would observe his laws. The archbishop being consequently overcome by the entreaties of such great men, came to the king, and in the presence of the clergy and the people, said that he had acceded to those laws which the king called those of his grandfather. He also conceded that the bishops should receive those laws and promise to observe them. Upon this, the king gave orders to all the earls and barons of the realm, that they should go out and call to remembrance the laws of King Henry his grandfather, and reduce them to writing. When this had been done, the king commanded the archbishops and bishops to annex their seals to the said writing; but, while the others were ready so to do, the archbishop of Canterbury swore that he would never annex his seal to that writing or confirm those laws.

When the king saw that he could not by these means attain his object, he ordered a written copy of these laws to be made, and gave a duplicate of it to the archbishop of Canterbury, which he, in spite of the prohibition of the whole of the clergy, received from the king's hand, and turning to the clergy, exclaimed, "Courage, brethren! by means of this writing we shall be enabled to discover the evil intentions of the king, and against whom we ought to be on our guard!" After which he retired from the court, and was unable by any means to recover the king's favour. And because he had acted unadvisedly in this matter, he suspended himself from the celebration of divine service from that hour, until such time as he, himself, or his messenger, should have spoken thereon with our lord the pope.

The Ascetic Life

After this, there came to England Rotrod, archbishop of Rouen, on behalf of our lord the pope, for the purpose of effecting a reconciliation between the king and the archbishop of Canterbury; to which, however, the king would on no account consent, unless our lord the pope should, by his bull, confirm those laws. When this could be in nowise effected, the king sent John of Oxford and Geoffrey Riddel, his clerks, to the pope Alexander, requesting him to give the legateship of the whole of England to Roger, that archbishop of York, that so through his means he might be able to confound the archbishop of Canterbury. But our lord the pope would not, as this part of it, listen to the king's request. However, upon the petition of the king's clerks, our lord the pope conceded that the king himself should be legate for the whole of England; on such terms however, that he could do nothing offensive to the archbishop of Canterbury. The king, on seeing this, in his indignation sent back to our lord the pope the letters appointing him legate, which John of Oxford and Geoffrey Riddel had brought. . . . Thereupon, at the commencement of the seventh year of his banishment, when he was now beloved by God and sanctified by spiritual exercises, the archbishop of Canterbury hastened with all speed to return to his see. For the pious father was unwilling any longer to leave the church of Canterbury desolate; or else it was, because, as some believe, he has seen in the spirit the glories of his contest drawing to a close, or through a fear that, by dying elsewhere, he might be depriving his own see of the honor of his martyrdom.

As for his life, it was perfectly unimpeachable before God and man. To arise before daybreak did not seem to him a vain thing, as he knew that the Lord has promised it crown to the watchful. For every day he arose before daybreak, while all the rest were asleep, and entering his oratory would awake his chaplains and clerks from their slumbers, and, the matins and the hours of the day being chaunted, devoutly celebrate the mass; and every day and night he received three or five flagellations from the hand of a priest. After the celebration of the mass, every day he reentered his oratory, and, shutting the door after him, devoted himself to prayer with abundant tears; and no one but God alone knew the manner in which he afflicted his flesh. And thus did he do daily unto his flesh until the hour for dining, unless some unusual solemnity or remarkable cause prevented it. On coming forth from his oratory he would come to dine among his people, not that he might sate his body with costly food, but that he might make his household cheerful thereby, and that he might fill the poor ones of the Lord with good things, whom, according to his means, he daily increased in numbers. And although costly and exquisite food and drink were set before him, still, his only food and drink were bread and water.

One day, while the archbishop was sitting at the table of Alexander, the Supreme Pontiff, a person who was aware of this secret, placed before him a cup full of water. On the Supreme Pontiff taking it up, and tasting it, he found it to be the purest wine, and delicious to drink; on which he said: "I thought that this was water;" and on replacing the cup before the archbishop, the wine immediately returned to its former taste of water. Oh wondrous change by the right hand of the Most High! Every day, when the archbishop arose from dinner, unless more important business prevented him, he always devoted himself to reading the Scriptures until the hour of vespers, at the time of sunset. His bed was covered with soft coverlets and cloths of silk, embroidered on the surface with gold wrought therein; and while other persons were asleep, he alone used to lie on the bare floor before his bed, repeating psalms and hymns, and never ceasing from prayers, until at last, overcome with fatigue, he would gradually recline his head upon a stone put beneath it in place of a pillow: and thus would his eyes enjoy sleep while his heart was ever watchful for the Lord. His inner garment was of course sackcloth made of goats' hair; with which his whole body was covered from the arms down the knees. But his outer garments were remarkable for their splendour and extreme costliness, to the end that, thus deceiving human eyes, he might please the sight of God. There was no individual acquainted with this secret of his way of living, with the exception of two—one of whom was Robert, canon of Merton, his chaplain, and the name of the other was Brun, who had charge of his sackcloth garments, and washed them when necessary; and they were bound by their words and oaths that, during his life, they would disclose these facts to no one. . . .

Accordingly, again was this champion of Christ afflicted with injuries and hardships still more atrocious, beyond measure and number, and, by public proclamation, enjoined not to go beyond the limits of his church. Whoever showed to him, or to any one of his household, a cheerful countenance, was held to be a public enemy. However, all these things the man of God endured with great patience, and staying among those of his own household, edified them all with his conversation and with words of exhortation: and once more the archbishop took his seat in his church, fearless, and awaiting the hour at which he should receive from God the crown of martyrdom. For, being warned by many beforehand, he knew that his life would be but short, and that death was at the gates [at the hands of assassins loyal to the king]. . . .

Martyrdom and Miracles

Thus it was that, at the beginning of the seventh year of his exile, the above-named martyr Thomas struggled even unto the death for the love of God and the liberties of the Church, which had almost entirely perished as regards the English Church. He did not stand in fear of the words of the unrighteous; but having his foundation upon a firm rock, that is, upon Christ, for the name of Christ, and in the Church of Christ, by the swords of the wicked, on the fifth day of the Nativity of our Lord, being the day after Innocents's day, he himself an innocent, died. His innocent life and his death, as being precious in the eyes of God, innumerable miracles deservedly bespeak, which, not only in the place where he rested, but in divers nations and kingdoms, were wondrously shown.

On the same day the passion of the blessed Thomas was revealed by the Holy Ghost to the blessed Godric, the anchorite, at Finchale, a place which is distant from Canterbury more than a hundred and sixty miles. The monks of the church of Canterbury, on this, shut the doors of the church, and so the church remained with the celebration of the mass suspended for nearly a whole year, until they had received a reconciliation of the church from our lord the pope Alexander. But the monks took up the body of their martyr, and the first night placed it in the choir, performing around it the service for the dead. It is also said, and with truthfulness, that when they had completed around the body the obsequies of mortality, and while he was lying on the bier in the choir, about daybreak he raised his left hand and gave them the benediction; after which, they buried him in the crypt.

Henry II: Conflict with the Church

John Harvey

John Harvey is the author of several books on the Middle Ages including *Cathedrals of England and Wales* and *The Gothic World—1100–1600— A Survey of Art and Architecture*. As a contemporary scholar interested in medieval England, Harvey has written an account of the Becket controversy in which he sympathizes with his subject—King Henry II of England—rather than with the archbishop Thomas Becket who quarreled with the king. Henry II—who reigned from 1154 to 1189—ruled over the largest territory in Europe in the twelfth century. He married Eleanor of Aquitaine and sired two future kings, Richard I and John. According to Harvey, Henry was a strong, fair, and effective ruler who showed compassion and tolerance for others, but who was unfairly vilified for his role in the assassination of Saint Thomas Becket, archbishop of Canterbury. The conflict centers on church power: Henry decreed that clergymen who were accused of crimes must be tried in secular courts; Becket, on the other hand, argued that the accused clergy should be tried only by ecclesiastical courts. Harvey argues that Henry's position on the issue was reasonable: he was concerned about the growing power of the church and its abuses. But the stubborn Becket would not capitulate and went into exile. When he returned to his church in Canterbury seven years later, Becket was assassinated by men loyal to the king. Henry's critics contended that his treatment of the archbishop paved the way for the assassination, but in truth, it was Becket who made the assassination happen by manipulating the king into the conflict, the result of which he knew would be martyrdom and sainthood for himself.

The descriptions of Henry II . . . give us a clear picture of the man: he was strongly built, with a large, leonine head, freckled fiery face, and red hair cut short. His eyes were grey, and we are told that his voice was harsh and cracked, possibly because of the amount of open-air exercise he took. He would walk or ride until his attendants and courtiers were worn out and his feet and legs covered with blisters and sores. This terrifying energy was the key-note of his whole character, and must have shone in his face, for it was said that men flocked to gaze upon him, though they had seen him a thousand times already. He could perform all athletic feats, but what was far more remarkable in his day was his knowledge of polite accomplishments and letters. He was a gifted linguist, for he had knowledge of all the languages "from the French sea to the Jordan", though he spoke only Latin and French. His knowledge of law was very extensive, and he adhered to the ancient custom of sitting in judgment in person, though he instituted the legal circuits with their justices of assize able to decide cases remote from the King.

He was sparing in diet and frugal in personal expenditure; careless of his dress, though it was always made of fine materials. Walter Map [a contemporary of the king] praised his lack of pride: ". . . he does not take upon himself to think high thoughts; his tongue never swells with elated language; he does not magnify himself as more than man; but there is always in his speech that cleanness which is seen in his dress . . . he comes nearer to admitting himself to be despicable than to making himself a despiser." This was the more surprising in a man of such varied ability; his legal knowledge was not merely general: he was accustomed to settle questions of disputed charters, where forgery was suspected, by personal examination—dubious cases that came before his justiciars were referred to his more acute judgment. His memory was exceptional: he never failed to recognize a man he had once seen, nor to remember anything which might be of use. More deeply learned than any king of his time in the western world, he was appealed to from all quarters; the summit of his power was reached in 1173, when he was called in as arbitrator between Toulouse and Aragon, and in 1177, when at a council held at London he determined the ancient quarrel between Alfonso IX of Castile and Sancho VI of Navarre. That he was thus able to supplant the Court of Rome in international affairs is indeed an extraordinary tribute to his personality and his justice.

Map tells us that his mother taught him to prolong everybody's affairs and keep men dangling in hope while he filled his own purse, and that in respect to cases in his court, which went on "so that many die before they get their matters settled, or leave the court driven by hunger", he followed this maternal counsel only too well. Yet Map's own statement that "whoever has a good case is anxious to try it before him; whoever has a bad one will not come to him unless he is dragged", must be placed on the other side. As to another of his failings, Map is inconsistent, for he accuses Henry of shutting himself up, away from honest men, accessible only to the unworthy; yet goes on to say that whenever the King went out he was seized upon by the crowds and buffeted hither and thither, even assaulted with shouts and rough pullings and pushings, in spite of which he never complained or showed anger, but listened to every man patiently, and if mishandled beyond bearing, retreated to some place out of reach.

Generous and Fair

The story of one of his judgments needs to be told in full, as Map tells it. " It was the custom of our court that sealed briefs containing their names and duties were drawn up and delivered to the ministers of the court gratis. Now the King's dispenser laid an information against a sealer, that he had refused to deliver him a brief containing his name and duties without payment. Turstin FitzSimon was the dispenser, Adam of Yarmouth the sealer. The court after hearing them was in doubt, and called in the King; he first heard Turstin, and then Adam, who said: 'I had received some guests, and I sent a man to beg the lord Turstin to give me two cakes of your own royal sort. He answered, "No." Afterwards, when he wanted his brief, I remembered that "No", and in like manner I said "No."' The king decided against him who had said 'No' first. He made Adam sit at the bench with the seal and Turstin's brief placed before him; and he compelled Turstin to put off his mantle, and on bended knee present Adam with two royal cakes, decently wrapped in a white napkin, and when the present had been received ordered Adam to deliver him the brief, and so reconciled them; and he added that his officers ought not only to help each other from their own stock or the treasury, but also to help anyone of the household, and even outsiders who were pressed by necessity."

His generosity was on a grand scale; but he kept the secret of his "large and fat almsdeeds, lest it should be known to his left hand what his right hand gave"; and in the hope of reaching even those of the poor whose complaints did not come to him personally, he appointed a Templar as his almoner, to distribute a tenth of all the food and drink that came into the King's house to the destitute. In this respect Henry was the forerunner of vast and warm-hearted charity displayed by his whole line, all of whom were better fitted to bring a personal touch into the distribution of wealth than are the impersonal officials of the Treasury. Nor did his charity reflect a lavish outlook: his personal outlay was most moderate. Gerald the Welshman used to be fond of telling how the monks of St. Swithin at Winchester grovelled in the mud before the King, complaining to him even with tears that their Bishop, Richard Tocilve, had deprived them of three dishes at their meals. Henry asked how many dishes they had left, and they answered " Ten." " In my court," said the King, "I am satisfied with three. Perish your Bishop, if he doesn't cut your dishes down to the same."

Henry and Religion

At other occasions he took pleasure in egging on the religious to mild dissipation, and travelling incognito was once entertained to a drinking bout by the Abbot of a Cistercian house [monastery], which should, of course, have most rigidly debarred such excesses. But even then Cistercian austerity was greatly relaxed, though within a few years of the death of St. Bernard,[1] for the monks had their own private toasts of "Pril" and "Vril", answering to the "Washeil" and "Drinkheil" of the lay banqueter. Into all this the Abbot initiated his guest. Later on, the Abbot visited court and as he reached the presence was greeted with " Pril " by the King, who made him perform the whole ritual of the toast, to the amusement of everybody but the unfortunate ecclesiastic himself. Henry's respect for the cloth was not exaggerated: in 1157, long before the great quarrel with Becket[2] over the rights of the Church, Bishop Hilary of Chichester, whose jurisdiction over the Abbots of Battle was on trial, objected that the secular authority could not deal with a spiritual jurisdiction, or depose any bishop or other ecclesiastic without leave from the Pope. The King's reply was "True enough, he cannot be 'deposed', but he can be quite shoved out with a push like this", suiting the action to the word.

While attending church services the King used to spend his time "doodling" or sketching, or in whispered conversation; but he was not indifferent to the sanctity of such a man as Hugh of Avalon. One Brother Girard was once taking Henry to task for his sin, while Prior Hugh waited silently with his head bowed. Taking no notice of the monk, the King turned to Hugh and asked what he was thinking of: "Are you making ready to leave our kingdom?" Hugh answered gently that he did not despair of the King, but was rather sorry for the troubles and labours which hindered the care of his soul. "You are busy now, but some day, when the Lord helps, we will finish the good work begun." At this the King burst into tears and embraced Hugh, swearing that he should not depart from the kingdom while he lived: "With you I will hold wise counsel, and with you I will take heed for my soul!"

Hugh once excommunicated one of Henry's foresters, and was summoned to the royal presence at Woodstock, where he found

1. French monastic reformer who lived from 1090 to 1153. 2. Thomas Becket, archbishop of Canterbury.

Henry and his courtiers sitting on the grass in a circle. The King took no notice of Hugh's greeting but remained in a sulky silence. Hugh pushed aside an earl and sat down at the King's side; Henry, too restless to stay quiet, called for needle and thread and began to stitch a leather finger-stall which he was wearing on his left hand. After a minute Hugh said: "How like you are now to your cousins of Falaise", alluding to William the Bastard's mother, the tanner's daughter. Overcome by the joke and the Prior's sly impudence, the King rocked with laughter, and then explained the allusion to those who had not grasped it. Not only could Henry take a joke in good part; he could also show remarkable

Henry II

delicacy. Map tells how he was riding at the head of a body of knights and clerks, talking with a distinguished monk, Dom Reric. There was a high wind at the time, and just as the cavalcade appeared a white monk was walking along the street, looked round, and tried to get out of the way. "He dashed his foot against a stone, and as angels were not bearing him up at the moment, fell in front of the king's horse, the wind blowing his habit right over his neck, so that he was entirely exposed to the eyes of the lord King and Reric. The King feigned to see nothing and kept silence; but Reric muttered: 'Curse that religion that reveals the arse.'"

The Becket Controversy

Henry's relations with Thomas Becket have overshadowed all his other dealings, not only concerning religion, but in his whole life and reign. Nothing could be more misleading than the notion of a saintly man of God ill-treated by a tyrannical potentate.[3] It was said that Henry was never known to choose an unworthy friend, but Becket's worthiness is a matter of opinion. Extraordinary mixture of well-to-do man-about-town, witty and extravagant, and self-willed, self-torturing, and it must be said, self-advertising churchman, Thomas Becket won for himself an outstanding place in history by his genius for manoeuvring other parties into the wrong.

---

3. Henry ordered that clergymen accused of crime should be tried in secular courts; Becket would not agree and lived in exile for seven years.

As the child of wealthy parents, young Thomas was weighed by his mother against money, clothes, and food. This equipoise of commodities Rohesia, a Norman from Caen, not the Saracen of legend, gave away to the poor, just as at the present day Indian poor benefit from the birthday weighing in diamonds of the Aga Khan. In his roaring days, as Henry's boon companion, Becket was far from sharing the King's real charity towards the poor and outcast. Riding together through London in midwinter, they saw an old man shivering in his rags. Henry turned to his friend, asking: "Would it not be a meritorious act to give that poor old man a warm cloak?" Becket, then chancellor, agreed, whereupon the King called out "Yours be the merit, then!" and seized Becket's splendid furred cloak, which after a short struggle he wrested from Thomas's grasp and threw to the beggar.

Green remarked that Becket was not abreast of the highest level of thought of his own time. When Hugh of Avalon, as Bishop of Lincoln, forbade his archdeacons and their officials to take fines instead of inflicting penance, they defended themselves on the ground that the blessed martyr Thomas had done the same. "Believe me," said Hugh, "not for that was he a saint; he showed other marks of holiness, by another title he won the martyr's palm." In alms-giving also it is easy to see an element of vainglory in Becket's behaviour. Archbishop Theobald had doubled the amount of the regular archiepiscopal alms; Thomas on his accession doubled the amounts which had been given by Theobald. But when, the day after his consecration, some minstrels and jugglers who had performed before him when he was chancellor came to him for their usual rewards he refused them, saying that his possessions were a sacred trust from henceforward, not to be spent upon actors and jesters. About all this there is a sad atmosphere of cant.

The martyrdom of Thomas Becket was a martyrdom which he had repeatedly gone out of his way to seek, and while it is impossible to condone the savage folly of his murderers, one cannot but feel sympathy towards Henry, thus placed in a position of responsibility for the death of a man [at the hands of assassins loyal to the King] who in happier days had, after all, been his friend. Becket got what he asked for, but Henry, as generous and as just as he was free from petty spite, was left burdened with murder and sacrilege for the remaining twenty years of his life. It is a major irony of history that Becket should be regarded as a martyr for the cause of freedom from a state tyranny largely imaginary, and against which Henry and the like strong kings formed the greatest bulwark. The dubious character of Church interference in policy did not escape Henry: when in 1185 the Patriarch Heraclius visited him to launch a new crusade,[4] Gerald the Welshman suggested that it was a great honour to the King that he should have been chosen out by the Patriarch above all

4. military expeditions to recover the Holy Lands from Moslems

the Kings of the earth. Henry retorted: "The clergy may well call us to arms and peril, seeing they will take no blows in the fray nor shoulder any burdens they can avoid." Even as regarded war against the infidel, the principle of pacifism was recognized, for Walter Map, writing of the Templars [an order of knights active in the crusades] about 1186, says: "They take the sword and perish by the sword. But, say they, all laws and all codes permit the repelling of force by force. Yet He renounced that law who when Peter struck a blow, would not call out the legions of angels. It does seem as if these Templars had not chosen the better part, when we see that under their protection our boundaries in the Holy Land are always being narrowed, and those of our enemies enlarged."

Upstanding Among Men

Gerald, some fifteen years later, went further in accusing the Archbishop of Canterbury, Hubert Walter, of correspondence with the enemy (France), of sending food to the enemy for his own personal gain, and of making a corner in the grain market. "Moreover, knowing as well he might, since it was done by his advice, that owing to the war between the Kings an order had been issued that a search for arms should be made in England, he caused all arms that were anywhere for sale to be purchased, and collected a vast number in a very short time. Then as soon as a further order was made that arms should be procured throughout the realm, he forthwith offered his store of arms for sale and made a vast profit." It is clear that though kings were to blame in their almost incessant warfare, there were few, if any, others who could lay claim to a higher morality.

It is, however, easy to find fault, and Henry himself rebuked one who sought to curry favour by abusing the Bishop of Worcester, who had been criticizing the King for having his son crowned and for seizing Church sees into his own hands. "Do you think, you scoundrel, if I say what I choose to my kinsman and my bishop, that you or anyone else are free to dishonour him with words and persecute him with threats? Scarce can I keep my hands from thy eyes!" In such a scene we can sense Henry's sincerity, and his loathing of the carping critic and the toady. His fairness can also be seen in his unpopular refusal to join in persecution of the Jews, and his setting open his dominions as a refuge for the Albigenses[5] when they were being harried in southern France. In a positive sense, too, he maintained human rights; he put down the barbarous treatment of shipwrecked sailors, and repressed plunder and outrage. Even natural calamities he did what he could to mitigate: Map once crossed the Channel with him in a fleet of twenty-five ships which had the oblig-

5. A collective denomination for the members of the Catharist religious sect.

ation of carrying over the King and his household free of charge. All but the ship in which Henry and Map were travelling were wrecked, though the crews were saved. In the morning the King called the wrecked sailors together and paid the estimated amount of their losses, coming to a large total, though he was not in any way responsible. His faithfulness to his pledged word was famous.

The
Crusades

PREFACE

The Crusades were a series of military expeditions to the lands around Jerusalem in an effort to wrest control of the Holy Land from the Muslims. The crusaders' main intent was to ensure safe passage to European Christian pilgrims who traveled to Jerusalem to visit and worship at sacred places. Pilgrimage to the Holy Land in medieval times was considered virtuous, and pilgrims needed protection from Muslim persecution. But the Western Church, based in Rome, had even more lofty goals: It desired a reunification of the Western and Eastern Churches and an increase in its own power and influence.

When the Roman Empire fell, the Roman church was split in two. The Eastern Church established its base in Constantinople and performed its masses in Greek. The Western Church was based in Rome and conducted its masses in Latin. When Europe began to recover from the tumultuous era that proceeded the twelfth century, the popes of the Western Church began to desire a reunification that would significantly increase the church's wealth and range of influence. When word came from the Eastern Church at Constantinople that the Seljuk Turks—who had newly converted to Islam—had overtaken the Holy Land and conquered most of the Byzantine Empire, Pope Urban II of Rome saw a divine opportunity. When the Eastern Church pleaded with the pope for help in defeating the Turks, Urban was happy to give it. The First Crusade was launched.

The First Crusade—which began in 1096—was the only one of the Crusades that was successful. After several years of fighting the Muslims, the Christian crusaders finally captured the city of Acre in 1104. Soon after, they ousted the Muslim Turks from the region. The Christians then established strongholds throughout the Holy Land, and Christians were once again safe in Jerusalem. But peace did not last long. Although the Christians and Muslims usually got along well, discord occasionally developed between the two religious factions. Beginning in 1128, a Turkish ruler named Zengi began taking advantage of this friction and recaptured areas of the Holy Land. When the king of Jerusalem appealed to the pope in Rome for help in defeating Zengi, the pope called for the Second Crusade.

In 1147, St. Bernard of Clairvaux, a prominent monk from the Cistercian order, preached the merits of the Second Crusade. Upon hearing the powerful speaker describe Muslim atrocities against the Christians in the Holy Land, people throughout Europe took arms and joined in the expedition. The Second Crusade was led by France's King Louis VII and Germany's Conrad III. Foolishly, these military leaders decided to reclaim Damascus from the Muslims. Damascus, however, had been an ally of the Christians because it too had been threatened by Zengi. Once attacked by its supposed friends, Muslim leaders in Damascus made a call to arms, and Louis and Conrad were soundly defeated. The Second Crusade was a failure.

Zengi's successor, Nur al-Din, made further inroads into Christian territory, but he was constantly distracted by simultaneous conflicts with Egyptian Muslims. His successor, Saladin, also fought the Egyptians and succeeded in having himself named king of Egypt and Syria. In 1187, Saladin began a military siege of the Christian kingdom in the Holy Land and succeeded in overthrowing the Christian forces. News of the loss of Jerusalem shocked western Europe, and in 1189, the pope declared a Third Crusade. Richard I of England, Philip II of France, and Frederick I Barbarossa of Germany each vowed to join the crusade. Barbarossa fell into a river and drowned midroute, however, and Philip quickly tired of the fighting and went home. Richard, however, stayed. The Third Crusade is perhaps best known for the rivalry between Richard and Saladin, respected rivals who fought each other ruthlessly. The result of the Third Crusade was limited victory for the Christians: Saladin allowed Richard to claim a thin portion of land along the Mediterranean coast, but the rest of the Holy Land belonged to the Muslims.

Pope Innocent III was not satisfied with limited success, however, and in 1198 he announced the Fourth Crusade. But the Fourth Crusade would turn out to be the most brutal and corrupt of all the Crusades, and it failed disastrously. On their way to the Holy Land, the crusaders stopped for the winter in Byzantine territory and soon got involved in political infighting in Constantinople. The ruler Isaac II was overthrown by his brother, who had himself crowned as Alexius III. Isaac's son, Alexius Angelus, managed to escape to the west and convince the crusaders to help him overthrow his uncle in exchange for money to cover the cost of the Crusades. The crusaders agreed to the bargain and Alexius Angelus was established as the new emperor. It quickly became clear, however, that Alexius was incompetent, and the Greeks rose up against him. The crusaders, who were Alexius's allies, also came under attack. Unpaid by Alexius and tired of persecution by the Greeks, the crusaders vowed revenge. In 1204, they terminated their expedition to the Holy Land and instead sacked the city of Constantinople. Their barbaric conduct during the raid—including rape, pillage, and murder—destroyed many Europeans' faith in the holiness of the Crusades.

Many minor crusades followed the Fourth, including a Children's Crusade in which thirty thousand children from France and Germany embarked for the Holy Land. The Children's Crusade ended in failure, also, with over half of the children sold into slavery. The minor crusades occurred sporadically until the 1300s, and all failed to reclaim the Holy Land from the Muslims. But even though the Crusades failed in their immediate objectives, they did succeed in producing some positive outcomes for Europe. Historians argue that the Crusades increased trade throughout Europe and facilitated the exchange of new ideas and technology. Many contend that the Crusades made possible the period of learning and creativity known as the twelfth-century renaissance. Others argue that the Crusades brought Europe wealth and influence. The Crusades also facilitated an exchange of power that would have enormous consequences for Europe. As the papacy weakened due to increasing disillusionment over the Crusades, kings wrested power from the church. This transference of power from ecclesiastical into secular hands paved the way for the formation of modern European nations.

But the Crusades resulted in many negative consequences as well. Many historians contend that the Crusades increased religious intolerance. They maintain that the Crusades made permanent the break between the Eastern and Western Churches and left lasting discord between them. Some historians contend that the Crusades also set in motion the religious turmoil that has plagued the Middle East since the twelfth century. Karen Armstrong, a writer and teacher, argues that the holy wars in the Middle East today "are the latest round in a conflict that began when the Christian West persecuted and massacred Jews and Muslims in the First Crusade." Other historians point out that when each new crusade began, religious fervor incited Europeans to persecute and slaughter European Jews. Ronald C. Finucane, a professor of history at Oakland University in Rochester, Michigan, argues that the hatred toward Jews that flared up during the First Crusade established a tradition of European anti-Semitism. He contends that "the slaughter of the First Crusade . . . remained the blackest memory for the Jews of Europe until overshadowed by the even greater slaughter of our own age." That is, Finucane suggests that the anti-Semitism produced by the Crusades led to the Holocaust persecution of the Jews under Hitler during World War II.

The Crusades had far-reaching consequences not only for Europe and the Middle East but the world. The crusading movement led to European imperialism and made possible the discovery of the New World by the Europeans. The Crusades had an enormous impact on the world's three major religions—Christianity, Judaism, and Islam. In spite of their failures, the Crusades established Europe as a major world player in the centuries to come.

The Holy Crusades

Sidney Packard

The Crusades were a series of European military actions against the Moslems in Palestine to win back the Holy Land from Islamic occupation. Sidney Packard argues that the Crusades were dominated by the Roman Church which wanted the Greek Orthodox Church to come under the power of the Papacy. To gain support for the wars, the church granted favors to those who participated, and, as more people joined and became beholden to the church, the power of the papacy increased. According to Packard, some of the benefits that accrued from the Crusades included an expansion of European influence, enhanced trade, urban development, and enriched cultural exchange. The Crusades, however, failed to accomplish the Church's goals. The wars actually hastened the separation between the Eastern and Western churches, Packard maintains, and the Christians were not able to maintain control of the Holy Lands. The Crusades also resulted in increased intolerance, fanaticism, anti-Semitism, and brutal imperialistic practices in the name of religion. Sidney Packard is a professor of history at Johns Hopkins University.

Where does one put the Crusades in an essay on the European twelfth century? A major and a unique factor in the whole of European history, the crusading movement was largely religious in its origin and in its objectives but certainly was never at any time an exclusively religious enterprise. The Crusades had their heyday in the twelfth century: their greatest successes and some of their greatest failures belong to this period. Although the crusading movement stumbled along until the late thirteenth century, was revived frequently and spasmodically thereafter, and is even thought to have inspired both

Excerpted from *Twelfth Century Europe: An Interpretive Essay,* by Sidney Packard. Copyright © 1973 by the University of Massachusetts Press. Reprinted with permission from the University of Massachusetts Press.

Columbus in the fifteenth century and Allenby[1] in the twentieth, the Crusades, seen in full perspective, were a gigantic fiasco, as [historian] Steven Runciman has pointed out. They can only be understood against the background of the century as here defined in which they originated and developed.

European Expansion

The Crusades were a popular and a comprehensive European movement, involving practically every facet of European life, thought, and feeling. They constitute chapter one in the history of European expansion and colonization. They served as a needed safety valve for the untamed energies of the younger sons, the disinherited younger brothers, and the progressively unemployed members of the warrior class of feudal Europe, who found less and less opportunity for gainful and appropriate activities on the home estates. They gave increased scope for both feudal kings and lesser feudal lords for combining holy purposes with private gains. They stimulated trade and traders, at first in the Mediterranean area but in the end in all Europe. Some have thought them responsible for the remarkable growth of towns in the twelfth century, especially in Italy, although in some cases, and notably in Italy, the stream of influence seems to have run, in part at least, the other way.

Thus some have thought the Crusades to have been largely economic in character, a judgment which is supported by the increasingly important role of economic factors in the later Crusades, notably in the Fourth, which seems to have been almost completely controlled by Venice. Certainly the economic boom of the twelfth century was not unconnected with the Crusades. Others prefer to look upon the Crusades as another chapter in the long rivalry of east and west which started with the Trojan War and has not yet run its full course. Others see the Crusades as another wing of the *Drang nach Osten*.[2] Still others see the Crusades as primarily a demonstration of European strength against the Moslem invader, whether in the eastern Mediterranean, in Spain and Sicily, or elsewhere, a demonstration which was more powerful and more popular because of the conviction of many that all Christendom in this instance faced a deadly peril, the military strength of an aggressive alien religion whose members could not be converted and therefore must be conquered. (Is a comparison with the modern world valid, substituting communism for Islam?)

Expansion of Papal Power

The Crusades are usually thought of as a great religious movement having the many and extensive pilgrimages of the earlier period as

---

1. British commander of Egyptian Expeditionary Force 2. "Drive to the East;" a reference to European Colonialism.

their background but called into action and dominated by the popes. Their professed objective was always the restoration of the holy places in Palestine to Christian control, but their real but less advertised objective seems to have been the reunion of the Greek Orthodox Church with the Roman, under papal control. Other interests of the popes were connected with their growing weakness in Italy, surrounded as they were by Normans in the south, by Moslems in Spain and in the Mediterranean, and by both city-states and German emperors in northern Italy. There may even have been papal desire, conscious or not, to provide some diversion from various activities in western Europe, monastic and secular, even including the increasingly popular pilgrimages to Saint James of Compostella.

In any case the popes spurred on the faithful, especially kings and princes, throughout the twelfth century, to go on crusade and furnished papal legates for leadership. It was generally believed that participation in the conquest of the earthly Jerusalem was one way, and perhaps the surest way, to qualify for the heavenly one. Crusaders received indulgences, protection for their property while absent, and the right to be tried only in ecclesiastical courts. Even the monastic energies of the period were provided for in the military orders, which managed a rather incredible and certainly an uneasy combination of monasticism and militarism. Saint Bernard, who felt as did Anselm[3] that monks should stay in their monasteries, not only preached the Second Crusade (in a spectacular setting at Vézelay), but also wrote the charter for the Templars.[4] The exploits of the other well-known orders, such as the Hospitallers and the Teutonic Knights, were matched in smaller areas by the lesser known Spanish orders of Calatrava, Santiago, and Alcantara. Thus the scope of the Crusades became broader geographically than the conquest of Palestine. All of this redounded to the prestige of the Church under papal leadership. The contrast between the status of Pope Urban II in 1096 and that of Pope Innocent III in 1215 is explained to a significant degree by the Crusades.

It is true of course that the Crusades were never wholly religious at any time and were much less so by the middle of the twelfth century and very nearly entirely secular by its end. But this was true of Europe as a whole, which was becoming more secular with each passing generation. The fanatical zeal of the Gregorian [monastic] movement was wearing rather thin by the end of the century and had itself been altered in both objectives and procedures. Some of this may have been due to mounting criticism of the Crusades as such; some of it was probably the result of much opposition to the Church itself. Some of it was surely caused by the universal dislike of taxa-

3. Saint Anselm was archbishop of Canterbury from 1093 to 1109. 4. Knights of a religious order who protected the Crusader States in Palestine from the Moslems.

tion, ecclesiastical and secular, much of it necessitated by the Crusades. How much of it was disillusion resulting from the deflection of the crusading spirit to political objectives nearer home, in southern France, in the Germanies, and elsewhere, is more problematical. The twelfth-century intelligentsia was still mainly clerical, but a literate laity was growing rapidly. By 1200 there was at least some idea of converting the infidel as against military action, as the early career of Saint Francis [of Assisi] indicates.

The Dark Side of the Crusades

The results of the Crusades in expanding the European horizon, in the development of trade and the towns, in the increasingly successful formation of bureaucratic secular states due in part to the absence, sometimes permanently, of powerful lords and other privileged persons, in the development of heraldry, and in the introduction of new tastes in food, clothing, and musical instruments, together with a new awareness of various creature comforts—all these things and much else have found their way long since into most of our books. The suggestion that the silver mines of Germany and Hungary financed the Crusades has been made more than once. But the unfortunate results of the Crusades are less often stressed sufficiently. The Crusades, over the two hundred years of their major activities, gave to Europe and the European world a legacy of intolerance, fanaticism, anti-Semitism, brutality, and political and military conquest in the name of religion.

The sack of Jerusalem in the First Crusade and of Constantinople in the Fourth, almost incredible in their well-documented details even to readers well acquainted with twentieth-century exploits of the same kind, were not isolated events. Crusading armies, saturated with religious fanaticism and human greed, spread rape and rapine all over Europe, at their point of departure upon many occasions, often along the route to their objectives: Palestine, southern France, Spain, the Germanies and the Baltic lands, and many parts of Hungary and the Balkans. These things may not have been new, but the Crusades gave them a vigor which ensured their continuation in European history. The use of assassination for both political and religious purposes was not unknown in European Christendom, but the contacts of the Crusaders with the sizable group in Asia Minor called "The Assassins" may have perfected European techniques in such procedures.

Other aspects of the Crusades have been too much neglected in all books written in western languages. This is notably true in regard to the results of the Crusades in eastern Europe and in the Slavic world generally. It is true that the Mongol invasions of the early thirteenth century were mainly responsible for the practically complete destruction of the Kievan state [present-day Russia], which had earlier been in fairly active communication with the west by monastic contacts through Poland and Hungary, by economic contacts via Regensburg and Bari, and by matrimonial alliances with almost every royal court in western Europe and even with some ducal families. But the Crusades had already by the late twelfth century seriously diminished all these contacts. The Crusaders preferred more and more the Mediterranean Sea routes to the Near East, thus ruling out to a large extent the work of the Jewish merchants in maintaining and developing western overland trade with the east, mainly through Regensburg.

The Crusades built up enormously the previous antagonisms of the Greek and Roman Churches, partly by keeping alive and continually fomenting the mutual suspicion and contempt of both sides prior to 1204, and, finally, by that catastrophic event. The east never forgot or forgave the sack of Constantinople in that year.

Furthermore, the partial destruction of the Byzantine Empire, culminating in 1204 after more than a half century of stress and turmoil within and without the imperial boundaries, broke the main contacts of the Slavs of eastern Europe with the Mediterranean area. The result was that Russia went its separate way for a long time, escaping complete subjection to the Moslems only by shifting the center of gravity of the Russian state from the southwest to the Muscovite northeast, leaving the other Slavic states, Bohemia, Poland, and the Balkan states very much to their own devices as border states of both the east and the west. Muscovite Russia built up new contacts with the west via Novgorod and the Hanseatic cities of northern Germany, a very different area from the Mediterranean with which Kievan Russia had had such a close relationship.

Many Changes

Many other features of the Crusades call for attention and are revealing as to twelfth-century European life. Even a list is impressive: the absence of kings on the First Crusade and the presence of three on the Third; the governmental arrangements in the Latin Kingdom of Jerusalem, which indicate the concept of feudalism in the minds of twelfth-century warriors and clerics, however unsuitable and unworkable on the Palestinian terrain; the foundation of a greater France along the routes of the Crusaders in the eastern Mediterranean (dukes of Athens and counts of Thermopylae); and the foundation of a Venetian empire, maritime and economic rather than territorial, on the eastern shores of the Adriatic and in Constantinople.

Other features would be the military exploits of the Crusaders, including the numberless castles, some of which still stand as a grim reminder of heroic twelfth-century European efforts to conquer in the east by methods which were western. Failure was due partly to insoluble logistical problems, partly to the lack of any properly unified command,

and partly to a combination of faith, greed, and folly on the one side and the great momentum of the Moslem adversary on the other. The variation in the routes of the Crusaders had long range consequences for European commercial and maritime activities, especially in naval expertise and architecture. There were some faint beginnings of toleration for the infidel among some of the Frankish soldiers who remained for more than one generation in the Latin crusading states of Palestine. The creation of the kingdom of Cyprus has been called the only permanent territorial conquest of the Crusades.

Other aspects of the Crusades which must be reckoned with by the historian would be their role in the emergence of France as the dominant country in western Europe in the next century, their effect upon the writing of history and on literature generally, and the consequences of their introduction into western Europe of some at least of the sensuality and the eroticism of the east. The aftermath of the Crusades on European soil was a crucial factor in the history of both Church and state in the thirteenth century. This included the Albigensian Crusade, the continuing Crusades in Spain, but also the smaller Crusades in Italy and the Germanies, frequently fought for private reasons under the aegis of the crusading idea, whether against heretics, rival cities, papal or imperial enemies, or against pagans, as in the case of the Wends and Prussians on the northeastern boundaries of the Germanies. Perhaps the most important aspect of the Crusades was that strength they gave to the papacy during most of the twelfth century which goes far to explain the ecclesiastical monarchy which reached its height at the end of the real crusading period under [Pope] Innocent III. . . .

The Crusades were not only the greatest achievement of the medieval papacy, but the First Crusade was also the first and possibly the only near approach to a united action by all Europe in its recorded history. That Crusade included the west and Byzantium. The popes then and later sent bulls to eastern and even northeastern Europe urging the Crusade against pagans and Moslems and offered the usual concessions to Crusaders, although they must have realized that such crusading action would not reach Palestine except under very special conditions. The fear of the Moslem may actually have been exaggerated through ignorance of all the facts, but it was there and, combined with other factors already alluded to, made the Crusades an enormously popular enterprise. That it satisfied the curiosity of all classes and gave them an opportunity for travel were valuable extra dividends.

A Colossal Failure

Then why did the Crusades fail? Only the First had any real success, and this was temporary. When the Crusades were over, Cyprus remained as the only permanent conquest. Professor Constable, in his examination of the Second Crusade, has stressed the breadth of the operations involved—five expeditions against the Moslems of Palestine, four against the pagan Wends across the Elbe, four campaigns against the Moslems in Spain, the conquest of Tripoli and Tunis by Roger of Sicily (who cared little for the Crusade but much for a bridge to north Africa)—all carried on simultaneously in the years from 1146 to 1148. Yet ten years later only Lisbon and Tortosa were still held by Christian rulers. He also points out that the Crusade was preached by Saint Bernard, was supported by the powerful Cistercian Order, and had the blessing of all the higher clergy and the cooperation of most of the rulers of Europe.

Failure seems to have come from the facts that there never was a unified command, that papal legates accompanying the crusading armies had too much authority and too little military expertise, and that there were always too many side issues, both in Palestine and in Europe. Campaigns in Spain, in Germany, and even in England (Anglo-Norman versus the Irish) and antagonism of the north against the south in France certainly overextended western European energy and resources that might have been directed to the Crusade in the eastern Mediterranean. The resources of a really united Christian Europe might have checked the Moslems significantly.

Main reasons for the failure of the Crusades in Palestine may have been that they always fought a limited war there and that they always used the strategy, the tactics, and even the weapons to which they were accustomed on their own home grounds against an enemy skilled in other methods and differently equipped. And the Crusaders made the same mistakes, again and again. They never constituted a really professional army. They never had troops enough. There was always too much reliance on mercenaries. They never understood the Moslems, considering them violent, brutal, deceitful, sexually immoral, and chained to the Koran, which they thought to be fictitious, confused, and full of error. Some tolerance was forthcoming for the Moslem by those who remained long in the country, but there was none evidenced by those, the great majority, who went home as soon as the campaign was over.

More important for the modern student is the obvious fact that the Crusaders in the end destroyed the thing they came to save and left the Christians of Palestine to more complete control by the Moslem. They also helped powerfully in the virtual destruction of the Byzantine Empire and, in the process, made the separation of the two Churches substantially final.

Contact with another culture was something the Crusades did produce, but the results for Europe were mainly in wider geographical knowledge, in acquaintance with vegetables and gardens previously unknown in western Europe, and in some new ideas in clothing, music, and architecture. A military expedition is not a good channel for intellectual and cultural transmission: most of the Byzantine and Moslem contribution along these lines actually came to Europe through Spain and, to a lesser degree, through southern Italy. There were new words in all European languages because of the Crusades, and there was much new material for the writing of history and for vernacular literatures. There was, in fact, hardly a household in Europe even at the end of the Middle Ages which did not possess some object "liberated" from the Moslem in the twelfth century and hardly a church in Christendom that did not possess at least one holy relic probably rescued from the hands of schismatics at Constantinople in 1204.

The Crusades were neither pure idealism nor unadulterated cynicism. They were in a sense a papal and a Frankish solution for what the modern world would call the Eastern Question. They may have given Europeans their first idea of territorial unity, but the concept was fragile and without sustained emotional content.

Crusading Knights: Knights Templar and Hospitaler

Frances Gies

Frances Gies and her husband, Joseph Gies, have written numerous books together on the Middle Ages including *Life in the Medieval Castle, Marriage and the Family in the Middle Ages*, and *Life in the Medieval City*. According to Gies, the Order of the Knights Templar was established to protect pilgrims traveling from Europe to the Holy Land. During the Crusades, however, the Templars' mission expanded to protect the Christian strongholds that were erected around Jerusalem. The Templars were recognized by the church and enjoyed widespread popularity throughout Europe. Gies claims that numerous establishments were founded in Europe to raise money and volunteers for the Order. Because of the Templars' popularity, other knights like the Hospitalers began to imitate them, according to Gies. The Hospitalers first established a hospital to aid pilgrims traveling to Jerusalem, but when the Crusades began, they became a military order and—like the Templars—protected Christian strongholds in Moslem territory. Gies maintains that the Templars and Hospitalers were so powerful that they were successful for many years in frustrating the Moslem leader Saladin's efforts to reclaim the Holy Land for the Moslems.

After the First Crusade, the bulk of the responsibility for maintaining the Christian presence in the Holy Land was borne by members of the Military Orders. In the eyes of the Church, the brother knights of these institutions were par excellence "soldiers of Christ," the epitome of chivalry.

Holy Knights

The Orders' original mission was the protection of pilgrims visiting the shrines of the Holy Land. To this duty was soon added what became their chief purpose: garrisoning the conquered land against a persistent and numerous enemy. The Order of the Temple was founded in about 1119 by two knights, Hugues de Payns, from Champagne, and Geoffrey de St. Omer, from Artois. The two men swore poverty, chastity, and obedience before the patriarch of Jerusalem and announced their mission of protecting and aiding pilgrims. First known as "the poor knights of the Temple of Solomon," from its location in Jerusalem, the Order was supported by two great Crusading lords, Hugues, count of Champagne, and Fulk, count of Anjou, and it was recognized by the Church at the Council of Troyes in 1128, which commissioned Bernard of Clairvaux, founder of the Cistercian Order, to draw up a Rule for it. After the Council, a group of Templars led by the two founders toured France and England soliciting recruits and grants of land. Bernard's Rule, adapted from that of the Cistercians, proved exceptionally appropriate for a military order. The Templars' discipline on the march and in battle quickly marked them as the elite troops in any Crusading army.

Largely thanks to the support of Bernard of Clairvaux, the Order soon enjoyed a popularity in Europe beyond its founders' dreams. At the request of Hugues de Payns in the early 1130s, St. Bernard wrote a tract, *In Praise of the New Chivalry*, acclaiming the concept of a fighting brotherhood dedicated to Christ. The worldly chivalry of the past was sinful—"*non dico militiae, sed malitiae*," "I do not call it a militia but an evil." He drew a vivid picture: worldly knights covered themselves with ornaments like women—silk cloths for their horses; tunics for their hauberks; painted lances, shields, and saddles; and reins and spurs decorated with gold, silver, and precious stones. "Clad in such pomp, in shameless fury and thoughtless stupidity you hasten to your deaths," and all for a cause "so light and frivolous that it terrifies the conscience." In contrast, the Templars risked no sin in killing since their enemies were enemies of Christ; their killing was "not homicide but malicide." Their lives were governed by discipline that Bernard himself had prescribed; they owned no private possessions, avoided all excess in food and clothing, and lived "as a single community in a single house, eager to preserve unity of spirit in a bond of peace." Besides shunning such vanities and follies as gaming, hunting, storytelling, and worldly entertainment, they scorned the care for personal appearance that other knights affected, wearing their hair cut short, leaving their beards un-combed, and riding to battle shaggy, dusty, darkened by sunburn, to "seek not glory but victory . . . meeker than lambs and fiercer than lions." At once monks and knights, "they vigilantly and faithfully guard . . . the Holy Sepulchre."

Influential Knights

The Temple won a succession of exemptions and privileges, financial, spiritual, and administrative, that freed it of numerous taxes and even-tually made it independent of all ecclesiastical authority except that of the pope, indeed, immune from all jurisdiction other than papal. Its in-creasing privilege followed and accompanied its growing wealth. Indi-vidual Templars owned nothing, but gifts and bequests of every de-scription poured in to the Order in Europe and the Holy Land: lands, serfs, cattle, mills, winepresses, money, and goods. "Temples," estab-lishments in the form of fortified structures, often of masonry, were founded throughout France, England, Spain, Germany, and Italy. Ma-jor facilities were built in the cities, smaller centers in the countryside. All were organized into provinces, each with its Master and Comman-der. The purpose of these European establishments was to supply the Temple in the Holy Land with two things: money and soldiers.

Most of the rural establishments were headed by two or three members of the Order, who were not knights but minor officials called *frères casaliers*, and who administered the local estates and supervised the agricultural laborers. The urban centers were manned by knights, sergeants, and priests, as well as servants. The largest and most important in Europe was the commandery in Paris, a strong ma-sonry keep with towers, located on the Right Bank. Its spacious walls enclosed a chapel built with a rotunda in imitation of the Church of the Holy Sepulchre in Jerusalem. Besides the Temple Enclosure, the Paris commandery owned entire streets in the city. In London the Templars built a commandery and a church with a rotunda in Hol-born, then in the middle of the twelfth century moved south to the bank of the Thames, where they constructed the New Temple in the form of a large church in Gothic style but, like other Templar churches, distinctively round in form. The establishment eventually included several small chapels and two large halls, one, a "hall of priests" used for meetings of the chapter, connected to the church by a cloister, the other a "hall of knights," where the knights lived; across the Thames was a fifteen–acre field used by the Templars for military exercises. Most towns, in England as in Europe, had a Tem-plar commandery, usually with a round church about which clustered the Templar community.

But the vital center of the vast network remained the house in Jerusalem, near the Golden Gate and the Dome of the Rock. A German pilgrim of 1165, John of Würzburg, was impressed by the great stables that could lodge "more than two thousand horses or a thousand five hundred camels," and the "new and magnificent church which was not finished when I visited it"—St. Mary Lateran. The refectory, which the Templars called the "palace," was a huge Gothic structure, its vaulted roof supported by columns, its walls covered with trophies taken from the enemy: swords, helmets, painted shields, and gilded coats of mail. At mealtimes trestle tables were set up and spread with linen cloths; the flagstone floor was covered with rushes. Between the palace and the church stood the dormitories, corridors of monkish cells furnished with a chair or stool, a chest, and a bed with mattress, bolster, sheet, and blanket.The sergeants slept in a common room. The complex included an infirmary; individual houses for the officers; a "marshalsy" or armory where weapons, armor, and harness were kept and where mail and helmets were forged and horses shod; tile draper's establishment, where cloth was stored and clothing and shoes made; and the kitchens. Excavated into the rock were deep wells, and there were vast cellars for the storage of grain and fodder. Outside the city the Temple maintained cattle, horse, and sheep farms.

The Templar organization created an incessant traffic between Europe and the Holy Land, shipping gold, silver, cloth, armor, and horses to the East, whence returned brothers on missions to the West, sick or elderly knights on leave, visiting officers on tours of inspection. A stream of messengers traveled in both directions.

The total number of Knights Templars in the Holy Land at any one time was never large. Figures in the thousands given by the chroniclers for battles were typically exaggerated and included sergeants, vassals, mercenaries, and native auxiliaries called Turcopoles. The number of knights engaged in a single battle rarely exceeded four hundred. The total of Templars in Europe also was numbered in the hundreds, at most one or two thousand.

Knights Hospitalers

The extraordinary success of the Templars and St. Bernard's promotion of the Order soon led to imitations. The Hospital of St. John of Jerusalem, founded before the First Crusade by merchants from Amalfi as a hospice for pilgrims, staffed by Benedictine monks, began during the Second Crusade (1146–1149) to take part in fighting. By the mid–twelfth century it had become a Military Order, while retaining its philanthropic character, and the dual role was formalized in 1206. Between 1164 and 1170 the Orders of Calatrava, Santiago, and Alcantara were established to fight the Moors in Spain and Portugal. A hospital set up in Acre by German merchants from Lübeck and Bremen in 1190, during the Third Crusade, adopted the

Rule of the Hospitalers and was recognized as an independent order. In 1198 it was transformed into the Order of Teutonic Knights, which, however, did most of its fighting in Europe, in the Baltic region.

For a century and a half the defense of the Christian European bridgehead in Asia Minor was primarily in the hands of the garrisons of Templars, Hospitalers, and Teutonic Knights. But whenever a new Crusade was undertaken, the knights of the Orders were obliged to submit to the leadership, usually royal or imperial, of the expedition's head. The arrangement did not always work smoothly. Men who spent their lives in the Holy Land often had a differ-

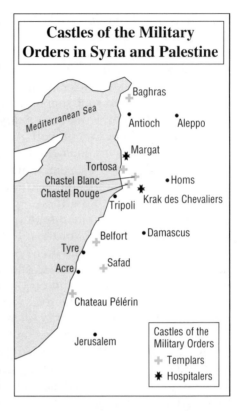

Castles of the Military Orders in Syria and Palestine

Baghras

Mediterranean Sea

Antioch   Aleppo

Margat

Tortosa

Chastel Blanc

Chastel Rouge

Homs

Tripoli   Krak des Chevaliers

Belfort   • Damascus

Tyre

Acre   Safad

Chateau Pélérin

Jerusalem

Castles of the Military Orders

✚ Templars

✱ Hospitalers

ent perception of the military and political situation from the leaders of the Crusade and therefore favored a different strategy. More, their self-interest might diverge from that of Crusaders bent on achieving an immediate and perhaps chimerical objective. An ill-conceived Crusading operation might end by leaving the permanent garrison of the country worse off than it had been to start with. Crusaders returned home, but the Military Orders remained, a small Christian island in a stormy Muslim sea. Often, however, the superior experience of the Orders was recognized and deferred to. In 1148, in the Second Crusade, Louis VII of France prevailed upon his knights to place themselves under the orders of the Templar officers, who divided them into squadrons and trained them to endure attack without being drawn into pursuit, to attack only under orders, to rally to the main body of the army on signal, and to maintain a fixed order of march.

The Military Orders and Saladin

The Orders were prominent in the Christian resistance against Saladin, the great sultan who united the Muslims in the last quarter of the twelfth century for a major Islamic offensive. Checked at Ascalon in 1177 and a year later at Jacob's Ford on the northern frontier of the Kingdom of Jerusalem, Saladin gained a decisive victory at Hattin in 1187. Some two hundred Templar and Hospitaler prisoners, including the Masters of both Orders, were executed at Saladin's command because they were "the firebrands of the Franks," and "these more than all the other Franks destroy the Arab religion and slaughter us." Jerusalem fell at once, and the Third Crusade was organized in Europe in an attempt to recover it. When the Crusaders arrived, the Military Orders placed themselves formally under the command of Richard Lionheart, but actually they served as the English king's chief advisers. Though the Crusade failed to recover Jerusalem, it established the Military Orders as major powers in Syria. Once again, the Crusaders, French, English, and German, went home, and the Templars and Hospitalers remained.

But unlike most of the handful of European settlers, with the exception of the Italian merchant colonies on the coast, they were backed by important resources in Europe, and Saladin and his successors had no easy time dislodging them. The most significant contribution the three great Orders made to the defense of the Holy Land was to build (or rebuild), maintain, and garrison the frontier castles. These massive masonry fortresses represented the full development of medieval military science. Only the Military Orders were rich and powerful enough to keep them constantly manned and in fighting trim. At most strategic points, strongholds, perhaps in ruins, already existed. These were taken over, enlarged, and given the most up-to-date elaboration. Where necessary, castles were built from scratch. The Templars' largest fortress, the castle of Tortosa, in the county of Tripoli, was part of the defenses of the city of Tortosa, its concentric curtain walls overlooking the Mediterranean. It withstood Saladin's attack in 1188. Second in importance, Chateau Pélérin (Pilgrim Castle) was built in 1218 with the aid of the Teutonic Knights on a rocky promontory south of Acre. Surrounded on three sides by the sea, it was protected toward the mainland by three lines of defense, a moat with a low wall, a second wall with three rectangular towers, and a bailey (courtyard) defended by two towers 110 feet high in a massive curtain wall. Chateau Pélérin was never taken by the Muslims. Other Templar castles included Safad, east of Acre, Belfort, Chastel Rouge, Chastel Blanc, Baghras, and La Roche Guillaume.

The most famous of all the Crusader castles was the Krak des Chevaliers, northeast of Tripoli. An Arab castle on the site was captured by the Crusaders in 1110. A vassal of the count of Tripoli occupied it until 1142, when the count ceded it to the Hospitalers, who built a huge concentric fortress, its two rings of massive walls dominated by great towers and separated by a wide moat. The Hospitalers' other important castle, Margat, between Latakia and Tripoli,

ceded to them by its baronial owner in 1186, was built on a mountain spur, with a double line of fortifications and a great circular
tower that a thirteenth–century pilgrim described as seeming "to support the heavens, rather than exist for defense." Saladin found both
the Krak des Chevaliers and Margat too strong to attack.

Ties to the Holy Land

The Orders' military power inevitably involved them in the politics of
the Crusader states. They took sides in the successional disputes of the
Holy Land and in political conflicts imported from Europe. Usually the
Hospitalers and Templars were ranged on opposite sides. In the early
thirteenth century, when the Guelf-Ghibelline (papal-imperial) quarrel
manifested itself in Syria, the Templars were Guelf, the Hospitalers
Ghibelline. Sometimes the quarrel went beyond words, as in the 1240s
when the Orders battled alongside members of the Italian merchant
communes, the Templars on the side of the Guelf Genoese and Vene-
tians, the Hospitalers on that of the Ghibelline Pisans.

The Templars' fund-raising activities led them into an incongru-
ous enterprise: banking. They began by lending money to finance
pilgrims and Crusaders. The first record of a Templar loan is in 1135,
to a couple who turned over their property in Saragossa, "houses,
lands, vineyards, gardens, and all that we possess," against a loan
that would allow them to make their pilgrimage to the Holy Sepulchre. The land was to be returned when the debt was repaid, the Templars realizing the revenues of the property in the meantime. Thus
despite the Church's prohibition of usury, the Order received disguised interest. From this modest beginning, it was only a decade to
a huge loan to Louis VII for the Second Crusade. Besides lending
money to clients, the Templars guarded and transported money and
valuables. Monasteries had traditionally filled these roles of money-
lender and safety deposit, but the Templars, with their estates and
alms, their commandery-fortresses and military strength, soon pre-
empted the business, contributing, in the view of some historians, to
the development of modern credit practices.

In Europe, both Templars and Hospitalers served as advisers, messengers, envoys, and sometimes arbiters for the kings of France, England, and Germany. In the Holy Land they practiced diplomacy not
only among the Christian states, but with the Muslim powers, for
others and on their own behalf. As permanent residents in Asia Minor, the Military Orders had an interest in the balance-of-power politics of strong Muslim states such as Damascus and Egypt, and did
not scruple to form alliances with one or another. Consequently, despite their undisputed military skill and valor, they were often regarded with suspicion in Europe. A chronicler reported French prince
Robert of Artois exclaiming, "See the ancient treachery of the Tem-

plars! The long-known sedition of the Hospitalers!" The Orders' advice in councils of war often conflicted with the very aims of the Crusaders. In the Third Crusade they actually dissuaded Richard Lionheart from attempting to retake Jerusalem, and when German emperor Frederick II successfully treatied with Egypt in 1229 for the peaceful return of the Holy City, Templars and Hospitalers opposed the move. The recovery of Jerusalem was actually undesirable to them because the city, no longer fortified, was difficult to defend. Their position was somewhat vindicated when on the expiration of a truce in 1239 the Muslims easily took back the city, but in Europe the Orders were widely perceived as having "gone native."

Some Templars and Hospitalers indeed had learned Arabic, and both Orders maintained friendly relations with Arab informants. The Syrian writer Usama (1095–1188) recounted an incident: "Whenever I went into [the al-Aqsa Mosque], which was in the hands of Templars who were friends of mine, they would put [a little chapel] at my disposal, so that I could say my prayers there. One day I had gone in, said the Allah akhbar, and risen to begin my prayers, when a Frank [Crusader] threw himself on me from behind, lifted me up, and turned me so that I was facing east. 'That is the way to pray!' he said. Some Templars at once intervened, seized the man, and took him out of my way, while I resumed my prayer. But the moment they stopped watching him he seized me again and forced me to face east, repeating that this was the way to pray. Again the Templars intervened and took him away. They apologized to me and said: 'He is a foreigner who has just arrived today from his homeland in the north, and he has never seen anyone pray facing any other direction than east.' 'I have finished my prayers,' I said, and left, stupefied by the fanatic who had been so perturbed and upset to see someone praying facing [Mecca]!"

The Islamic Reaction to the Crusades

P.H. Newby

The European Christians who embarked on the first Crusades in order to reclaim the Holy Land from the Moslems were motivated by political, economic, and religious concerns. One of their most important aims in securing the Holy Land, according to P.H. Newby, was to protect the European Christians who were making pilgrimages to Jerusalem. The Moslems also viewed the region around Jerusalem as holy, but they did not at first see European Christians as a threat. Newby argues that it was not until the brutal Turkish ruler Zengi, initiated a counter-crusade and reclaimed the city of Edessa that Moslems began to consider the Christians who made pilgrimages to Edessa and the other holy lands around Jerusalem as enemies. After his death, his son continued to fight the Christians, but Nur al-Din was motivated by purer and largely religious concerns. Nur al-Din succeeded in taking Damascus in the second Crusade, according to Newby. After his death, his lieutenant—Saladin—continued the battle against the Christians. By unifying Syria and Egypt and relying on them for money and soldiers, Saladin was able to reclaim the Holy Land for the Moslems in 1187. P.H. Newby is the author of several books about the Middle East and Egypt including *Warrior Pharaohs: The Rise and Fall of the Egyptian Empire*.

Excerpted from *Saladin in His Time* (London: Faber & Faber, 1983) by P.H. Newby. Copyright © 1983 by P.H. Newby. Reprinted with permission from David Higham Associates.

The success of the First Crusade in 1097 did not cause as much despondency among Moslems as a whole as might be expected, although the butchering of the inhabitants of Jerusalem [by European Christians] was not forgotten. Little was known in Baghdad about Western Europe. At first the Crusade was thought of as just another of the Byzantine Emperor's forays. Even the Fatimids,[1] who had once counted Sicily as their province, still traded extensively with the Italian states and should therefore have known better, misunderstood the invaders' intentions and tried to negotiate a division of territory in Syria and Palestine with them. Moslems thought they were threatened more by divisions within their own world than by this attack from the West. What is evident from the Western point of view is that the Crusaders were lucky in their timing.

Had they arrived a few years earlier the formidable Seljuk[2] Sultan Malik Shah would have been alive and events might have turned out differently. But Malik Shah died in 1092 and his sons fought for the succession in a way that showed they were indifferent to anything but securing the real centres of power which they located in Iraq and Persia. By the time the various Turkish successors to the Seljuks had established themselves as independent rulers in such centres as Mosul and Aleppo, the Crusaders were in firm possession of conquered territories: the Principality of Edessa (dangerously far to the east), Antioch, Tripoli and the Kingdom of Jerusalem itself. Even so they never succeeded in taking that key military city in North Syria, Aleppo, nor the rich city of Damascus, and so controlling the trading and military routes across the desert between Mesopotamia and the Nile valley.

The first Crusaders had many motives, political and economic as well as religious, but the one with broadest appeal was the securing of freedom for Christian pilgrims to visit the Holy Places. In earlier times this had not been a great issue. Except for the period of the mad Fatimid Caliph al-Hakim (996–1021) who demolished the Holy Sepulchre in 1009, pilgrims were welcomed and money made out of them; but when the Turks took over from the Fatimids a new spirit of intolerance was shown and pilgrims had a rough time, particularly those from the West. The Church of the Holy Sepulchre (rebuilt by the Byzantine Emperor) and the Holy Places at Bethlehem and Nazareth had, after a period when the Latin Church controlled them, now reverted to the guardianship of the Byzantine Emperor and the Orthodox Church, and they had their own reasons for treating pilgrims who observed the Roman rite as not being fully Christian. Under Turkish overlords the Relic of the True Cross, part of

1. a Moslem dynasty that ruled over northern Africa and parts of Egypt between A.D. 909 and 1171
2. The Seljuks were members of several Turkish dynasties ruling over Asia from the eleventh to the thirteenth century.

that discovered in the time of the Emperor Constantine, was carried through the streets of Jerusalem during festivals while pilgrims of whatever Christian persuasion, Latin, Orthodox, Armenian, Coptic, Jacobite, Maronite, prostrated themselves in the dust, much to the scorn of the Turkish and other Moslem soldiers who regarded them as idolators and spat accordingly.

There is not much evidence in the early years of the twelfth century, when a Christian king reigned in Jerusalem, that Moslems regarded the recovery of that city as a great religious duty. To Western Christendom it had been intolerable that the land of Christ's ministry, and particularly the city of his death and resurrection, should be in the hands of Moslems. It was intolerable, too, for Jews that the site of Solomon's temple should be profaned by the rituals of all alien creed. But although Moslems venerated the city because of the references to it in the Koran and in certain Traditions they did not, to begin with, yearn to possess it as a religious necessity, as they would have yearned to repossess Mecca and Medina if those holy cities had been in infidel hands.

Nevertheless Jerusalem and the Sahil (which was the rest of Palestine extending up and into modern Lebanon) was holy to Moslems for the same reason it was holy to the Jews and the Christians; it was the land of the patriarchs and the prophets. The three religions are rooted in the history of the Semitic peoples, and Mohammed, who at first hoped to persuade the Jews of Medina to accept the Koran as God's ultimate revelation of the truths imparted to Abraham and Moses, originally turned to face in the direction of Jerusalem, not Mecca, to pray. Abraham was the first Moslem, the first, that is to say, who testified to the One God who then tested his submission (the word Moslem means 'submitted') by asking him to sacrifice his son Isaac, traditionally on the sacred rock of Moriah. To this rock Mohammed was miraculously transported one night on the steed Al-Burak in the company of the Angel Gabriel. By means of a ladder of light Mohammed ascended into heaven and eventually found himself in the presence of God who gave instructions on the devotions his followers should perform. The magnificent Dome of the Rock had been built over Moriah nearly 500 years before Saladin's time by the Caliph Abd al-Malik. The scarcely less ancient Al-Aqsa Mosque (the 'farther' mosque) ranks only after the mosques at Mecca and Medina. Another place of special sanctity was the Cave of Machpelah at Hebron where Abraham, Sarah, Isaac, Rebecca, Jacob and Leah were buried. All that land between the Euphrates and the so-called River of Egypt (a wadi running down to the sea near El Arish) was regarded as having been specially blessed by God; Mohammed, according to tradition, had said it was of particular holiness, 'that is to say, purity'. It was that part of the world where for Moslems it was best to live and die.

Zengi and Nur al-Din

The man who is usually given the credit for starting the Holy War, the counter-Crusade, to recover this territory for the Moslems was Zengi, the ruler of Mosul. In 1130 he gained a bloody victory over the Crusaders just south of Aleppo. In 1144 he recovered the rich and ancient city of Edessa from the Franks [European Christians] mainly because they had dropped their guard and the city was there for the taking. It was not primarily an act of religious fervour on his part; he had spent a lot of energy not on attacking the Franks but on an abortive attempt to seize Damascus, now an independent Moslem city.

Zengi was a brutal and intemperate Turk who had shown himself an effective military leader. He had been an administrator in the service of the Caliph but his campaigning had been as a vassal of one or other of the successors to the Seljuk Sultanate, mostly against fellow-Moslems. The taking of Damascus seems to have been the height of his ambition. Then he would have been master of the three key cities of Damascus, Aleppo and Mosul, controlling movement between Mesopotamia on the one hand and the lands of Egypt, the Seljuk Sultanate of Rum and the Crusader states on the other. Thereafter he might, who knows, have attacked the Latin Kingdom but not, one feels, out of religious enthusiasm. The son who succeeded him in 1146 was, however, a very different man from his ferocious father. Nur al-Din turned out to be the ideal Moslem prince; devout, a great believer in the equality of all men before God and the law, of simple even austere tastes, and a good soldier. It was in his time that the idea of recovering Jerusalem so that it could be purified of the unbelievers gained momentum. Christian reverence for the Holy Places to some extent fed Moslem reverence for their sacred precinct there, the *haram*. Nur al-Din ordered a pulpit to be made against the day he entered Jerusalem in triumph and could install it in the Al-Aqsa Mosque. But the time was not ripe, partly because the Franks had good leadership and partly because Nur al-Din could not keep a sufficiently large fighting force together for any length of time.

Zengi's other sons acknowledged Nur al-Din's suzerainty and ruled in their various cities in North Syria and in the 'island' (Jezireh) between the great bend of the Euphrates and the Tigris. The Turkish emirs who served them and their overlord had been well rewarded for their loyalty. They were proud of being Turkish and proud of serving such a successful family as the Zengids. This did not prevent them from siding with one brother against another when quarrels broke out, or even changing sides to secure some advantage. But it was a more settled world than the one Zengi himself had been born into. There was more money about, trade began to prosper again and the Turkish emirs saw these benefits as the natural consequence of Zengid power. To usurp the Zengid succession would cause resentment and it was Saladin's destiny to do just that.

Nur al-Din and the other Zengids had no support from Egypt where the once powerful Fatimid Caliphate had degenerated to the point where an individual caliph might rule little more than his own Twin Palaces and viziers fought civil wars. The political divide between Egypt and Syria was a source of strength to the Frankish states. They could agree to a truce with one of them and attack the other, usually Egypt because it was such a rich and vulnerable country. In later years Egypt was seen by the Crusaders as the key to power in the Middle East. But not yet. Their eyes were too firmly fixed on the Holy Places. The Moslems also, even in Nur al-Din's time when a Holy War to drive the Franks out of Palestine began to grip their imagination, had no grand strategy. Nur al-Din had no thought of invading Egypt as a preliminary to an attack on Jerusalem. If he marched on the Nile the Franks, as he saw it, would march into Syria behind his back. He could not fight both the Fatimids and the Franks at the same time. When it did come, the Syrian take-over of Egypt was reluctant.

Saladin and the Crusader States

In the middle of the century the Crusader states were reasonably well united under good leadership while the Moslems were divided. As time went by these positions were reversed. The Franks ran into trouble over the succession in the Latin Kingdom, there was tension between the old families established there since the First Crusade and newcomers from Europe; power was increasingly assumed by the military orders, the [knights] Templars and Hospitallers, who acknowledged no authority but the pope and quarrelled with each other. The Moslems, however, moved from disunity to unity and this was largely due to Zengi and his son Nur al-Din. The case of Damascus is instructive. The city was so independent it regularly collaborated with the Franks and presented no great threat to them. But after the Second Crusade of 1147 which, ironically, had the city as its principal objective, it was taken over by Nur al-Din. After that, first of all under Nur al-Din and even more so under Saladin it was a main base in the fight to drive the Franks out.

The most dramatic step towards mobilizing Moslem resources against the Franks was the hesitant annexation of Egypt by Syria and the end of the Fatimid Caliphate in 1171. For the first time it was possible to think of the Latin Kingdom of Jerusalem being caught in Moslem pincers. Saladin's part in this, as Nur al-Din's lieutenant, set him on the road to empire. He had no thought of it before going down to Egypt where it was almost as though he stumbled on the realities of power. The security of his own position among the Moslems actually required a war against the Latin Kingdom; and the wealth of Egypt, in men and materials and gold, was necessary to wage it successfully. The unexpected death of Nur al-Din meant that Saladin's main hope of holding Egypt and Syria together was as Nur al-Din's spiritual successor; it was politically necessary for him to establish the same kind of moral ascendancy. His advantage over Nur al-Din was his ability to command the wealth of Egypt as well as the regiments of Syria and the Jezireh.

It detracts in no way from Saladin's achievement that the wind veered in favour of the Moslems and against the Franks during his lifetime. A lesser man could not have held together the sometimes conflicting ambitions of his supporters or won enemies over to his side. His triumph was personal and darkened at the end only by the sober expectation that it was too personal to be lasting.

The romantic Western legend of Saladin was given a new impetus by Sir Walter Scott's *The Talisman*, and even Lane-Poole's scholarly biography of 1898 is under its influence. It has provoked modern historians into a certain amount of debunking. So far from being the noble champion of Islam he was, they say, an ambitious and ruthless man whose main purpose was to establish an empire for himself and members of his family, even if it meant fighting fellow-Moslems as vigorously as he fought the Franks. Up to a point this is feasible but it leaves the near anarchy of the time out of the reckoning. Saladin was only reluctantly ambitious to begin with. Once having established himself he could survive only by anticipating the inevitable threats to his position. A leader could not be virtuously passive and remain a leader, or even alive. Saladin is a more credible personality if he is seen as a man with the wit and ability to maintain the initiative, admittedly in a way that served his own interests, while serving genuinely the interests of Islam as a whole. As Sir John Hackett has said in a review of the most recent work of scholarship, *Saladin: The Politics of the Holy War*, by M.C. Lyons and D.E.P. Jackson: 'In the bloodstained jungle of twelfth-century Syria the Saladin of *The Talisman* would hardly have stood a chance.'

The Crusaders Through the Eyes of a Muslim

Usama ibn Munqidh

Usama ibn Munqidh was a cultured Muslim whose life spanned almost the whole of the twelfth century. Usama wrote memoirs in which he recorded his encounters with the Christians—also called Franks—who occupied the Holy Land during the era of the Crusades. His memoirs consist of both anecdotes and references to historical events that portray Christians as pious, and Christian knights as well-respected and powerful. Usama also recounts a darker side of the Crusaders that includes cruelty, religious intolerance, and dishonesty. In general, Usama had respect for the Christians who had been living with the Muslims the longest—for they adopted many local customs and made friends with the Islamic people—but held contempt for the Christians newly arrived to the Holy Land. The newcomers, according to Usama, had no respect for the Muslims and treated them poorly.

A mong the Franks—God damn them!—no quality is more highly esteemed in a man than military prowess. The knights have a monopoly of the positions of honour and importance among them, and no one else has any prestige in their eyes. They are the men who give counsel, pass judgment and command the armies. On one occasion I went to law with one of them about some herds that the

Prince of Baniyās seized in a wood; this was at a time when there was a truce between us, and I was living in Damascus. I said to King Fulk, the son of Fulk: 'This man attacked and seized my herd. This is the season when the cows are in calf; their young died at birth, and he has returned the herd to me completely ruined.' The King turned to six or seven of his knights and said: 'Come, give a judgment on this man's case.' They retired from the audience chamber and discussed the matter until they all agreed. Then they returned to the King's presence and said: 'We have decided that the Prince of Baniyās should indemnify this man for the cattle that he has ruined.' The King ordered that the indemnity should be paid, but such was the pressure put on me and the courtesy shown me that in the end I accepted four hundred *dinar*[1] from the Prince. Once the knights have given their judgment neither the King nor any other commander can alter or annul it, so great an influence do their knights have in their society. On this occasion the King swore to me that he had been made very happy the day before. When I asked him what had made him happy he said: 'They told me that you were a great knight, but I did not believe that you would be chivalrous.' 'Your Majesty', I replied, 'I am a knight of my race and my people.'[2] When a knight is tall and well-built they admire him all the more.

Frankish Piracy

I entered the service of the just King Nur ad Din—God have mercy on him!—and he wrote to al-Malik as-Salih[3] asking him to send my household and my sons out to me; they were in Egypt, under his patronage. Al-Malik as-Salih wrote back that he was unable to comply because he feared that they might fall into Frankish hands. He invited me instead to return to Egypt myself:[4] 'You know,' he wrote, 'how strong the friendship is between us. If you have reason to mistrust the Palace, you could go to Mecca, and I would send you the appointment to the governorship of Aswān and the means to combat the Abyssinians. Aswān is on the frontier of the Islamic empire. I would send your household and your sons to you there.' I spoke to Nur ad-Din about this, and asked his advice, which was that he would certainly not choose to return to Egypt once he had extricated himself. 'Life is too short!' he said. 'It would be better if I sent to the Frankish King for a safe-conduct for your family, and gave them

1. The basic monetary unit of Iraq, Kuwait, and southern Yemen. The Dinar is approximately equivalent to three and a half U.S. dollars. 2. This exchange, and the whole paragraph, depends on a play on the terms 'chivalry' and 'cavalry', for which Arabic has only one word. 3. In spite of his title ('the good king') al-Malik as-Salih was in fact the Fatimid vizier Tala'i' ibn Ruzzik, who ruled Egypt under its Caliph al-Fa'iz and died in 1161. 4. Usama was deeply implicated in the intrigues and bloody revolutions of Muslim politics; this explains the reference in one of the letters mentioned in the text to his fear of 'the Palace'.

an escort to bring them here safely.' This he did—God have mercy on him!—and the Frankish King gave him his cross, which ensures the bearer's safety by land and sea. I sent it by a young slave of mine, together with letters to al-Malik as-Salih from Nur ad-Din and myself. My family were dispatched for Damietta on a ship of the vizier's private fleet, under his protection and provided with everything they might need.

At Damietta they transferred to a Frankish ship and set sail, but when they neared Acre, where the Frankish King[5] was—God punish him for his sins—he sent out a boatload of men to break up the ship with hatchets before the eyes of my family, while he rode down to the beach and claimed everything that came ashore as booty. My young slave swam ashore with the safe-conduct, and said: 'My Lord King, is not this your safe conduct?' 'Indeed it is,' he replied, 'But surely it is a Muslim custom that when a ship is wrecked close to land the local people pillage it?' 'So you are going to make us your captives?' 'Certainly not.' He had my family escorted to a house, and the women searched. Everything they had was taken; the ship had been loaded with women's trinkets, clothes, jewels, swords and other arms, and gold and silver to the value of about 30,000 *dinar*. The King took it all, and then handed five hundred *dinar* back to them and said: 'Make your arrangements to continue your journey with this money.' And there were fifty of them altogether! At the time I was with Nur ad-Din in the realm of King Mas 'ūd,[6] at Ru-'bān and Kaisūn; compared with the safety of my sons, my brother and our women, the loss of the rest meant little to me, except for my books. There had been 4,000 fine volumes on board, and their destruction has been a cruel loss to me for the rest of my life.

Frankish Medicine

The ruler of Munáitira[7] wrote to my uncle asking him to send a doctor to treat some of his followers who were ill. My uncle sent a Christian called Thabit. After only ten days he returned and we said 'You cured them quickly!' This was his story: They took me to see a knight who had an abscess on his leg, and a woman with consumption. I applied a poultice to the leg, and the abscess opened and began to heal. I prescribed a cleansing and refreshing diet for the woman. Then there appeared a Frankish doctor, who said: 'This man has no idea how to cure these people!' He turned to the knight and said: 'Which would you prefer, to live with one leg or to die with two?' When the knight replied that he would prefer to live with one

---

5. Baldwin III (1143–62). 6. The Seljuqid Sultan of Iconium. The two forts are in the region of Samosata. These events took place in about 1155. 7. The Crusaders' *Moinestre*, in Lebanon about ten miles east of Jubáil.

leg, he sent for a strong man and a sharp axe. They arrived, and I stood by to watch. The doctor supported the leg on a block of wood, and said to the man: 'Strike a mighty blow, and cut cleanly!' And there, before my eyes, the fellow struck the knight one blow, and then another, for the first had not finished the job. The marrow spurted out of the leg, and the patient died instantaneously. Then the doctor examined the woman and said; 'She has a devil in her head who is in love with her. Cut her hair off!' This was done, and she went back to eating her usual Frankish food, garlic and mustard, which made her illness worse. 'The devil has got into her brain,' pronounced the doctor. He took a razor and cut a cross on her head, and removed the brain so that the inside of the skull was laid bare. This he rubbed with salt; the woman died instantly. At this juncture I asked whether they had any further need of me, and as they had none I came away, having learnt things about medical methods that I never knew before.[8]

The Franks and Marital Jealousy

The Franks are without any vestige of a sense of honour and jealousy. If one of them goes along the street with his wife and meets a friend, this man will take the woman's hand and lead her aside to talk, while the husband stands by waiting until she has finished her conversation. If she takes too long about it he leaves her with the other man and goes on his way. Here is an example of this from my personal experience: while I was in Nablus I stayed with a man called Mu'ízz, whose house served as an inn for Muslim travellers. Its windows overlooked the street. On the other side of the road lived a Frank who sold wine for the merchants; he would take a bottle of wine from one of them and publicize it, announcing that such-and-such a merchant had just opened a hogshead of it, and could be found at such-and-such a place by anyone wishing to buy some; '. . . and I will give him the first right to the wine in this bottle.'

Now this man returned home one day and found a man in bed with his wife. 'What are you doing here with my wife?' he demanded. 'I was tired,' replied the man, 'and so I came in to rest.' 'And how do you come to be in my bed?' 'I found the bed made up, and lay down to sleep.' 'And this woman slept with you, I suppose?' 'The bed,' he replied, 'is hers. How could I prevent her getting into her own bed?' 'I swear if you do it again I shall take you to court!'— and this was his only reaction, the height of his outburst of jealousy!

I heard a similar case from a bath attendant called Salim from Ma'arra, who worked in one of my father's bath-houses. This is his

8. Not all Frankish doctors were butchers like the fiend portrayed here, but the air of ironic superiority that this passage conveys was justified by the supremacy of the great medical tradition of the East at that time.

tale: I earned my living in Ma'arra by opening a bath-house. One day a Frankish knight came in. They do not follow our custom of wearing a cloth round their waist while they are at the baths, and this fellow put out his hand, snatched off my loin-cloth and threw it away. He saw at once that I had just recently shaved my pubic hair. 'Salim!' he exclaimed. I came toward him and he pointed to that part of me. 'Salim! It's magnificent! You shall certainly do the same for me!' And he lay down flat on his back. His hair there was as long as his beard. I shaved him, and when he had felt the place with his hand and found it agreeably smooth he said: 'Salim, you must certainly do the same for my *Dama*.' In their language *Dama* means lady, or wife. He sent his valet to fetch his wife, and when they arrived and the valet had brought her in, she lay down on her back, and he said to me: 'Do to her what you did to me.' So I shaved her pubic hair, while her husband stood by watching me. Then he thanked me and paid me for my services.

You will observe a strange contradiction in their character: they are without jealousy or a sense of honour, and yet at the same time they have the courage that as a rule springs only from the sense of honour and a readiness to take offense.

Orientalized Franks

There are some Franks who have settled in our land and taken to living like Muslims. These are better than those who have just arrived from their homelands, but they are the exception, and cannot be taken as typical. I came across one of them once when I sent a friend on business to Antioch, which was governed by Todros ibn as-Safi,[9] a friend of mine. One day he said to my friend: 'A Frankish friend has invited me to visit him; come with me so that you can see how they live.' 'I went with him,' said my friend, 'and we came to the house of one of the old knights who came with the first expedition. This man had retired from the army, and was living on the income of the property he owned in Antioch. He had a fine table brought out, spread with a splendid selection of appetizing food. He saw that I was not eating, and said: 'Don't worry, please; eat what you like, for I don't eat Frankish food. I have Egyptian cooks and eat only what they serve. No pig's flesh ever comes into my house!'[10] So I ate, although cautiously, and then we left. Another day, as I was passing through the market, a Frankish woman advanced on me, addressing me in her barbaric language with words I found incomprehensible. A crowd of Franks gathered round us and I gave myself up for lost, when suddenly this knight appeared, saw me and came up. 'What do

---

9. Theodore Sophianos, the Greek commander (*ra'is*) of the municipality of Antioch. 10. It is fear of this 'unclean' food that troubles the Muslim guest, who even when reassured eats cautiously.

you want with this man?' 'This man,' she replied, 'killed my brother Urso.' This Urso was a knight from Apamea who was killed by a soldier from Hamāt. The old man scolded the woman. 'This man is a merchant, a city man, not a fighter, and he lives nowhere near where your brother was killed.' Then he turned on the crowd, which melted away, and shook hands with me. Thus the fact that I ate at his table saved my life.

The Templars at Jerusalem

This is an example of Frankish barbarism, God damn them! When I was in Jerusalem I used to go to the Masjid al-Aqsa, beside which is a small oratory which the Franks have made into a church. Whenever I went into the mosque, which was in the hands of Templars who were friends of mine, they would put the little oratory at my disposal, so that I could say my prayers there. One day I had gone in, said the *Allāh akhbar*[11] and risen to begin my prayers, when a Frank threw himself on me from behind, lifted me up and turned me so that I was facing east. 'That is the way to pray!' he said. Some Templars at once intervened, seized the man and took him out of my way, while I resumed my prayer. But the moment they stopped watching him he seized me again and forced me to face east, repeating that this was the way to pray. Again the Templars intervened and took him away. They apologized to me and said: 'He is a foreigner who has just arrived today from his homeland in the north, and he has never seen anyone pray facing any other direction than east.' 'I have finished my prayers,' I said, and left, stupefied by the fanatic who had been so perturbed and upset to see someone praying facing the *qibla!*[12]

I was present myself when one of them came up to the amīr Mu'īn ad-Dīn—God have mercy on him—in the Dome of the Rock, and said to him: 'Would you like to see God as a baby?' The amīr said that he would, and the fellow proceeded to show us a picture of Mary with the infant Messiah on her lap. 'This,' he said, 'is God as a baby.' Almighty God is greater than the infidels' concept of him![13]

The Ransoming of Prisoners

I had sought an opportunity to visit the King of the Franks to sue for peace between him and Jamāl ad-Din Muhammad ibn Taj al-Mulūk[14]—God have mercy on him!—basing my hopes of success on a service that my late father had once performed for King Baldwin, the father of King Fulk's wife.[15] The Franks brought their pris-

11. The beginning of the canonic sequence of prayers. 12. The Muslim at prayer must face the *qibla*, the direction of Mecca. The custom of facing east to pray was widespread among mediaeval Christians. 13. A Qur'anic formula, used with particular relevance here in reporting what is to a Muslim a blasphemy. 14. The treaty of 1140 between Damascus and the Franks (see above). This passage suggests that the author had a hand in drafting the treaty. 15. Baldwin II had been the guest of the amīr of Shaizar during one of his periods of captivity, as Usama himself informs us elsewhere.

oners for me to ransom, and I ransomed those whose survival was God's will. There was a fanatic called William Jibā who had gone off to sea as a pirate in his own ship and captured a vessel carrying four hundred men and women who were coming from the Maghrib on the Pilgrimage. Some were brought before me with their owners, and I ransomed as many as I could. Among them was a young man who greeted me and then sat without speaking. I asked who he was, and was told that he was a young devout, who was owned by a tanner. 'How much do you want for this one?' I asked. 'Well,' he said, 'I shall only sell him if you buy this old man as well, for I bought them together. The price is forty-three *dinar*.' I redeemed a certain number on my own account, and another group for Mu'īn ad-Din—God have mercy on him—for a hundred and twenty *dinar*. I paid in cash as much as I had on me, and gave guarantees for the rest. On my return to Damascus I said to Mu'īn ad-Dīn: 'I redeemed some captives on your behalf for whom I could not pay cash. Now that I am back, you can pay for them yourself if you like, or if not then I will pay for them.' 'No,' he said, 'I insist on paying, for my dearest wish is to gain merit in God's eyes.' He was outstanding in his eagerness to do good and earn a heavenly reward. He paid the sum I owed the Franks, and I returned to Acre a few days later. William Jibā had thirty–two prisoners left, among them the wife of one of the men I had been able to ransom. I bought her, but did not pay for her at once. Later that day I rode to his house—God damn him!—and said to him: 'Sell me ten of these.' He swore that he would only sell the whole lot together. 'I have not brought enough money for all of them,' I said; 'I will buy some of them now and the rest later.' But he insisted that he would sell the whole group together, so I went away. That night, by God's will, they all escaped, and the inhabitants of that quarter of Acre, who were all Muslims, sheltered them and helped them to reach Muslim territory. The accursed Jibā searched for them in vain, for God in his mercy saved them all. Then Jibā began to demand the money from me for the woman whom I had bought from him but not yet paid for, and who had fled with the rest. I said: 'Hand her over, and I will give you the money for her.' 'The money was due to me yesterday, before she escaped,' he said, and forced me to pay. But it meant little to me beside the joy of knowing that these poor things were safe.

A Proposal to Send My Son to Europe

A very important Frankish knight was staying in the camp of King Fulk, the son of Fulk. He had come on a pilgrimage and was going home again. We got to know one another, and became firm friends. He called me 'brother' and an affectionate friendship grew up between us. When he was due to embark for the return journey he said

to me: 'My brother, as I am about to return home, I should be happy
if you would send your son with me,' (the boy, who was about fourteen years old, was beside me at the time), 'so that he could meet the
noblemen of the realm and learn the arts of politics and chivalry. On
his return home he would be a truly cultivated man.' A truly cultivated man would never be guilty of such a suggestion; my son might
as well be taken prisoner as go off into the land of the Franks. I
turned to my friend and said: 'I assure you that I could desire nothing better for my son, but unfortunately the boy's grandmother, my
mother, is very attached to him, and she would not even let him
come away with me without extracting a promise from me that I
would bring him back to her.' 'Your mother is still alive?' 'Yes.'
'Then she must have her way.'[16]

The Falcon of Acre

I went to Acre with the amīr Mu'īn ad-Dīn—God have mercy on
him—to visit the court of the Frankish King Fulk, the son of Fulk.[17]
There we met a Genoese who had brought from the land of the
Franks a great falcon on a lure. It worked together with a young
bitch, hunting crane. When the bird was set at a crane the dog ran
behind, and as soon as the bird had attacked the crane and struck it
down, she seized it so that it could not escape. The amīr asked the
King to give him the falcon, and the King took the bird and the dog
from the Genoese and gave it to him. They travelled back with us,
and on the road to Damascus I saw the falcon savaging gazelles as
it did the food we gave it. We brought it back to Damascus, but it did
not survive long enough to be taken out hunting.

Christian Piety and Muslim Piety

I paid a visit to the tomb of John the son of Zechariah—God's blessing on both of them![18]—in the village of Sebastea in the province of
Nablus. After saying my prayers, I came out into the square that was
bounded on one side by the Holy Precinct. I found a half-closed
gate, opened it and entered a church. Inside were about ten old men,
their bare heads as white as combed cotton. They were facing the
east,[19] and wore (embroidered?) on their breasts staves ending in
crossbars turned up like the rear of a saddle. They took their oath on
this sign, and gave hospitality to those who needed it.[20] The sight of

---

16. It is characteristic of the mediaeval Muslim family that in the excuses he invents Usama in-
vokes not the boy's mother but his grandmother. What a pity that he did not agree to the proposal;
Usama's son, visiting the Christian world, might have left us some fascinating comparisons between the two civilizations. 17. See above. 18. Both Zechariah and John the Baptist were believed
to be prophets and venerated as such by the Muslims. 19. Normal practice among Christians of
the time (see above). 20. The text and meaning of the last words here are uncertain: the cross in
the form of staves was probably on the habits of these monks of the chapter of St. John.

their piety touched my heart, but at the same time it displeased and saddened me, for I had never seen such zeal and devotion among the Muslims. For some time I brooded on this experience, until one day, as Mu'in ad-Din and I were passing the Peacock House[21] (*Dar at-Tawawis*), he said to me: 'I want to dismount here and visit the Old Men (the ascetics).' 'Certainly,' I replied, and we dismounted and went into a long building set at an angle to the road. For the moment I thought there was no one there. Then I saw about a hundred prayer-mats, and on each a sufi, his face expressing peaceful serenity, and his body humble devotion. This was a reassuring sight, and I gave thanks to Almighty God that there were among the Muslims men of even more zealous devotion than those Christian priests. Before this I had never seen sufis in their monastery, and was ignorant of the way they lived.

21. A monastery (*khanqā*) belonging to an order of Muslim mystics, or sufis.

Chivalry and Courtly Love

The mysterious knight gently removed the long strands of hair that were entwined in the comb. He nearly fainted and fell off his horse as he caressed the strands. He "began to adore the hair, touching it a hundred thousand times to his eye, his mouth, his forehead and his cheeks." Finally, the knight "placed the hair on his breast near his heart" and continued on his way.

This passage about the mysterious knight depicts the romantic side of knighthood that is probably familiar to most modern readers. Modern readers would also be familiar with portrayals of knights as fierce warriors engaged in bloody battles. Knights are depicted as courageous and athletic, willing to enter into frays with other knights in service of their lords. In fact, real knights were more practical than romantic. They did perform brave feats out of loyalty to their lords during the 1100s, but they were obligated to do so. Under feudalism, lords granted knights land in exchange for their services during wars. Knights had to be loyal or they would break the feudal contract with their lords and lose their land. Because inheritance customs at that time dictated that only the eldest born son would inherit his father's property, all other sons were effectively disenfranchised. For most young men, becoming a knight was the only option open to them, unless they wanted to enter into service of the church. So knights were loyal out of necessity, but only toward their lords. Their relationships with others were ungoverned by any laws, and knights were often lawless. Kings in the early part of the twelfth century were not yet powerful enough to enforce laws against knightly transgressions, and knights' misbehavior continued unchecked. Gradually, however, a political and cultural backlash formed to oppose knightly anarchy.

As kings began to enjoy more power and influence as a result of booming economic expansion, they were able to afford their own armies and did not have to rely on knights to protect their territories. Knights, in consequence, became increasingly unnecessary, and their prestige declined. As a result of their declining reputation, knights found that people whom they used to treat with abandon were less tolerant of their behavior and now had the kings' laws to protect them. Affluent people of the court also began to expect a higher code of knightly behavior and began to commission works of literature that depicted knights as thoughtful, generous, and above all, chivalrous toward women. Influential women like Eleanor of Aquitaine—who was the duchess of Normandy and then the queen of England—patronized the arts and encouraged writers to pen romantic stories of knights and other young men in love. The troubadours—poets who lived in the castles of France—helped to popularize courtly love. Other writers, like Chrétien de Troyes, popularized the notions of chivalry. These depictions in stories and songs helped set a standard for behavior that real knights were encouraged to live up to.

The knight who lovingly placed the strands of his beloved's hair next to his heart is Sir Lancelot and his beloved is Queen Guinevere, the wife of King Arthur. This depiction of the chivalrous knight is found in Chrétien de Troyes's tale, "The Knight of the Cart." Chrétien was the inventor of Arthurian romance as we know it, and he did much to shape contemporary conceptions of romantic love. Lancelot undertakes a quest to win the queen's adoration, and for her he suffers humiliation, physical hardship, and exhaustion. He endures many trials during his adventures, but his loyalty to his beloved remains unshaken.

Feudalism and Knightly Ethics

Fred A. Cazel

The feudal system was based on a contract between a knight and his lord. The lord gave the knight a plot of land called a fief and promised to protect it in exchange for the knight's service during wars. Fred A. Cazel argues that this arrangement was essentially democratic since the lord and his knight and their vassals were in attendance when any major decisions—personal or professional—were made. The obligations between the knights and lords did not extend beyond the feudal contact, however, so anarchy characterized human activity outside the feudal bond. As kings began to claim certain privileges not outlined in feudal contracts, Cazel maintains, feudal monarchies developed. These new feudal systems helped to create order since increasingly powerful kings were able to enforce laws that protected the public good. Another feudal development that helped establish order was the creation of a system of ethics designed to temper the conduct of knights. Under the new code of ethics, knights were to be brave, loyal, and generous at all times. Most important, according to Cazel, knights were expected to treat ladies with respect and adoration—an ethic called chivalry which defined romantic love. Fred A. Cazel is professor emeritus at the University of Connecticut and chair of the Mansfield Historical Society.

I can only describe the feudal *system* in the briefest possible manner. Its base was the fully armed warrior—the knight. He had a fief which consisted of enough land and labor to support him. When he received his fief, the knight did homage to a lord. The lord was bound

Excerpted from *Feudalism and Liberty: Articles and Addresses of Sidney Painter,* edited by Fred A. Cazel Jr. Copyright © 1961 by the Johns Hopkins University Press. Reprinted with permission from the Johns Hopkins University Press.

to protect the knight, his family, and his fief. In return the knight was bound to be faithful to his lord and do him service. When the lord needed soldiers for war in the field or to garrison his castle, the knight had to appear in full armor. When the lord summoned his vassals to court, the knight was bound to attend. When a vassal died, his heir owed the lord a money payment called relief and the vassal was expected to aid the lord financially on certain occasions such as the wedding of his eldest daughter or the knighting of his eldest son. The rights and duties of lord and vassals were set in the lord's court—and assembly of vassals presided over by the lord. These definitions of rights and duties were feudal law or custom and differed from fief to fief. Thus for example two fiefs lying side by side might have entirely different laws governing inheritance.

Democracy and Anarchy

The feudal system provided for military and political cooperation between members of the knightly class with the least possible restraint on individual liberty. A knight had certain definite personal obligations toward his lord and his own vassals. He had rather more vague ones toward other vassals of his lord. But toward all other men he was a free agent who could do what he pleased. Thus it was a serious offence for him to rape the daughter of his lord or of one of his own vassals, but he could rape anyone else's daughter with impunity if he was powerful enough to ignore the ire of her relatives. Outside the bounds of feudal custom, the vassal was unrestrained. And within the feudal class the system was completely democratic—custom was set and enforced by the vassals.

Thus the feudal relationship was essentially a contract between lord and vassals which was defined and enforced by mutual agreement. The system operated in the same manner. It was assumed that lord and vassals had a common interest—the welfare of the fief. No lord was expected to make a serious decision, such as choosing a wife or going to war, without asking counsel of his vassals.

As a political system pure feudalism was little removed from anarchy. It assumed a more-or-less permanent state of war. While it provided machinery for the peaceful settling of most disputes, it did not *compel* men to settle their disputes peacefully. Thus if two knights quarrelled, they could always find a feudal court competent to hear the case, but if they preferred to wage war on each other, and they usually did, feudal custom did not hinder them. France in the eleventh and early twelfth centuries, and parts of Germany in the fourteenth and fifteenth, are prime examples of feudalism uncontrolled by public authority. In England from the beginning, in France after 1150, and in Germany before the downfall of the Hohenstaufen dynasty, royal authority based on the traditions of Germanic monarchy, mingled vaguely with those of Imperial Rome, curbed feudal anarchy to some extent. Because these kings ruled through a combination of royal and feudal institutions—were both kings and feudal suzerains—historians call them "feudal monarchs."

Feudal Monarchies

Feudal monarchy reached its apex in the twelfth and thirteenth centuries. Feudal institutions were in full vigor and organized into comprehensive systems with the kings at the summits. Feudal custom governed the relations between the kings and their vassals—the public law of the kingdoms was essentially feudal law. Yet the kings had sources of power independent of their vassals. These centuries saw a rapid development of trade and towns. From these sources the kings drew revenues which enabled them to hire soldiers and pay officials. Hence they could oblige their vassals to fulfill their obligation, force them to settle their disputes in court, and punish them if their offences against the general criminal law became too outrageous. By the thirteenth century a knight who committed murder or rape would have to pay a heavy fine. A very insignificant knight might even be hanged. Obviously the feudal monarchs were faced with the temptation to use their new power to ignore feudal custom or alter it in their own favor without seeking their vassals' consent. But here they met firm resistance. King John in Magna Carta and the sons of Philippe le Bel in their great series of provincial charters of liberties definitely admitted that they were bound by the feudal customs of their realms.

Before leaving our discussion of the feudal system at its height it might be well to say something of its geographical extent. As we have seen, early feudal institutions existed in the major part of the Carolingian Empire,[1] newly conquered Saxony being the only exception. Feudalism as an organized system embracing all or nearly all the land first appeared in Northern France and the adjacent German districts of Lorraine and Franconia. In 1066 the Norman Conquest completely feudalized England. In the last half of the eleventh century the Norman conquerors of Southern Italy and Sicily established feudalism in those regions. In 1100 the completely feudal kingdom of Jerusalem was founded in Palestine. Meanwhile the feudal system had spread to Southern France and the Spanish states of Barcelona and Aragon. Feudal institutions gained ground rapidly in parts of Germany such as Bavaria, Swabia, and Saxony during the period of confusion marking the end of the Salian[2] dynasty and were systematized in the late twelfth and early thirteenth centuries by the Hohenstaufen emperors. In the eleventh century the Byzantine Empire had developed institutions very

---

1. Frankish dynasty founded in 751 that lasted until 987 in France and 911 in Germany. 2. A tribe of Franks who settled in the Rhine region of the Netherlands in the fourth century.

similar to Western European feudalism, and a feudal system on the French model existed there during the brief life of the Latin Empire. While Scandinavia, Russia, and the Spanish states of Leon and Castile had some institutions reminiscent of feudalism, they never developed a feudal system.

Knightly Ethics

During the centuries in which feudalism was taking shape as a political system, the feudal class was developing its ethical conceptions. If feudalism was to be effective, certain virtues were required of the knight. He had to have the warrior's qualities of courage, skill in fighting, and cunning—in the terminology of the day bravery, prowess, and wisdom. It was also necessary that he fulfill his feudal obligations—that he be loyal. Another virtue, generosity, which has always been valued by warrior classes living at least partly by plunder, was greatly admired, especially by the various groups of attendants who profited from it. Needless to say, generosity was highly praised by the reciters of tales of war-like deeds who depended on it for their living. Then a class which makes war both its vocation and avocation is bound to develop rules to alleviate its unpleasant features. Knightly armor was heavy and hot—one hated to wear it except when necessary. When a knight traveled, he preferred to carry his armor on a pack horse. Hence custom soon demanded that a knight should give his enemy time to get into his armor before attacking him. The fortunes of war are fickle and the victor of one day might well be the prisoner of the next. It was to every knight's interest that noble prisoners be treated as honored guests and allowed to go free on parole to collect their ransoms. Thus the feudal environment gradually created knightly ethics. And no knight who listened to tales of Charlemagne, Arthur, and the knights who followed them could fail to know the nature of this ethical system.

Another set of ethical ideas which gradually gained ground in the minds of the knightly class represented a reaction against the feudal environment. The feudal system had no place for anyone who could not fight. The women of the feudal class were valued for their marriage portions, their housekeeping abilities, and their fertility. A woman could not rule a fief or testify in a court. She was always in the custody of some male—her father, her husband, or her eldest son. Yet women as housekeepers were powerful and could command the services of hungry bards. Hence, it occurred to some women that they could invent and propagate ideas which would raise their status and make life more pleasant. For this purpose they invented love or, perhaps more correctly, romantic love—historians call it courtly love. Sometimes, it meant simply adoration of a lady's beauty, accomplishments, and virtues. At other times it meant something far more concrete and more easily comprehended by the feudal male. But whatever the precise meaning given to the term, love was thought of as something ennobling. It made a knight a better ruler, a better fighter, and obviously a more pleasant companion. And this love was voluntary, a common fire which consumed both parties. It was far removed from the businesslike and formal arrangements which produced feudal matrimony. Courtly love found its most complete expression in some of the troubador lyrics and in Chrétien de Troyes' "Lancelot,"[3] but it was an important element in much of the literature produced for the entertainment of the feudal class. The knight was taught to treat ladies with at least a modicum of courtesy and to seduce them to the accompaniment of music and song.

The effectiveness of feudalism as a group of political and social institutions came to an end in France and England during the fourteenth and fifteenth centuries.

---

3. French writer of the twelfth century who wrote romances about knights and chivalry; Lancelot was a knight in Chrétien's tales.

The World of Knights: Fact and Fiction

Andrea Hopkins

Andrea Hopkins argues that the image of the knight has pervaded popular imagination since medieval times. The knight in medieval romances such as those written about King Arthur and the Round Table is portrayed as courageous, generous, and honorable, and at all times chivalrous to women. This model of knightly behavior, however, was not always followed by real knights who lived in the twelfth and thirteenth centuries. Hopkins maintains that real knights could be savage and sometimes slaughtered thousands of people for religious causes. Moreover, knighthood was expensive, inconvenient, and dangerous: at short notice, a knight had to obey his lord and head off to war riding an expensive horse, wearing expensive and heavy armor, and risking financial ruin should he be captured and have to buy his way to freedom. According to Hopkins, real knights experienced a decline in their status in the fourteenth century. As the financial costs of knighthood increased, kings were forced to pay for their knights' service or promise a share in any booty collected from wars. Rather than serving a higher moral cause, therefore, knights became motivated by gain, which led them to commit atrocities such as sacking cities and slaughtering innocents for money.

Shortly after the death of T. E. Lawrence (Lawrence of Arabia)[1] in a motorcycle accident in 1935, the following obituary appeared in the *Montreal Daily Herald:*

> Lawrence belonged to the era of chain-mail and broadswords, when men broke their lances in impossible quests, and to the age of the troubadours when men boasted of their deeds under one moon and under the next covered their vanity with sackcloth . . . One cannot dictate to posterity, but we hope that a few generations will remember him, if only as a baffling and arresting figure—a knight in shining armour in an age of colored shirts.

This response to the growing legend of Lawrence's exploits in the Arabian desert was typical. Visitors to St Martin's Church, Wareham, in Dorset, can see a splendid medieval-style tomb effigy of Lawrence as a crusader knight.

Forty years later, one of the most popular films of all time, *Star Wars*, though ostensibly a work of science fiction, told of a group of warrior heroes known as the Jedi Knights. These men fought with "light sabres" to protect the weak against unjust oppression, and their behaviour, in accordance with disciplines taught them by "masters", enabled them to perform superhuman feats with the aid of a mystical "Force". These examples alone suffice to demonstrate the extraordinary influence that the concept of knights continues to have, centuries after there had ceased to be any real knights left in Europe.

Fact or Fiction

But what was a "real" knight? The modern conception of a medieval knight, or what he aspired to be, is familiar to everyone. He was a tall, strong, handsome man on a large white horse, clad in mid–fifteenth-century plate armour with a shield, banner and surcoat, while his horse's caparison displayed his coat of arms. He was characterized by such personal qualities as courage and prowess, and was jealous of his honour. Most important of all, he was dedicated to the service of an ideal, a code which dictated his behaviour in specific, predictable ways. We know, for example, that he would always come to the aid of a damsel in distress, and that he would never refuse a fight simply because the odds were greatly against him. In fact, he was more likely to engage in combat on that account, like Sir Lancelot who, in some medieval romances, refused to fight fewer than four men at once on the grounds that otherwise it would be unfair to his opponents. No consideration of personal advantage, in short, could sway him from adherence to his beliefs and loyalties. Excellence in combat and absolute integrity—these were the chief characteristics of that paragon, the knight in shining armour, who embodies the ideal of medieval chivalry in twentieth–century films, popular fiction, cartoons, and even advertisements. . . .

1. British soldier and writer born in 1888.

[The reality of the knight's identity] is difficult to identify, not least because in the Middle Ages the image of the noble knight was inspired almost from the first by the ideal of knighthood portrayed in the great medieval romances. These romances were extremely pervasive, so that even those sources where one would normally expect to find facts rather than fantasy (histories, chronicles, personal biographies and so on) are, in the Middle Ages, strongly flavoured with the exotic spices of romance.

In any case, the distinction between fact and fiction in literature was by no means so clear cut in the Middle Ages as it is today. History and romance were inextricably intertwined, and both were seen as vessels of truth. In the Middle Ages, there was no such thing as "only a story". To discover the truth about medieval knights, we need to look closely at the ideal to which they aspired, as described in romances, as codified in treatises such as the *Ordene de Chevalerie*, and as celebrated in the biographies of great and famous knights, such as William the Marshal or Don Pero Nino.

A high standard was set, and history shows us that it was rarely attained in practice. Knights were primarily men who were trained to fight and they inhabited a violent world. But what distinguished a medieval knight from his predecessor, the mounted warrior of the early Middle Ages, was his consciousness of the ideal, including those aspects which were the hardest to live up to, and his desire for honour.

Chivalry

For a medieval knight, "honour" meant far more than mere courage and the skill of a warrior. The concept of chivalry developed, within a fairly brief period, from a simple warrior's code to a sophisticated system of values in which the principles of personal integrity, the duty to defend the weak from oppression, and the practice of knightly virtues, such as *largesse* (generosity), *pité* (compassion), *franchise* (a free and frank spirit) and *courtoisie* (courtliness, especially to women), combined with the more traditional virtues of loyalty and prowess. These qualities are repeatedly stressed in medieval accounts of knights, where the conduct of both real knights and fictional heroes is measured against this standard.

The chivalrous ideal as portrayed in literature is, of course, only one side of the coin. Equally, the conclusions of modern historians about the grim realities of medieval knighthood produce an incomplete and distorted picture. Fictional ideal and historical reality must be seen together. Medieval commentators were themselves aware that there were bad knights, who brought knighthood into disrepute. In romances, too, the hero knights encountered their sinister mirror images, the wicked knights who terrorized the helpless peasants, dishonoured ladies, even desecrated churches. Just as these "black knights" certainly had their counterparts in real life among the robber barons, freebooters and mercenaries of medieval Europe, so too it is clear that thousands of knights felt themselves contributing to a tradition of chivalry stretching back hundreds of years.

Here is one of the few instances in which it can be clearly seen that life imitated art. As early as 1223 we hear of knights taking part in a tournament in Arthurian dress[2] in Cyprus to celebrate the knighting of the son of the crusader baron, John of Ibelin; the first of many such tournaments in costume. The aristocracy and gentry of medieval Europe were fascinated by the idea of chivalry, even though many of its most popular and enduring literary expressions, such as the romances of Chrétien de Troyes, showed knights in a context far removed from the actual function of the warrior élite, that is, making war. Equally the rulers of medieval Europe exploited the desire of their retainers to emulate this ideal, organizing rituals and ceremonies, designing vows and accoutrements intended to enhance the allure of knighthood, despite its attendant obligations of military service and the sometimes crippling expense it entailed. Thus in 1306 we hear of the Feast of the Swans, held by King Edward I of England, a magnificent and highly romantic ceremony at which the king knighted his eldest son, together with 300 or so other young men of noble birth. After the dubbing ceremony there was a great banquet, during which

> . . . two swans were brought before King Edward I in pomp and splendour, adorned with golden nets and gilded reeds, the most astounding sight to the onlookers. Having seen them, the king swore by the God of Heaven and by the swans that he wished to set out for Scotland and, whether he lived or died, to avenge . . . the breach of faith by the Scots.

This same oath was then pledged by all the other nobles present, and the newly created knights, thus providing Edward with a substantial number of fighting men for his intended campaign against the Scots. It also provided him with an excellent opportunity to levy a special tax: the same chronicler, the anonymous author of *Flores historiarum*, records that "for the knighting of the king's son, the clergy and people ceded a thirtieth part of their goods to the king, and the merchants a twentieth".

The Savage Knight

In contrast to the high ideals which are constantly honoured in romance and chronicle, and in the grand rituals and ceremonies with which knights celebrated their deeds and their station, history also provides us with tales of savagery perpetrated by knights throughout the Middle Ages. Thus, when the First Crusade reached its triumphant conclusion in 1099 with the recapture of Jerusalem from the Seljuk Turks, the great

2. Dressed in the helmet and shield associated with King Arthur and his Knights of the Round Table.

crusader lord, Godfrey of Bouillon, was chosen as its first ruler. He was honoured from the early fourteenth century onwards by being considered the ninth of the Nine Worthies. (The Nine Worthies were a collection of biblical, classical and historical heroes supposed to be the greatest examples of chivalry and they included Alexander the Great, Julius Caesar, [King] Arthur and Charlemagne.) Yet we now know that, at the taking of Jerusalem in 1099, he presided over the massacre of every single person in the city, with the exception of the Saracen [Moslem] commander and his personal retinue who were given a safe conduct.

We can see, also, as the medieval period went on, that there were forces at work which undermined any idealism or high-mindedness associated with the practice of knighthood. Knights in romances spent much time engaged in quests designed to test their knightly qualities, or prove them worthy of their ladies, rather than fighting battles to protect or advance their society or serve their lord. Real knights, unlike their literary counterparts, were obliged to be in the field at short notice, heavily armed and mounted on an expensive horse. If a knight was captured, he could expect to pay a huge ransom, in addition to losing his horse and his armour, the legitimate prize of his captor. More important knights, especially those with estates of their own, were expected to maintain their position with style. This involved supporting other knights in their retinue, as well as squires, pages and perhaps a herald, all of whom had to be fed, clothed, armed and given costly gifts from time to time. A successful knight could make an immense fortune, as we shall see from the example of William the Marshal and others, but for ordinary knights it could be an expensive calling.

One or two romances touch on the financial problems experienced by knights. Examples include Marie de France's *Lanval*, in which the knight's poverty is magically relieved by his fairy mistress, or the anonymous Middle English *Sir Amadace*, who, having been all but bankrupted by his knightly generosity, sets forth to repair his fortunes by adventure, only to spend his last forty pounds on a deed of charity—burying the decaying corpse of an indebted merchant whose creditors are denying him burial. For this, of course, he is later rewarded.

Mercenary Knights

During the thirteenth and fourteenth centuries it became more difficult, and then impossible, for kings and great magnates to maintain armies in the field comprising men motivated solely by their desire to fulfil their feudal obligations to their lords. The cost of a knight's equipment and horses had become prohibitive and, increasingly, it became necessary to pay knights for their service, or at least to tempt them to fight with promises of great booty to be looted from the vanquished.

The later Middle Ages saw the rise of a new kind of "knight" who was a professional adventurer, motivated by nothing higher than gain—a mercenary, in fact. By the mid–fourteenth century there were large numbers of these men in Europe, with no place in society other than as soldiers of fortune. One of the greatest scandals of the age resulted from the recruitment of such men into the army of King Peter of Cyprus in his "Crusade" against the city of Alexandria in 1365. The mercenaries sacked the city, slaughtered thousands of its inhabitants (including many Christians), stole as much loot as they could carry and then went home, with the result that the city fell back into the hands of "the Infidel" within days of its conquest.

So, after the rise of chivalry and its "golden age" in the eleventh and twelfth centuries, we see the operation of two conflicting trends. On the one hand are the efforts of knights themselves and their lords and kings to glorify and elevate the status of knights, and make knighthood more socially exclusive; on the other, social and political pressures which tended to debase and brutalize knights. But in searching for the truth behind the glittering image, we shall see that the exacting concept of knighthood, which was early recorded in the *Ordene de Chevalerie*, was a real influence on the knights of the time.

Many of the medieval romances, from all the countries and languages of Europe, were largely drawn from three great cycles: the *Matter of Rome*, whose stories were drawn from classical antiquity ("Rome" referred to the supposed "authority" from whose works the tale had been drawn, rather than the subject matter—the stories themselves came equally often from Greek literature or myth); the *Matter of France*, which concerned the deeds of Charlemagne and his twelve "peers" in their eighth–century conquests of the Saracens; and the *Matter of Britain*, which was the story cycle of King Arthur and his knights of the Round Table in sixth–century Britain. Thus, most of the romances written from 1150 to 1450 were set in the distant past. Those lords and knights who participated in the Arthurian dress tournaments which achieved such a vogue in the thirteenth and fourteenth centuries were looking to the past just as surely as were the Victorian ladies and gentlemen who, inspired largely by the medieval romances of Sir Walter Scott, took part in the disastrous medieval tournament held at Eglinton castle in 1839 when heavy rain turned the lists into a bog.

The difference was that, in the Middle Ages, people did not view themselves, as we do now, as the culmination of centuries of civilized development, but rather as the degenerate remnants of a far greater past. They did not, however, see the past as essentially different from their own time, only better. The past was in most respects an ideal mirror of present society. This is why we find in medieval illustrations the heroes of the Trojan war represented in contemporaneous dress and arms, and even fighting with the latest medieval battle techniques.

Medieval knights—their aspirations, their experiences, their stories—are familiar to us. This is partly because many of their values have been incorporated into the ethos of the "gentleman" in western culture, but it is partly because the natural desire to form, and to be seen as, an élite group, bound by common goals and acknowledging certain rules of behaviour, has resulted in the creation of similar groups at other times and in other societies. The most striking analogy is of course the Samurai of medieval Japan.

Chrétien de Troyes and Courtly Love

Peter S. Noble

Peter S. Noble is the author of several books on medieval literature including *The Character of Guinevere in the Arthurian Romances of Chrétien de Troyes.* Noble argues that the romances of Chrétien de Troyes establish for the first time a code of courtly love—the highly romanticized
love between high-born persons in medieval courts. Although Chrétien
had earlier literary models to draw from—such as the songs of the troubadours—he presented an original and daring interpretation of courtly
love through his tales of King Arthur and the Knights of the Round Table.
While the troubadours believed that only love outside of marriage could
be true romance, Chrétien repudiated adultery and endorsed marriage as
ennobling. According to Noble, Chrétien was certainly responding to the
interests and needs of his audience who at that time were primarily high-
born women of the court. They knew firsthand the suffering caused by
their husband's infidelities, their second-class status, and the isolation of
life within medieval castles. Noble contends that by placing a lady as the
center of the knight's existence in his romances, Chrétien helped raise the
status of women and left for future generations an enduring model of what
romantic love should be.

In the late eleventh century a variety of social and intellectual currents were jointly bringing about changes in people's attitudes to
many things, not least the relationship between the sexes. One of the
most important of these elements was the changing position of
women. The widening horizons of the eleventh and early twelfth cen-

Excerpted from *Love and Marriage in Chrétien de Troyes*, by Peter S. Noble. Copyright © 1982
by the University of Wales. Reprinted with permission from the University of Wales Press.

turies opened new paths; many women rebelled against their enslavement to the marriage bed and their social inferiority, and in an age in which the celibate ideal flourished as never before or since in western Europe they sought escape in ways ascetic as well as carnal.[1]

Women no longer accepted the secondary role assigned to them in society quite so passively, and this was certain to be reflected in the literature as well. 'Yet it [the twelfth century] was also the age which saw the rise of the romantic tradition, of courtly love and literature. Whatever its origin and background, however much its sentiments may be paralleled in earlier literature in Christendom and Islam, as a fashion generating a vast and flourishing literature it was something new and reflects the inventiveness and variety of fashion and sentiment in the late twelfth and early thirteenth centuries.'[2] Much of the credit for the success of the romantic tradition of this period must be attributed to Chrétien de Troyes whose works are the earliest surviving Arthurian romances and, in the eyes of most critics, reached a standard not to be equalled in verse. Chrétien undoubtedly knew the Provençal tradition.[3] His own surviving lyric poetry contains clear references to Bernart de Ventadorn.[4] He also knew well the Tristan legend[5] against which he reacted with some vigour. There must also have been an already existing tradition in the north on which Chrétien could draw.[6]

What seems equally certain is that there was no codified system, no strict set of rules prescribing the appropriate behaviour for the lover at the time when Chrétien was writing. The troubadours of the south were individualists, whose songs cannot be confined within such a restrictive term as *amour courtois* [courtly love] . . . .

Nevertheless there are certain generalisations which can be made, perhaps the most important being the very secular nature of the love. . . . Not only was it secular but it was hostile to marriage . . . and of necessity adulterous. . . . Love of this type should be ennobling . . . as well].

Such concepts are clearly in circulation and well known before Chrétien, but they are not more than that. 'A distinction must be made between the established doctrine, a rigid system of rules of behaviour, which did not exist, and a mode of thought, expressed in literary conventions, which can be traced through so much medieval literature . . .'[7] Chrétien had at his disposal the southern tradition of adulterous love for a lady, probably socially superior, who might or might not choose to reward her lover, whose love was in no way platonic but

---

1. C. Brooke, Introduction in *Medieval Women*, ed. D. Baker (Oxford, 1978), 5. 2. Ibid. 7. 3. The literary language of the troubadours—Lyric poets who composed songs about love. ed. 4. M-C Zai, *Les Chansons courtoises de Chrétien de Troyes* (Berne and Frankfurt, 1974), 95. 5. The legend recounts the story of a prince who falls in love with an Irish princess and dies with her. ed. 6. J. Frappier, 'Vues sur les conceptions courtoises dans les littératures d'oc et d'oïl au xiie siècle, *Cahiers de Civilisation médiévale*, 2 (1959) 154–56. 7. J. Ferrante and G. Economou, editors *In Pursuit of Perfection* (Port Washington, N.Y., 1975), 3.

full of sensuality and longing. The lover hoped to earn an improvement in his position by his patient devotion but he was not prepared to be faithful for ever. The love of the troubadours was of necessity self-centred. As they were rarely close to or in contact with the beloved they had to concentrate on their own thoughts and feelings. In addition there was the Tristan legend, already well-known on the continent, with its theme of all-consuming passion imposed by fate, a direct contrast to the reasoned and measured (in theory at least) love of the troubadours. There are also, as already suggested, some independent northern traditions harking back to Geoffrey of Monmouth and Wace [collectors of Arthurian legends]. Finally there is the whole mass of Celtic legend apart from Tristan.

Chrétien and Andreas

There was no code of love, however, and the introduction of Andreas Capellanus seems of dubious value with reference to Chrétien. Andreas almost certainly was writing after Chrétien, and it is highly uncertain whether they even knew each other.[8] The date most favoured for the writing of Andreas' text is 1186,[9] when it seems likely that Andreas was not in the service of the Countess Marie, if he ever had been,[10] and may not have been writing for her.[11] His usefulness in interpreting Chrétien can therefore be easily overestimated. Whatever dates one accepts for the romances of Chrétien, by 1186 his work was, if not complete, at least well advanced. Andreas may be drawing on Chrétien, but Chrétien is certainly not drawing on Andreas. Further as John Stevens has pointed out, the existence of Andreas' book proves very little, '. . . the existence of Andreas Capellanus's treatis, *De Amore*, does not prove the existence of a "code of courtly love". It simply establishes the existence of experiences which could be codified and that there was a fashion for codification.[12]

Coupled with this is the whole problem of the interpretation of Andreas. Stevens is inclined to dismiss any claim that the writer may have to be taken seriously.[13] For Robertson the work is ironic,[14] but others

8. J. F. Benton, 'The Court of Champagne as a Literary Center', *Speculum*, 36 (1961), 578. 'The weightiest evidence, therefore, places the author [Andreas] at the royal court.' 9. Ibid. 580. 10. Ibid. 551. 'Andreas Capellanus may have been Countess Marie's chaplain . . .' This cautious attitude of Benton is rejected by H. A. Kelly who asserts that Andreas was not at Marie's court. *Love and Marriage in the Age of Chaucer* (Ithaca, 1975), 36. 11. Benton, op. cit. 586–87. 'The question of Marie's Latinity bears on the intended audience of Andreas' *De Amore*; for if Marie could not understand *De Amore* without the help of a translation, there is little reason to think that it was written for her delectation. The obvious audience for a Latin Treatise would be clerics and a few well-educated laymen, who might have found the first two books of *De Amore* amusing rather than instructive.' 12. John Stevens, *Medieval Romance* (London, 1973), 33. 13. Ibid. 32. 'The moral opportunism of this opening paragraph [of Book 111] is hard to beat. It certainly does not encourage us to take the pious recantation of Book III very seriously—indeed it does not encourage us to take anything seriously that Andreas has written.' 14. D. W. Robertson, jnr., 'The Subject of the *De Amore* of Andreas Capellanus', *Modern Philology*, 50 (1952–53), 145–61.

have taken it at face value, '. . . his . . . is a simple manual for those who wanted to love *honeste*, that is, like gentlemen.[15] Barbara Nelson Sargent has shown, moreover, that it would be wrong to assume that all medieval readers automatically interpreted the *De Amore* ironically.[16] Father Foster would accept the work as a reliable witness to twelfth–century attitudes.[17]

The scope for argument is limitless, but what Andreas' *De Amore*, whether it is ironical or not, does bear witness to is the intense interest in educated circles in love and more particularly in a sophisticated love which '. . . reflects an enhancement of the position and influence of women in medieval society, in the sphere of sexual relations.'[18] Any links between Andreas and Chrétien de Troyes remain to be proven, and his doctrines cannot be shown to have influenced Chrétien. They do, however, presumably reflect some of the fashionable ideas which were currently in circulation, the chief of which seems to be that love could only be adulterous.[19] This was, of course, in direct conflict with the reality of the period.[20] 'Whether *De Amore* was intended literally or satirically, a point still debated, its ideology, like that of the troubadours is in unmistakable conflict with medieval living realities which stoutly upheld the ancient double standard in respect to adultery.[21] Reality may well be better depicted in the *chanson de toile* as J-C Payen has suggested,[22] but there love is seen as brutal, a source of pain and tears to the woman, who nearly always has to submit to and justify herself before the man. Nevertheless such poems would also help to arouse public interest in emotional problems and relationships.[23]

Romance, the genre which concentrates above all on love, particularly on the awakening of love, makes little pretence of being realistic. The background of the Arthurian court in some Celtic region, remote in both time and distance from the courts of Champagne and

15. W. T. H. Jackson, 'The *De Amore* of Andreas Capellanus and the practice of love at court', *Romanic Review*, 49 (1958), 244. 16. Barbara Nelson Sargent, 'A Medieval Commentary on Andreas Capellanus', *Romania*, 94 (1973), 541. 'I can only conclude that, whatever may have been the Chaplain's intentions, the assertions that any and all medieval readers must have found it humorous, as an ironical presentation of the wrong kind of love, and that Drouart de la Vache's comments prove this, do not stand up under examination.' 17. K. Foster, 'Courtly Love and Christianity', *Aquinas Paper* 39 (London, 1963), 6. 'Andreas was evidently something of an extremist. He liked to push ideas as far as they would go . . . The tone and allusions of his work make it clear that he wrote within and for a definite aristocratic "set", the countess of Champagne's in fact; and she was one of the greatest ladies of her time . . . Moreover the ideas of Andreas are broadly in harmony with those of the twelfth century troubadours, so far as ideas of any kind are discernible in their lyrics. In this sense, at least, the *De Amore* is certainly a representative document.' 18. Ibid. 16. 19. Lazar, op. cit. 136. 'La *fin'amors* est un amour caché, adultère, dominé par l'appétit de la chair.' 20. It was permissible for husbands to have extra-marital affairs but not wives. ed. 21. Frances and Joseph Gies, *Women in the Middle Ages* (New York, 1978), 46. 22. J-C Payen, *Le Motif du repentir dans la littérature francaise médiévale* (Geneva, 1968), 262. 'Or la chanson de toile nous donne, certainement, de la réalité médiévale une image plus juste que la poésie des trouvères . . .' 23. Ibid. 263. 'Peut-être autant que l'art raffiné des trouvéres la chanson de toile a contribué à éveiller le public médiéval aux problèmes du cœur.'

Flanders [in France], gives freedom to writers to meet the wishes and fantasies of their audience, which in the case of women are clearly escapist, seeking a world in which they do exercise authority over men in the sphere of emotions at least. They escape too from the sordid reality of unfaithful husbands, regular child-birth with all its attendant risks and the diseases and dirt of their own, often far from comfortable or glamorous, castles. This unreality becomes clearer and more stressed as the genre continues into the thirteenth century. Chrétien, on the whole, reduces the role of the Celtic *merveilleux* [that which inspires wonder] and indeed does not treat it with the seriousness of some of his followers.[24] This means that the Celtic background on which he draws so heavily remains just that, an exotic background, against which his characters can experience recognisable emotions and grapple with recognisable problems. The audience is forced to concentrate on the main character or characters, although there are passages where the emotional tension is relaxed through the use of description or the *merveilleux*.

An Audience of Women

If we accept that Chrétien was writing for the court of the Countess Marie, as we presumably must, except for *Le Conte du Graal* [The Story of the Grail], then he is writing for a court with a sophisticated audience of high-born women whose many connections with other courts might make them familiar with the material on which he was drawing. They would also know from first hand experience or observation the sort of problems which women had to face. One can surely assume that the life of Eleanor of Aquitaine [Queen of France] with its many storms would be familiar to all of them. Her need, after her divorce from Louis of France, to secure a husband quickly to defend her immense possessions would be obvious to all of them, not least because they would remember the attempts to kidnap and abduct her on her way south from Paris. Her problems with Henry's[25] infidelities would also be common knowledge. With examples like this from the lives of people they knew or to whom they were related upper class women would be glad to find release and escape in stories where they were not mere pawns, but could exercise control and influence.

Lyric poetry would already have made them familiar with many of the concepts of love as treated by the troubadours. The *romans d'antiquité* [ancient romantics] had moved away from the masculine dominated view of life offered by epic and the audience was ready for the next step in the treatment of women and love, which would be taken by the authors of Arthurian romance. Chrétien therefore can be seen

24. Lucienne Carasso-Bulow, *The Merveilleux in Chrétien de Troyes' Romances* (Geneva, 1976). 143.
25. Henry II of England married Eleanor of Aquitaine in order to procure parts of France for his empire. ed.

to be responding to the interests and the wishes of his time and of the society for which he was writing, but his treatment of love is unexpected given the background against which he was writing and the attitudes expressed by many of his predecessors. . . .

Love and Morality

Chrétien is not just an apologist for marriage and love in marriage, he is their advocate,[26] constructing three of his romances round this theme and showing the disadvantages of other relationships based, as he sees it, on a less stable foundation. The *Chevalier de la Charrete* [the knight of the cart], according to Chrétien himself, was not entirely of his own choosing, and he may not have had a wholly free hand in the treatment either, but in it too it is possible to detect an attitude not inconsistent with the attitude of *Erec et Enide, Cligés* and the *Chevalier au Lion.*[27] *Le Conte du Graal*, was written for another patron, Philip of Flanders, a man with very different tastes from those of the Countess Marie, and this must be a factor in explaining the new type of story on which Chrétien had embarked. It may well be that he turned to religion, as he was dissatisfied with the values of earthly love,[28] but love is not absent from *Le Conte du Graal*, and as it is unfinished, we cannot be certain how Chrétien intended to resolve the various problems. Perceval might or might not have returned to marry Blancheflor, but the emphasis on the religious nature of Perceval's quest may well reflect Chrétien's realisation of where the interests of Philip of Flanders lay, while the minor characters and the adventures of Gauvain suggest that Chrétien had by no means lost interest in the problems of love.

Love and its problems are a constant theme in the works of Chrétien de Troyes, but a superficial reading of his work can leave the impression that his attitude changes with each poem. It develops, of course, and he has different things to say in each poem because he is examining different aspects of the relationship between men and women, but, as I have attempted to show elsewhere with regard to the characters who reappear in the romances, Chrétien develops and enriches his interpretation without altering his earlier ideas.[29] So with love he has a clear idea of what he wants to say, and his ideas, as I hope to show, are not those of either the real world where women remained on the whole down-trodden, inferior and abused, nor those of the fantasy world of many of his contemporaries where adultery or fornication were the norm. It is quite certain that Chrétien was

26. P. Haidu, *Aesthetic Distance in Chrétien de Troyes* (Geneva, 1968), 41, uses the following turns of phrase; 'Chrétien's prejudice in favor of married love . . .' and '. . his predilection for married love . . . 27. *Erec and Enide, cligés,* and *The Knight of the Lion.* ed. 28. Ferrante and Economou, op. cit., 159. 29. P. S. Noble, 'Kay the Seneschal in Chrétien de Troyes and his Predecessors', *Reading Medieval Studies,* 1 (1975), 55–70 and 'The Character of Guinevere in the Arthurian Romances of Chrétien de Troyes', *Modern Language Review,* 67 (1972), 524–35.

strongly opposed to adultery. Instead he puts forward his own ideas, a daring thing for a medieval writer to do in an age when no credit was given for originality. Luttrell has shown that Chrétien comes as near as he can to admitting that although he drew on sources, he used them for his own creations.[30] As a professional writer, presumably dependent on his writing for his living and therefore bound to please his patrons, Chrétien used the vocabulary, the ideas and the attitudes which were in vogue at the time, but like all truly great writers he has an extraordinary richness, so that his poems can be interpreted in many ways using the evidence provided by Chrétien.[31] Chrétien himself may not have realised fully just how much he was putting into his romances, but with regard to his treatment of the theme of love, I would suggest that he knew very well what he was doing. When necessary he might disguise his true ideas, but throughout his poetry he is opposed to contemporary, fashionable morality and attitudes, which may help to explain the apparent change of emphasis in *Le Conte du Graal*.

[Chrétien] has a clear concept of love and the morality linked with it and that he does more than just advance the case for the sort of married love which he seems to prefer to describe. By humour, irony and contrast he brings out the failings and the disadvantages of other sorts of love, particularly the adulterous or unmarried love advocated by some of his contemporaries, especially in the form of the passion experienced by Tristan and Iseult.[32] His answers may not always be wholly convincing but such are the tasks which he set himself.

30. Luttrell, op. cit. 253. 31. Jessie Crosland, *Medieval French Literature* (Oxford, 1956), 120. 32. P. Gallais, *Genèse du roman occidental; essais sur Tristan et Iseut* (Paris, 1974), 59. *Tristan doit être nié.* '*Tristan* est une tentation a laquelle il ne faut pas succomber.'

Lancelot and Guinevere

Chrétien de Troyes

Writing in France during the second half of the twelfth century, Chrétien de Troyes was the inventor of Arthurian courtly romances. His tales of King Arthur and the Knights of the Round Table recount the love adventures of knights and their polished manners when before the ladies of the courts. In *The Knight of the Cart*, Chrétien tells the story about the knight Lancelot's adventures to prove his undying love for Arthur's queen, Guinevere. Such adulterous love was a celebrated theme in most courtly romances, but Chrétien's ironic treatment of it shows that he does not approve of consummated love between men and women who are not married. In the following excerpt, the queen asks Lancelot to illustrate his love for her by performing poorly in a jousting tournament. Although he suffers humiliation before the other knights, Lancelot obeys Guinevere's every order, and she is convinced that he is her true lover.

A lready the crowds had assembled on every side: the queen with all her ladies and the knights with their many men-at-arms. The most magnificent, the largest, and the most splendid viewing stands ever seen had been built there on the tournament field, since the queen [Guinevere] and her ladies were to be in attendance. All the ladies followed the queen on to the platform, for they were eager to see who would do well or poorly in the combat. The knights arrived by tens, by twenties, by thirties—here eighty and there ninety, a hundred or more here, two hundred there. The crowd gathered before and around the stands was so great that the combat was begun.

Lancelot's Valor

Knights clashed whether or not they were already fully armed. There seemed to be a forest of lances there, for those who had come for the pleasure of the tourney had brought so many that, looking in every direction, one saw only lances, banners, and standards. Those who were to joust moved down the lists, where they encountered a great many companions with the same intent. Others, meanwhile, made ready to perform other deeds of knighthood. The meadows, fields, and clearings were so packed with knights that it was impossible to guess how many there were. Lancelot did not participate in this first encounter; but when he did cross the meadow and the herald saw him coming on to the field, he could not refrain from shouting: 'Behold the one who will take their measure! Behold the one who will take their measure!'

'Who is he?' they all asked. But the herald refused to answer.

When Lancelot entered the fray, he alone proved a match for twenty of the best. He began to do so well that no one could take their eyes from him, wherever he went. A bold and valiant knight was fighting for Pomelegoi, and his steed was spirited and swifter than a wild stag. He was the son of the king of Ireland, and he fought nobly and well, but the unknown knight pleased the onlookers four times as much. They were all troubled by the same question: 'Who is this knight who fights so well?'

The queen summoned a clever, pretty girl to her and whispered: 'Damsel, you must take a message, quickly and without wasting words. Hurry down from these stands and go at once to that knight bearing the red shield; tell him in secret that I bid him "do his worst".'

The girl swiftly and discreetly did as the queen asked. She hurried after the knight until she was near enough to tell him in a voice that no one could overhear: 'Sir, my lady the queen bids me tell you to "do your worst".'

Lancelot Does His Worst

The moment he heard her, Lancelot said that he would gladly do so, as one who wishes only to please the queen. Then he set out against a knight as fast as his horse would carry him, but when he should have struck him, be missed. From this moment until dark he did the worst he could, because it was the queen's pleasure. The other knight, attacking him in turn, did not miss, but struck Lancelot such a powerful blow that Lancelot wheeled and fled and did not turn his horse against any knight during the rest of that day. He would rather die than do anything unless he were sure that it would bring him shame, disgrace, and dishonour, and he pretended to be afraid of all those who approached him. The knights who had praised him before now laughed and joked at his expense. And the herald, who used to say, 'This one will beat them all, one after another!' was very dispirited and embarrassed at becoming the butt of the knights' gibes.

'Hold your peace now, friend,' they said mockingly. 'He won't be taking our measure any more. He's measured so much that he's broken that measuring stick you bragged so much about!'

'What is this?' many asked. 'He was so brave just a while ago; and now he's so cowardly that he doesn't dare face another knight. Perhaps he did so well at first because he'd never jousted before. He just flailed about like a madman and struck so wildly that no knight, however expert, could stand up to him. But now he's learned enough about fighting that he'll never want to bear arms again as long as he lives! His heart can no longer take it, for there's no bigger coward in the world!'

The queen was not upset by anything she heard. On the contrary, she was pleased and delighted, for now she knew for certain (though she kept it hidden) that this knight was truly Lancelot. Thus throughout the day until dark he let himself be taken for a coward. When darkness brought an end to the fighting, there was a lengthy discussion over who had fought best that day. The king of Ireland's son felt that beyond any doubt he himself deserved the esteem and renown; but he was terribly mistaken, since many there were equal to him. Even the red knight pleased the fairest and most beautiful of the ladies and maidens, for they had not kept their eyes as much on anyone that day as on him. They had seen how he had done at first—how brave and courageous he had been. But then he had become so cowardly that he dared not face another knight, and even the worst of them, had he wanted, could have defeated and captured him. So the ladies and knights all agreed that they would return to the lists the following day, and that the young girls would marry those who won honour then.

Slander and Gossip

Once this was settled, they all returned to their lodgings, where they gathered in little groups and began to ask: 'Where is the worst, the lowliest, the most despicable of knights? Where has he gone? Where has he hidden himself? Where might we find him? Where should we seek him? Cowardice has probably chased him away, and we'll never see him again. He's carried Cowardice off with himself, so that there cannot be another man in the world so lowly! And he's not wrong, for a coward is a hundred thousand times better off than a valorous, fighting knight. Cowardice is a wanton wench and that's why he's given her the kiss of peace and acquired from her everything he has. To be sure, Courage never lowered herself enough to try to find lodging in him. Cowardice owns him completely. She has found a host who loves and serves her so faithfully that he has lost all his honour for her sake.'

All night long those given to slander gossiped in this manner. Though the one who speaks ill of another is often far worse than the one he slanders and despises, this did not keep them from having their say. When day broke, all the knights donned their armour once more and returned to the fighting. The queen, with her ladies and maidens, came back to the stands, and together with them were many knights without armour who had either been captured on the first day or had taken the cross, and who were now explaining to them the heraldry of the knights they most admired.

'Do you see the knight with the gold band across a red shield?' they inquired. 'That's Governal of Roberdic. And do you see the one be-
hind him who has fixed a dragon and an eagle side by side on his shield? That's the king of Aragon's son, who's come into this land to win honour and renown. And do you see the one beside him who rides and jousts so well? One half of his shield is green with a leopard upon it, and the other half is azure. That's dearly loved Ignaurés, a handsome man who pleases the ladies. And the one with the pheasants painted beak to beak upon his shield? That is Coguillant of Mautirec. And do you see those two knights beside him on dappled horses, with dark lions on gilded shields? One is called Semiramis, the other is his companion—they have painted

Lancelot and Guinevere's relationship is perhaps the most famous example of courtly love.

their shields to match. And do you see the one whose shield has a gate painted upon it, through which a stag seems to be passing? On my word, that's King Yder.' Such was the talk in the stands.

'That shield was made in Limoges and was carried by Piladés, who is always eager for a good fight. That other shield, with matching bridle and breast-strap, was made in Toulouse and brought here by Sir Kay of Estrall. That one comes from Lyons on the Rhône—there's none so fine under heaven!—and was awarded to Sir Taulas of the Desert for a great service. He carries it well and uses it skilfully. And that other shield there, on which you see two swallows about to take flight, yet which stay fast to take many a blow of Poitevin steel, is an English model, made in London. Young Thoas is carrying it.'

The Queen Makes More Demands

In this manner they pointed out and described the arms of those they recognized; but they saw no sign of that knight whom they held in such low esteem, so they assumed that he had stolen off in the night, since he did not return that day to the combat. When the queen, too, did not see him, she determined to have someone search through the lists for him until he was found. She knew of no one she could trust more to find him than that girl she had sent the day before with her message. So she summoned her at once and said to her: 'Go, damsel, and mount your palfrey. I am sending you to that knight you spoke to yesterday. You must search until you find him. Make no delay! Then tell him once again to "do his worst". And when you have so instructed him, listen carefully to his reply.'

The girl set off without hesitation, for the evening before she had carefully taken note of the direction he went, knowing without a doubt that she would once again be sent to him. She rode through the lists until she saw the knight, then went at once to advise him to continue 'doing his worst' if he wished to have the love and favour of the queen, for such was her command. 'Since she so bids me,' he replied, 'I send her my thanks.' The girl left him at once.

As he entered the field, the young men, the squires, and men-at-arms began jeering: 'What a Surprise! The knight with the red armour has returned! But what can he want? There's no one in the world so lowly, so despicable, and so base. Cowardice has him so firmly in her grip that he can do nothing to escape her.'

The girl returned to the queen, who would not let her go until she had heard that reply which filled her heart with joy, for now she knew beyond a doubt that that knight was the one to whom she belonged completely; and she knew, too, that he was fully hers. She told the girl to return at once and tell him that she now ordered and urged him to 'do the best' that he could. The girl replied that she would go at once, without delay. She descended from the stands to where her groom was waiting for her, tending her palfrey. She mounted and rode until she found the knight, and she told him immediately: 'Sir, my lady now orders you to "do the best" you can.'

'Tell her that it would never displease me to do anything that might please her, for I am intent upon doing whatever she may desire.'

The girl hurried back as quickly as she could with her message, for she was certain that it would please the queen. As she approached the viewing stands, eager to deliver her message, the queen stood up and moved forward to meet her. The queen did not go down to her, but waited at the top of the steps. The girl started up the steps, and as she neared the queen she said: 'My lady, I have never seen a more agreeable knight, for he is perfectly willing to do whatever you command of him. And, if you ask me the truth, he accepts the good and the bad with equal pleasure.'

'In truth,' she replied, 'that may well be.'

Then the queen returned to the window to observe the knights. Without a moment's hesitation Lancelot thrust his arm through the shield-straps, for he was inflamed with a burning desire to show all his prowess. He neck-reined his horse and let it run between two ranks. Soon all those deluded, mocking men, who had spent much of the past night and day ridiculing him, would be astounded: they had laughed, sported, and had their fun long enough!

With his arm thrust through the straps of his shield, the son of the king of Ireland came charging headlong across the field at Lancelot. They met with such violence that the king of Ireland's son wished to joust no more, for his lance was splintered and broken, having struck not moss but firm dry shield-boards. Lancelot taught him a lesson in this joust: striking his shield from his arm, pinning his arm to his side, and then knocking him off his horse to the ground. Knights from both camps rushed forward at once, some to help the fallen knight and others to worsen his plight. Some, thinking to help their lords, knocked many knights from their saddles in the mêlée and skirmish. But Gawain, who was there with the others, never entered the fray all that day, for he was content to observe the prowess of the knight with the red shield, whose deeds seemed to make everything done by the other knights pale by comparison. The herald, too, found new cause for happiness and cried out for all to hear: 'The one has come who will take the measure! Today you will witness his deeds; today you will see his might!'

The Influence of the Troubadours

Raimon De Loi

According to Raimon De Loi, People in the Middle Ages didn't live long, so they lived—and loved—with intensity. The medieval conception of this intense love was shaped by the troubadours—lyric poets who traveled to various French courts and composed songs about love. De Loi argues that the influence of the troubadours on those who occupied the courts of France was so strong that a legal code developed to manage the behavior of lovers involved in courtly romance. The code stipulated that the male lover must be faithful to his lady. He must also be patient and meek, and defend his lady's honor. Most important, De Loi maintains, the lovers must never marry; since men and women in the twelfth-century courts usually wed for convenience in order to unite noble families, the troubadours believed that real love could not exist between married people. The problem of courtly love popularized by the troubadours played an important role in medieval life for two centuries, and has influenced all generations since. Raimon De Loi is the author of several books on literature, including *A Companion of Literatures*.

T he color of life in the Middle Ages was a deep, glaring, and unmitigated red. Life was fast; life was hard; life was for youth and lived with such energy and enthusiasm that whatever was done of good or bad was done with an absolute intensity. Richard the Lion-Heart, a writer of indifferent poems but a great patron of poets—particularly those who wrote poems in his honor—was dead when he was forty-one; before he was eighteen he had conquered a kingdom. At an

Excerpted from *Trails of the Troubadours* (Port Washington, NY: Kennikat Press, 1927) by Raimon De Loi.

age when our modern youth are being persuaded that virtue is its own reward, the medieval youth were proving that the essence of virtue is a strong arm, agile wit, and a cynically realistic conviction that the battle is, after all, to the swift, the strong, the sure. When they were not making war or playing at politics, they were playing at love or making poems; and they made love and poetry with the same ardor and ruthlessness that they displayed in the taking of cities and the killing of enemies.

Most of the evil they did has died with them, but the fruits of their slight leisure, their poetry, and their philosophy—both a kind of game picturing a make-believe world—have survived.

We of modern times frequently confuse the game with the candle. Because medieval wars were conducted on a small scale, we think they were of small importance to the men who were killed in them; because medieval poetry was very brilliant, we use it to cast a false light on medieval manners. Galahad[1] is a literary myth created by a popular novelist of the thirteenth century writing for medieval flappers. But because love and poetry were games, do not assume that they were frivolous pastimes. Time in those golden days was money and was created to be spent to good advantage. The troubadours worked hard at their play; they played hard at their work.

The "Gay Science"

A particular group of fashionable young men who frequented the courts in and about Marseilles, Toulouse, and Tours [in France] were called troubadours. They fashioned for us two arts: the art of lyric poetry and the art of love, which they referred to as the "gay science." Although there had been lyric poetry before the troubadours, it had never been raised to the perfection to which they raised it. Although there had been arts of love before the troubadours, they metamorphosed those arts and gave them the forms in which love is practiced today.

In modern times the art of love has fallen into a decay. Women are, I suppose, still beautiful, and passion is still a fluid force in the spirits of men; but in the affectation of a scientific interest in emotions we are apt to affect a superiority to the emotions we are analyzing. Whereas men in the twelfth century affected to be more moved by love than they could possibly have been, men of the twentieth century affect to be less moved than we know in fact that they actually are.

But despite our ingenuous affectation of dispassionateness, the medieval theory of love has become a real part of our being. It is on record that men, even in modern times, have compared the women they loved to all the flowers of the botanical dictionary, that they have

1. The purest of the knights of the Round Table as depicted in Arthurian legends.

insisted that these women were superior in wisdom to the wise women of the past, present, and future. Many of us still believe that the maiden should be coy and the lover despairing, although we know that lovers are more often despairing because maidens are not coy enough. The lover's humility which makes him the slave of the beloved, and his arrogance which makes him her defender, which we now consider the instinctive equipment of every civilized man, were formulated by the troubadours of the tenth to the thirteenth centuries.

These precepts are contained in exquisite poems, in lengthy philosophical dissertations on love, and in allegories. The philosophical dissertation on love has, in modern times, become a psychological monograph on immorality; for the allegory we no longer have sufficient intellectual industry; but the lyric poem remains now as it was then, a source of delight. For the troubadours sang of love in the springtime, of the passions and despairs of lovers, of the beauty and cruelty of women, themes which still retain for us an enduring interest.

The Code of Love

The strangely artificial relation which existed between the despairing lover and the charming lady, and between the charming lady and her heavy husband to whom she had been married for reasons of state, was soon regulated by a legal code. What this code was has been reported in many documents, but with particular charm in one called "The Art of Honest Loving" by Andreas, a chaplain. In general, the lover must be true to the king and queen of love; he must fast for love every other day; and he must stir up others to love.

In particular he must be discreet and secret, for true love is always clandestine. When the poet writes to his mistress he must refer to her under an assumed name. This name ultimately became an open secret in the court, yet it was considered bad form to address a lady with absolute frankness.

The lover must be constant to one lady; he must be patient with her moods; he must be meek and afraid of being over-bold; he must be conscious of his inferiority to his mistress; he must think of nothing unpleasant for her sake; he must be thoughtful to please her; he must think no evil of her; he must keep his person and his dress neat and clean for her sake; and finally, he must defend her honor and reputation at all costs. The observance of this rule led to innumerable difficulties. Frequently the ladies had no honor, which, as in the case of Loba de Perrautier, led to tragedy.

To these may be added several other customs. The lover was supposed to wander alone musing on his lady; he was supposed to be sleepless when she was cruel, to dream of enjoying her love, to be wretched in her absence, to be a master of the language of love and the signs of lovers, and to maintain his interest in love even when he had grown old.

Only knights, clerks, and ladies of gentle birth were citizens of the kingdom of love. These citizens were urged to love one another but, with peculiar naïveté, were prohibited from marrying each other. The authors are unanimous that love between husband and wife is impossible. "Though husband and wife be both citizens of the kingdom of love, they are citizens of different counties, and between these counties there is constant strife, and each must be faithful to serve the lord and mistress of his particular county who are also the vassals of the Lord of Love."

One of the subtleties of the gay science is illustrated in a story about Lancelot.[2] Lancelot was on his way to rescue Guinevere. Guinevere was a lady of questionable reputation who had the habit of getting kidnapped and always wanted rescuers. One biographer suspects her of being a shape-shifter who appeared during the day as a lady but could also assume the form of a snake. At a ford, Lancelot became engaged with an evil knight of the region (all knights who were your enemies were then, as they are today, evil knights) and lost his horse. He faced the problem of transporting himself for some distance clad in several tons of armor. A peasant with a cart gave him a lift, but when he appeared before his lady in this ignoble position she refused to receive him. This adventure was, for the Middle Ages, as much a social problem as the *Doll's House*[3] is for us. What is a lady to do when her knight presents himself in that way? How can one accept the love of a knight who does things as impossible as riding in a peasant's cart? Indeed could a modern lady love a man who eats with his knife, who is seen with vulgar companions, who is for good reason or bad transported to her house in a butcher's cart!

But these were refinements. . . .

The troubadours were sophisticated, subtle, and perverse, the color of their life was red, and, above all, they had a youth and a love of living which they imparted to the songs they sang and the trails they followed.

---

2. A knight of the Round Table in Arthurian Romances. 3. A play written by Henrik Ibsen in which the wife of a banker rebels against her domestic confinement.

Songs of a Troubadour

Bernart De Ventadorn

The troubadours were lyric poets of the twelfth and thirteenth centuries who were supported by the lords of French and Italian courts. Their songs of courtly love—the love between a knight or other male living in the court and the lady of the castle—helped shape romantic sensibilities in centuries to come and were the earliest modern poetry. The troubadour Bernart De Ventadorn was born in 1140 into a servant family, but he quickly won the favor of the lord of the castle by singing to him. His songs were composed in the French provencal language—which is an off-shoot of Latin—and are full of wit. Unfortunately, the troubadour fell in love with his lord's wife and was forced to leave the castle once the affair was discovered. Bernart fled to Eleanor of Aquitaine, the duchess of Normandy, who was a patron of the arts. He fell in love with her too, however, and he eventually retired to a monastery where he died in 1180. Bernart's poems illustrate a common paradox in troubadour poetry. The speaker in each poem is a tormented lover who laments his lady's indifference toward him. Since his lady is chaste like a good Christian, he admires her, but because she is beautiful, he desires her and urges her to consummate their love.

TANT AI MO COR PLE DE JOYA

1. I have a heart so filled with joy
   Everything changes its nature:
   Flowers white, crimson, and gold

Seems the frost,
For with the wind and the rain
    My fortune keeps on growing;
Ah yes, my worth keeps mounting,
    My song's improving too.
I have a heart so full of love
    And joy and sweetness,
That the ice appears to me a flower,
    And the snow lies green.

2. I can go out without my clothes,
    Naked in my shirt,
For fine, true love will keep me safe
    From wintry blasts.
But a man's a fool to lose measure
    And not to toe the line,
And so I've taken special care
    Ever since I fixed on
The most pretty love who ever lived,
    From whom I expect great honor.
For in place of the wealth of her
    I'd not take Pisa.

3. She can cut me off from her friendship,
    But I rest secure in my faith
That at least I've carried away
    The beautiful image of her.
And I have for my own devices
    Such a store of happiness
That until the day when I see her,
    I'll feel no anxiousness.
My heart lies close to Love and
    My spirit runs there too,
Though my body's anchored here, alas!
    Far from her, in France.

4. Still I have steady hope from her
    (Which does me little good),
For she holds me as if in a balance
    Like a ship upon the waves,
And I don't know where to hide myself
    From woes besetting my senses.
All night long I toss and I turn
    Heaving upon my mattress:
I suffer greater torment in love
    Than that arch-lover Tristan,
Who underwent so many pains
    To gain Isolde the Blonde.

5. 0 God! Why am I not a swallow
    Winging through the air,
Coming through the depths of night
    There inside her chamber?
My good, joy-bearing lady,
    Your lover here's expiring.
I'm afraid my heart may melt
    If things go on like this.
Lady, because of your love
    I join my hands and adore:
Beautiful body with healthy hues,
    You make me suffer great woe.

6. There isn't any affair of the world
    That can occupy me more
Than the mere mentioning of her;
    Then my heart leaps high
And light suffuses my face, and
    Whatever you hear me say of it,
It will always appear to you
    That I really want to laugh.
I love that woman with such good love
    That many a time I cry,
And to me my sighs contain
    A better savor.

7. Messenger, go on the run:
    Tell to my pretty one
The pain, 0 yes the grief
    I bear—and torment.

LO GENS TEMS DE PASCOR

1. The sweet season of rebirth
    With its freshening green
Draws for us flower and leaflet
    With many a different hue;
And therefore every lover
    Is gay and full of song—
But me, I cry and clamor
    Without a taste of joy.

2. To all I lament, good men,
    About Milordess and Love,
For I placed my faith in them—
    Those ever treacherous two—
And they've turned my life to grief;
    And the good and all the honor

I have rendered to the fairest
Counts for nothing, gives no aid.

3. Pain and grief and damage
   I've had, and I have a lot;
   And yet I've borne it all.
   And I don't even think they're harsh,
   For you've never seen any other lover
   Offer better without deceit:
   No, I don't go around changing
   The way those women do.

4. Since we both were children,
   I have loved her, courted her well,
   And my joy goes ever doubling
   Through each day of every year.
   And if she doesn't offer me
   A welcome-look and her love,
   Then when she's aging, let her beg
   Me to offer my desire then!

5. Woe's me! What good is living
   If I can't see day by day
   My fine, true, natural joy
   In her bed, stretched under a window,
   Body pure white head to toe
   Like the snow at Christmastide,
   So that we two lying together
   Can measure each other's sides?!

6. Never was loyal lover seen
   Who enjoyed a worse reward;
   For I love her with sincere love,
   And she says: "What do I care?"
   In fact, she says that's why
   She shows me her deadly rage,
   And if she hates me for this cause,
   Then *she's* guilty of a mortal sin.

7. Surely there'll some day be a time,
   My lady beautiful and good,
   When you can pass me secretly
   The sweet reward of a little kiss:
   Give it only on the grounds
   That I am taken with desire.
   One good is worth two others
   If the others are gained by force.

8. When I behold your features,

Those gorgeous eyes full of love,
I can't help wondering to myself
How you can answer me so vilely.
And I consider it high treason
When a person seems honest and pure
And turns out puffed with pride
In places where he is strong.

9. Pretty Face, if my above-all
Didn't stem from you alone,
I'd long ago have left my songs
Through the ill of the evil ones.

AMORS E QUE.US ES VEJAIRE?

1. Love, how does it seem to you?
Ever find a bigger fool than I?
Think that I'll always be a lover,
Yet never find a drop of grace?
Order me do whatever you will.
It's done; it's right for me.
But you! where O where's the good
In always working me some wrong?

2. I love the woman of fairest air
In all the world, none better;
But she doesn't care a jot,
And I don't know how it's happened.
Just when I think I'm breaking free,
I can't! Love's got me fast.
I'm betrayed because of my good faith.
Love! Surely I can accuse you of that!

3. And so I'll have to wrestle with Love
Since I can't seem to break away.
He's let me know I'm in a hold
Where I'll never have any hope of joy.
Far better perhaps to hang myself,
For having had the heart and nerve,
And yet I haven't got the strength
To ward away the work of Love.

4. Yet Love knows how to descend
Wherever he most wants to go,
And he knows how to grant good rewards
For his torments and his pain.
But so poorly can he buy and sell me
That he's no longer any good for me,

Unless milady should deign to see me
And listen to my words.

5. What a bother! O, what trouble
Every day begging for some grace,
But the love that's pent up inside me
I can't cover, I can't hide.
Woe's me! No sleep nor even pause,
And I can't even stand in one place,
And I know I can't keep on going
If the pain doesn't soon abate.

6. I know the reason, the cause,
And can prove it to Milord:
No man could, nor ever dared
Enter the lists against Lord Love,
For "Love conquers all"
And forces me to adore her;
And he could do the same to her
In just one little moment.

7. Lady, no one can say a single word
About the good heart and pure desire
I have when I consider them,
For I never loved anything so much.
Already a year ago my sighs
Would have murdered me, my lady,
If it wasn't for that gorgeous sight
That started my desires doubling.

8. Lady, you only scoff and laugh
Whenever I ask you for anything,
But if you learned to love enough,
You'd certainly talk a different line.

9. Nimblefoot (Alegret), learn to sing my song
And you, my trusty Iron-Heart (Ferran),
Carry it for me to my Tristan,
Who knows well how to scoff and laugh.

CAN L'ERBA FRESCH'E.LH FOLHA PAR

1. When grasses fresh and leaflets sprout
And the flower blossoms on the bough,
And the nightingale high-pitched and clear
Lifts his voice and moves his song,
I've joy from him and joy from the flower,
And joy from me and more from Milord;
From everywhere I'm circled round with joy,

And this is a joy that overcomes the rest.

2. Alas! and yet I'm dying of worry!
　　So often I stand in grievous thought
　　That thieves could carry me away
　　And I'd never know what happened.
By god, Love, you've found me your prey,
With too few friends and no other lord.
Why didn't you upset Milordess once
Before I was stricken with this desire?

3. I wonder how I can carry on
　　Without showing her my yearning.
　　For when I see her, just a glance,
　　Those eyes of hers so beauty-filled,
Scarcely can I stop from running toward her.
Yes, that I'd do, were it not for fear,
For never was body better painted or cut,
And yet so cruelly slow for the task of love.

4. I love Milordess and hold her dear,
　　I respect her and I give her praise,
　　So much that I dared not speak to her,
　　Not beg a thing, not even demand.
And yet she knows my ill and my grief;
And when she wants, she can yield me honor,
And when she wants, I'm content with less
So that she will never suffer blasphemy.

5. If I knew how to bewitch people,
　　My enemies I'd turn into babes,
　　So that they could never trap us
　　Or say a word to turn to damns.
And then I know I'd see my pretty one,
Those lovely eyes, her lively hue—
I'd kiss that mouth in every way
So that the marks would last a month!

6. Yes, I'd like to find her alone,
　　Asleep or just pretending,
　　So that I could steal one sweet kiss
　　(I'm not worth enough to openly beg).
By God, lady, we accomplish little in love!
Time's going by; we're losing the very best part.
We'd better talk with some secret signs:
If nerve won't help, then maybe cunning will!

7. It's right a man should blame a lady
　　Who keeps putting her good friend off:

A long sermon on the subject of love
Is just a big bore, and a cheap trick too,
For a man can love and make a pretense,
And sweetly lie with no witness around.
My good lady, if only you'd grant me your love,
Never would I be troubled again by lies.
8. Messenger, run, and please don't prize me less
    If I'm afraid to rush there to Milordess.

Romantic Legend: Eleanor of Aquitaine

D.D.R. Owen

Eleanor of Aquitaine lived from 1122 to 1204. Her life resembled in many ways the figure of the noble lady central to the legends of King Arthur and the Knights of the Round Table, according to D.D.R. Owen. Like Queen Guinevere, she encouraged chivalric practices, got involved in affairs of state, arbitrated sentimental issues that arose in the castle, searched for adventure, and encouraged the arts. According to Owen, Eleanor was married twice to kings and twice suffered the deterioration of romantic love. Her first marriage to King Louis VII of France was annulled after Eleanor was unable to produce a male heir to the throne. Her second marriage to King Henry II of England united portions of France that belonged to Eleanor with Henry's England, creating the Angevin Empire. When Eleanor moved to England to be with Henry, however, she found Henry impossible, and their marriage deteriorated. Owen argues that when Henry died, Eleanor resumed her quest for adventure in spite of the deaths of several of her children. A romantic legend in her time, Eleanor died in the convent of Fontevrault. D.D.R. Owen is the author of several books on medieval literature including *The Legend of Roland: A Pagent of the Middle Ages*. He also edited the book, *Arthurian Romance: Seven Essays*.

In the absence of reliable contemporary descriptions of Eleanor [of Aquitaine] the person, I would suggest that the nearest we could

Excerpted from *Eleanor of Aquitaine: Queen and Legend,* by D.D.R. Owen. Copyright © 1993 by D.D.R. Owen. Reprinted with permission from Blackwell UK.

come to seeing her as she was perceived in her heyday might be to as-
semble a composite picture of Henry's [King Henry II of England]
queen from the more sympathetic of the portrayals of Guenevere in
courtly romance.[1] As an exquisitely beautiful young girl, of noble
southern blood according to the chroniclers, she had made an ideal
match by marrying the most illustrious of kings, who ruled over
Britain and territories beyond the Channel. The great mutual love between the couple was to become eroded, though never entirely disap-
pear, in the course of their long reign. Even when her own affections
were divided, she continued to perform to the best of her ability her
duties as mistress of the royal court: to be the confidante and coun-
selor of its younger members, acting as intermediary, when the need
arose, between them and the king, encouraging chivalric practice,
while being prompt with sensible advice on wider matters of state. She
saw her special domain as the arbitration of sentimental issues, which
were always a potential source of discord in the close-knit social unit
of the royal entourage. She helped to make it a more civilized place
by encouraging the arts, including literature, which itself served as a
mirror of refined social intercourse; and she shared with her husband
the role of Maecenas. Generous in thought and dead, she usually managed to control her personal feelings except under the pressure of grief
and, on rare occasions, of jealousy. Her virtues earned for her universal affection; and her long life ended in pious seclusion.

If we find such a portrait too bland and vague, then we must exercise our privilege, as have most writers on Eleanor, of creating our
own picture by accommodating our personal vision of her to the
known facts of her life. Not only must we avoid the stereotypes of her
legend (fairy princess, devil's daughter, scheming witch and so forth),
but allowance must be made for the development of her character over
the course of her long life as it suffered the stress of circumstances and
personal relationships. So, . . . I shall offer a sketch of my own, on the
understanding that its authenticity is limited to the skeleton of fact that
underlies it.

The Real Eleanor

Let us accept that the young Eleanor was beautiful, but not with the
blonde radiance favoured by the medieval poets and rhetoricians: dark-
haired rather, and with a sparkle in her eyes. She had inherited the
family intelligence and interest in the arts that flourished around her;
and as heiress-apparent to her father's great duchy, she was well
schooled too in more practical matters. Passionate and adventurous as
a girl, when she was suddenly wrenched from the relaxed life of her
native south [of France] she took some time to adjust to the more

---

1. Stories of romantic love as depicted in legends of King Arthur and the Knights of the Round Table.

sober atmosphere of King Louis's Paris. But once she had found her feet as queen, she was not content to remain the passive ornament of her adoring husband's court. Leaned on by political favour-seekers on the one hand and by men of the Church on the other, she quickly gained a shrewd knowledge of and interest in state affairs, while being inclined to leave excessive devoutness to her pious husband.

When the crusade was called, she was only too eager to be free of tiresome political intrigue and participate in its adventure. But this turned out to be quite different from the romantic jaunt of her dreams; and the trials and disasters of the journey were for her a maturing experience. Yet they did not efface her nostalgia for the cultured gaiety of her childhood; and this was reawakened by the hospitality at Antioch of her dashing uncle Raymond of Poitiers. It made her restive under Louis's heavy-handed restraint, and especially resentful of the authority he so sternly imposed. On their homeward journey, she bore with the pope's well-intentioned admonitions, which reinforced her growing sense of inadequacy at her failure to produce a royal heir to the crown of France. By now, both she and her husband were becoming increasingly aware that their temperaments were seriously incompatible and that their continued partnership was in the best interests of neither themselves nor the French kingdom. Then Eleanor's natural inclinations towards romance, adventure and active statecraft led her to seize the chance of marriage to a more dynamic but potentially equally powerful man.

England and France United

A foreigner even in France, she viewed the prospect of Anglo-Norman England as no less attractive than Paris. Its reputation for learning may have been lower, but it was no cultural backwater. In any case, as a hardened traveller, she had no qualms about returning across the Channel as opportunity offered; so when, after spending the first eighteen months of her marriage on her native soil, she left for England and the crown, she was assured of the possibility of going back there from time to time. By then she had realized one of her dearest ambitions with the birth of her first son, William. True, he survived barely three years; but by then she had another boy, Henry, so although the loss hurt, she felt only passing sorrow, as when she had had to leave her daughters behind with Louis. Indeed, in thirteen years she presented Henry with eight children: five sons and three daughters. This fully satisfied her maternal instincts, which were strong; and she continued to care deeply for the welfare of her children, although the girls' marriage potential did not leave them under her wing for long.

Her early years as queen of England were fulfilling for her in other ways. Despite her frequent pregnancies, her existence was far from sedentary. Apart from several visits to the Continent, she was often found travelling about England with her restless husband. She retained too a lively interest in domestic and international affairs and always with an eye to her children's prospects. For she was not one to dwell on the past, but showed as much concern for the future as the present. Even her continuing interest in Fontevrault [a convent] was not entirely altruistic: it was only prudent in her day to prepare for some unfortunate contingency which would call for a secure refuge from the storm. In the meantime, though, she could not be bored when she had such an ambitious and dynamic husband; and besides, she found pleasure in receiving visitors at her court, patronizing its cultural life, and bringing some southern sparkle to what she must sometimes have felt as the dour materialism of Anglo-Norman society.

Problems with Henry

However, as with Louis though for different reasons, she had to reconcile herself to a slow deterioration in her marital relations with Henry. It was not just his notorious bouts of temper: she had soon learnt to side-step or otherwise deal with them. Nor was it his equally well-known infidelities which, as the much older partner, she had to tolerate. It was more that whereas he seemed to live mainly in a frantic present, the romantic dreams of her youth had now given way to long-term dynastic ambitions for her sons. While he acted, she planned her strategy for a more distant future. Although her patience with Henry became increasingly strained, she would not have contemplated making a break with him (the convent was still for her an unthinkable alternative) had he not caused the disaffection of her sons. For once, though, her plans misfired and she became her husband's captive.

Her frustration now was not as total as it might have been. Although her energies had not waned, confined as they now were by the restrictions on her movements, the time had come to harbour them until her freedom returned. In the meantime, she had become an interested spectator, kept in touch with affairs, but not participating in them. The change was not as drastic as it might seem, since she had long lost her influence over Henry in public matters. So for her this was a time for contemplation, refining her political judgement and waiting for a favourable turn of events. Feeling herself the widow of a still living husband, she could only look beyond him to a life still full of possibilities. During these long years her native intelligence matured into wisdom. And when at last he gradually allowed her back on the public scene, she was content to be used by him as a pawn until such time as she would be needed again to play an active role.

Her relief was tempered by tragedy with the deaths of her sons the young Henry and Geoffrey, with that of Matilda soon to follow. Perhaps the knighting of John heralded happier days to come; and there was still the promise of Richard, her favourite. Then came the further death, that of her husband, over which she found fewer tears to shed. Now in her late sixties, she felt herself revitalized; and indeed her remaining years were to be full of activity. It was not over calm seas that she was to sail to that long prepared last haven of Fontevrault. She felt keenly the deaths of more of her children: Marie her first–born, Alice, Richard, Joanna, but especially Richard. Yet she used her reserves of energy to the full, perhaps even relishing her last adventures as much as her first. As a final pleasure she was able to visit her dear Poitiers [a city in south-west France] once again, and possibly even died there before resting for ever in her equally cherished abbey of Fontevrault.

Few people of her age, and certainly few women, could have experienced more, learnt more of the ways of their pulsating world. A legend in her own lifetime, Eleanor of Aquitaine may not have been one of the great makers of history, but she was certainly one of the great livers of it.

The Twelfth-Century Renaissance

During the 1100s in Europe a twelfth-century renaissance occurred whose scholarship has astonished modern historians. After studying the period more closely, historians have come to reevaluate the belief that the medieval period in Europe was static and that the great Italian Renaissance of the fifteenth century was an awakening of imagination after a long period of intellectual stagnation. The roots of the Italian Renaissance, it now appears, can be traced to the twelfth century.

The twelfth-century renaissance was a revival of learning that looked both backward and forward in time. Scholars during this period were fortunate that enhanced trade with other regions brought ancient Greek manuscripts—which had been translated into Latin—into Europe. Students memorized many of the works of Aristotle and used his ideas about logic and argumentation to create a new method of learning called disputation. Using this method, a student would construct an argument and defend it against challenges from other students and his teacher. The new emphasis on logic was criticized by older teachers who decried its overuse at the expense of traditional subjects like rhetoric and grammar. Even emerging scholars such as Peter Abelard and John of Salisbury, who embraced logic, felt it was being overemphasized. Nevertheless, the focus on Aristotle and his tracts on logic illustrated a search for order and rationality that would characterize learning in subsequent centuries.

The disagreements that arose on the proper emphasis on logic in an academic curriculum were by no means the only controversies over scholarship. On the contrary, the intellectual movement of the period was characterized by conflict. Older teachers tended to support the traditional teaching method of memorization while their students demanded the new method of disputation. Schools began to divide along secular and religious lines as well. Many older teachers believed that only theology was a proper subject of study. Younger teachers felt that schools should teach subjects required for secular professions, and they left their posts to found new schools devoted to the teaching of law and other secular subjects. Finally, the intellectual movement of the twelfth century pitted reason against faith. The scholar Anselm, for example, used logic to defend the existence of God, but his dependence on reason to validate what was once taken on faith underscores the growing sense at that time that faith alone was not enough.

The renaissance of the twelfth century also looked ahead to the greater Italian Renaissance of the fifteenth century and to many modern institutions. While scholars studied the traditional seven liberal arts—rhetoric, grammar, logic, arithmetic, geometry, music, and astronomy—they also began to study secular subjects such as law, science, and medicine. Twelfth-century scholars brought Roman law to Europe, and their systematic application of this code to the relationships between individuals helped establish a model that many fledgling European nations followed. The renewed interest in science and mathematics during the 1100s also paved the way for later scientists such as Copernicus, who would eventually discredit many ancient Greek theories such as the Ptolemaic model of the solar system. During the 1100s both Latin and vernacular literature flourished as well, bequeathing to later generations some of the most eloquent Latin writings and establishing a tradition of literature written in ordinary language. The establishment of the first universities was one of the twelfth century's most important developments, and some of those schools, such as Oxford, still exist as a legacy of the period. The twelfth-century renaissance also saw astonishing architectural accomplishments such as Gothic cathedrals, many of which, like the first universities, still stand. While this earlier renaissance produced no great painter such as Michelangelo, skilled artists created spectacular stained glass windows with which to adorn new churches, a tradition that endures into modern times.

The students who were involved in the twelfth-century renaissance resurrected the ancient past through the works of Greek writers and helped establish the creative roots for important intellectual movements and social institutions to come.

Overview: The Twelfth-Century Renaissance

Marshall Clagett, Gaines Post, and Robert Reynolds, eds.

Marshall Clagett, Gaines Post, and Robert Reynolds describe the renaissance in twelfth-century Europe as a burst of creativity inspired by the recovery of ancient learning through the translation of Greek and Roman texts into Latin. Political and economic changes in the region made the renaissance possible. Traditional feudalism—a political and economic system wherein knights were given land by lords in exchange for their services during wars—created lawlessness because knights had no obligation to obey laws outside of the feudal contracts they made with their lords. Eventually, this version of feudalism was replaced by feudal monarchies in which kings had more power to enforce law and order, and stability increased. The editors argue that economic growth as a result of enhanced trade also aided stability because it channeled more money to the kings and helped them keep law and order. The church contributed to the stability of the region as well; as papal power and influence grew, church-sponsored schools were developed. The editors maintain that the institutions and practices that developed from this revival of learning became the foundations of the modern world. Marshall Clagett is professor emeritus of history of science and mathematics at the School of Historical Studies; Gaines Post was a medieval historian at Princeton University; and Robert Reynolds is a professor of medieval history.

There was, to be sure, a revival, a renaissance of importance—[historian] Charles Homer Haskins was right. In the monastic and cathedral schools of France and England men of learning, in secular as well as religious ways that belong to medieval humanism, read and cherished the Latin classics. Ancient philosophy in Augustinian and Neoplatonic[1] terms found a new home and interpretation in the school of Chartres. At Paris the study of Aristotle's logic resulted in a methodology that became fruitful in all fields of learning. In Sicily and Spain, Western Christian scholars found, in Arabic and Greek versions which were rapidly translated into Latin, the main body not only of Islamic but also of ancient Greek learning in Aristotelian[2] and Neoplatonic philosophy, and in medicine, mathematics, astronomy, and the natural sciences. Finally, the classical Roman law, in the *Corpus Juris Civilis,* was fully revived at Bologna and became the basis of our modern legal science. Of the classical tradition, only the belles-lettres of Greece, except Plato's *Meno* and *Phaedo,* and portions of the *Timaeus,* remained unknown in the West in the twelfth century. But if the direct knowledge of Greek literature had to wait for the fifteenth century, the twelfth century was the real beginning of the later Renaissance, and can be directly associated with the term because of the revival of interest in and extensive recovery of ancient learning.

The Development of Cities and States

More important, however, is the fact that the twelfth century was a great period of creative, even revolutionary, activity in all aspects of civilization—and Haskins would agree. This was particularly true in Latin western Europe, but partly true also in central and eastern Europe—less true in the Greek, Byzantine Empire, and in the world of Islam, for by the twelfth century the Greek and Islamic contributions were declining, yielding to the dynamic vigor of the West, as Professor von Grunebaum's paper at least partly reveals. The decline in the West that accompanied the end of the Roman Empire, the barbarian invasions, the Arabic-Moorish conquest of Spain, the failure of the Carolingian Empire,[3] and the anarchy of feudalism, was reversed by the appearance of a greater political stability in the rise of feudal monarchies, in the revival of the ideal of the Roman Empire in Germany and Italy, in the organization of the spiritual monarchy of the papacy over the Roman Church, and in the growth of communes which in Italy were becoming powerful city-states. If these states and the

1. Augustinian refers to any ideas pertaining to Saint Augustine—who lived in the period from 354 to 430—or his doctrines; Neoplatonic refers to the philosophical and religious system in Greece in the third century A.D. based on the doctrines of Plato and other eastern and western philosophers. 2. Pertaining to the Greek philosopher Aristotle—who lived in the period from 384 to 322 B.C.—or his doctrines. 3. The Frankish dynasty that was founded in 751 and lasted until 987 in France and 911 in Germany.

Church were often in conflict, partly as a result of their increasing strength and consciousness of their rights, and the Empire itself was to fail to become a state precisely because emperors like Frederick Barbarossa went beyond their resources in trying to recreate the Roman Empire as a universal state, nonetheless the gain in the direction of developing modern national states was greater than the loss. In England and France, and in Castile and Aragon, the monarchy was gradually able, with the aid of feudal custom and principles of public law deriving from ideas in the *Corpus Juris Civilis* and the legists of Bologna, to centralize their governments and territorial states as the basis for modern nations. The papers of Professors Kantorowicz and Strayer are of interest for theoretical and practical aspects of this centralization. Despite the traditional Christian ideal of the subordination of the state to moral ends and to God, the state was becoming a natural end in itself, and lawyers and kings were well aware of the necessity and "reason of State" as a justification for the growth of the central public authority.

This political development accompanied, in part drew aid from, a significant revival of economic activities. For a new activity in trade and industry created a money economy which furnished able kings with the means for enforcing law and order, organizing an army, persuading feudal lords to respect the public interest, and increasing the royal domain. At the same time the merchants and artisans in their guilds, with an ever larger population made possible by the new economic life and social and political order, became the bourgeoisie, the middle class, and organized town governments. Here was the beginning of our modern city institutions and civic life. With the growth of cities and the need of educated men for business, law and justice, and government, learning itself moved from monasteries to cathedral schools and universities, as Professor Holmes has shown in his paper, and naturally the new wealth and urban environment stimulated the revival of art and architecture, as they did the establishment of more parishes and church buildings to take care of the spiritual welfare of the people. Religion and culture alike found a home in the city. A new "civilization," in the literal sense of all that relates to the city and civil life, was at hand. Thus if in these studies Professor Krueger devotes his attention to northern economic growth, his paper is closely related to the other important aspects of the century.

The Power of the Church

The consequences of all these movements were tremendous for the Holy Roman Church. In our period the Church was a successful continuation of the ancient Roman tradition of unity and universalism in the Christian faith and in the body of the faithful. It was successful because a strong, centralized papal monarchy, from Pope Gregory VII to Pope Innocent III and beyond, staunchly defended and maintained the ideal of the supremacy of Church over State, of the spiritual realm over the secular, of the eternal welfare of the soul over the temporal, and temporary, welfare of the body. This supremacy extended likewise into the realm of culture: all learning and all schools were ultimately subject to the jurisdiction of the pope, whose duty it was, according to the divine command, to superintend all learning lest ideas contrary to the faith be taught. The pope, indeed, in the later twelfth and early thirteenth centuries, encouraged the rise and organization of the first universities, and protected their autonomy in relation to local ecclesiastical and secular authorities. As a result, if under the Church no complete academic freedom could be permitted, the papacy did protect, to a surprising degree, the right of the professors to study and teach pagan and Islamic thought and to discuss problems of philosophy and revelation in rational terms; and the popes encouraged the study and teaching of all fields of learning—there was no hostility to the sciences, medicine, and Roman law.

The centralization of the state of the Church, however, was not complete; nor was it aimed at the destruction of local customs and traditions. In fact, local popular religion, often stimulated by learned saints like Bernard of Clairvaux, might be more creative than papal leadership in the spiritual realm. The cult of the Virgin Mary reached a great climax in our century. It came in part from the people, in part from St. Bernard. It was expressed in popular devotion, in learned mysticism, in Latin hymns, and in the building of magnificent Romanesque and Gothic cathedrals dedicated to Our Lady. At the same time masters of theology in the cathedral school of Paris and elsewhere were actively debating problems relating to the sacraments. They prepared the way for the decrees of the Fourth Lateran Council, 1215, which established the number of sacraments at seven and promulgated the doctrine of transubstantiation. Because of crusades and the closer relations with the Greek Church and Constantinople, Western Latin theologians revived the old Christological debate about the divine and human natures in Christ. Such discussions, which Professor Anastos recounts, reflected both an important intellectual activity at Paris and the renewed unity of Mediterranean-European culture amid the diversity of opinions.

Great as the twelfth-century church was, however, as an institution embodying the ideal of unity in the faith and in culture under the leadership of popes like Gregory VII, Alexander III, and Innocent III, it contributed to the breakdown of medieval universalism in the Holy Roman Empire—or at least it recognized the inevitable in the new economic and social life, the communes, and the rising independent states. While opposing the German emperors who hoped to create a great state including Germany and Italy in the Empire, the papacy recognized kingdoms to the east and west of Germany as independent states, and in Italy supported the rise of the communes as city-states that in fact recognized no superior in the emperor. If the canonists and popes felt that unity was the more victorious as a Christian unity in the one Church and under a pope-emperor, or a pope who had the ultimate supreme authority over emperors and kings alike, in fact their policy helped create those national states which by 1300 were refusing obedience to Boniface VIII.

Despite these tendencies inherent in the circumstances of the age, despite all localism and diversities in learning, a remarkable unity prevailed in learning and culture and civilization. Christian ideals pervaded political, economic, social, and cultural developments. Latin was the universal, living language of government, law, business, religion, and education. Trade was free of national tariffs. Within this kind of universalism scholars, men of letters and artists and architects, using the subject matter and ideas inherited from Greece and Rome, and from Islam, laid the cultural foundations of modern European-American civilization.

The Universities

To repeat, and to elaborate what has been said above, they created a new kind of institution of higher education, the university, which is still the most characteristic center of learning in the modern world. At the University of Bologna professors of law began to develop a new legal science in adapting the revived Roman law to the medieval environment. The English common law, which was itself a great medieval achievement, profited from the Roman influences spreading from Bologna. While the English law contained the ideal of fair trial (as in Magna Carta[4]), the Roman law contributed a clear statement of the ideal in terms of the presumption of innocence and the right of all accused parties to be properly summoned and to enjoy a more adequate defense through a better system of court procedure. The public law of Rome greatly aided kings in "systematizing" feudalism and organizing a central government. The idea of the state, already becoming a national state, reappeared. Indeed, both "reason of state" and nationalism found early expression by 1200. But if the head of the new state, the king, was as a result more powerful, not only the old Christian-Augustinian ideal of law and justice, of the fundamental law of God, but also the Roman and feudal emphasis on equity, fair trial, and the legal rights of subjects, limited his power and prevented the early appearance of statism and absolutism.

Philosophy enjoyed a new period of creative activity in the University of Paris. The debates of realists and nominalists, the brilliance of Abelard,[5] and the recovery of Aristotelian philosophy culminated

---

4. The great charter of English political and civil liberties granted by King John of Runnymede on June 15, 1215. 5. Peter Abelard was a French philosopher and theologian who lived from 1079 to 1142.

in the great medieval synthesis achieved by Thomas Aquinas.[6] But it must be remembered that Aristotle did not completely triumph at the expense of Plato and Christian Neoplatonism. From [the school at] Chartres, as Professor Klibansky shows, came a deeper appreciation of nature which played an important role in art and architecture as well as literature and political and legal thought. For while God and divine reason and measure and number remained in nature, there was a stronger emphasis on studying nature and imitating nature, and on the naturalness of society and the state. The very stress on natural objects as symbols of God's plan in the creation of the world led to the study of physical light by means of mathematics and optics. Here medieval symbolism and the Neoplatonic and Augustinian doctrine of divine illumination made use of the newly received Greco-Islamic science, and in part contributed to the rise of modern science.

Math, Medicine, and Science

In the twelfth century we find the foundation laid for the first creative activity of European mathematics, medicine, and the natural sciences. The immature, practical geometry of the early Middle Ages was replaced in the course of the century by complete versions of Euclid's *Elements* introduced into the Latin educational community in some five different translations. Even the relatively complex geometry of Archimedes that was to be a crucial tool of the new science came to the attention of scholars for the first time in the twelfth century. At the same time, Latin mathematicians came into intimate contact in Arabic guise with the Indian system of numerals and calculation. With it came also Arabic algebra and trigonometry. In addition, the twelfth century saw the introduction of the best examples of the Greek efforts to use mathematics in the description of the physical world. Ptolemy's great *Mathematical Syntaxis* or *Almagest*—the final mature product of Greek astronomy—was translated and began to be followed by Western astronomers. It must be remembered that the later efforts of Copernicus toward reorienting astronomy are inconceivable without a prior mastery of Ptolemaic astronomy. Similar Greek treatises of a crucial nature for the development of the sciences of mechanics and optics passed into the Latin schools in this century. Finally, the Arabic-Greek medicine was absorbed in the school of Salerno to make Salerno the fountainhead of European medicine. It is thus evident in all areas of scientific activity that a virtual revolution took place in the twelfth century—a revolution marked by the transformation of the early medieval descriptive, compendious, and non-mathematical science into a more mature mathematical and experiential science on the lines of the

6. Saint Thomas Aquinas was an Italian Dominican monk, philosopher, and theologian who lived from 1225 to 1274.

Greek model. The extraordinary development of modern science came about, at least in part, as the result of the introduction of, and reaction to, the twin traditions of Greek philosophy and science that were transmitted to Europe in the twelfth century.

Outside the schools and universities, creative activities were perhaps equally important. But it must be remembered that frequently new technological developments as well as literature and art and architecture profited from the learning in the schools. Whether the ideas, however, came to artisans from contacts with the East in the crusades,[7] from masters who acquired the elements of physics and geometry in cathedral school or university, or from innate European inventiveness, the fact is that new machines, new technical processes like the refining of sugar, and new engineering skills, for example, in the building of castles and Gothic churches, made their appearance. Above all, Gothic architecture, scorned by men of the Italian Renaissance as barbarous, was a great and original contribution to the world. The Gothic church at its best was both a mighty symbol of religion and the divine plan, and a synthesis of academic learning and engineering technology. Further, it provided a stone framework for the stained glass windows which at Chartres are still incomparably beautiful; and it provided the background for the stone-carvers to create great sculpture, symbolic and naturalistic at the same time. Professor Katzenellenbogen's paper throws light on the artistic developments at Chartres.

Outside the schools too, although resulting in part from literacy in the Latin classics in the schools, the vernacular languages and literatures attained a surprising maturity. Inspired by local interests and stories of heroes, by pilgrimage and crusade, and by the desire to understand human nature, poets wrote feudal epics, Arthurian romances,[8] sagas, lyrics, and fabliaux,[9] and created French, Spanish, Italian, and German and Scandinavian literature. To be sure, some of the vernacular appeared earlier, particularly the Anglo-Saxon literature. But the twelfth century was the period of the real beginning of the modern national literatures, leading to Dante[10] and Chaucer.[11] It is interesting that the Jews were contributing to Italian literature in this period, as Professor Spitzer shows in analyzing an anonymous Judeo-Italian elegy.

---

7. Military expeditions undertaken by European Christians in the eleventh, twelfth, and thirteenth centuries to recover the Holy Land from the Moslems. 8. Arthurian romances recount the legends of King Arthur and the Knights of the Round Table. 9. A medieval verse tale characterized by comic and ribald treatment of themes drawn from life. 10. Dante Alighieri was an Italian poet and author of *Divine Comedy* who lived from 1265 to 1321. 11. Geoffrey Chaucer was an English poet and author of *The Canterbury Tales* who lived from 1340 to 1400.

The Rise of
Universities

Lawrence Cunningham and John Reich

Lawrence Cunningham is professor of humanities at Notre Dame. John
Reich is professor of humanities at Syracuse University. Cunningham
and Reich argue that our present universities can be traced back to the
schools that arose in the late twelfth and early thirteenth centuries. The
universities developed as cities spread and the need for educated work-
ers to handle the more complicated demands of urban institutions grew.
The discovery of classical texts also rejuvenated learning and animated
the university movement. According to Cunningham and Reich, schools
were formed either by teacher guilds or student unions, and curriculum
focused on arts, and later, theology. Although student life was harsh
compared to contemporary standards and women did not attend, strong
parallels exist between university life then and now such as the high
cost of textbooks and the scarcity of employment opportunities after
graduation.

A number of our contemporary institutions have roots in the Middle Ages. Trial by jury is one, constitutional monarchy another.
By far the best-known and most widely diffused cultural institution
that dates from the Middle Ages, however, is the university. In fact,
some of the most prestigious centers of European learning today
stand where they were founded eight hundred years ago: Oxford and
Cambridge in England; the University of Paris in France; the University of Bologna in Italy There is also a remarkable continuity be-

Excerpted from *Culture and Values: A Survey of the Western Humanities,* by Lawrence S. Cunningham and John J. Reich. Copyright © 1990 by Holt, Rinehart, and Winston. Reprinted with
permission from Harcourt, Inc.

tween the organization and purposes of the medieval university and our own, except that we have coeducation. The medieval student would be puzzled, to be sure, by the idea of football games, coeducation, degrees in business or agriculture, and well-manicured campuses, were he to visit a modern American university. Such a student would find himself at home with the idea of a liberal arts curriculum, the degrees from the baccalaureate through the master's to the doctorate, and the high cost of textbooks. At a less serious level, he would be well acquainted with drinking parties, fraternities, and friction between town and gown (the phrase itself has a medieval ring). The literature that has come down to us from the period is full of complaints about poor housing, high rents, terrible food, and lack of jobs after graduation. Letters from the Middle Ages between students and parents have an almost uncanny contemporaneity about them except for the fact that women did not study in the medieval universities.

Cities and Schools

European universities developed in the late 12th and early 13th centuries along with the emergence of city life. In the earlier medieval period schools were most often associated with the monasteries, which were perforce situated in rural areas. As cities grew in importance, schools also developed at urban monasteries or, increasingly, under the aegis of bishops whose cathedrals were in the towns. The episcopal or cathedral school was a direct offshoot of the increasing importance of towns and the increasing power of bishops, the spiritual leaders of town life. In Italy, where town life had been relatively strong throughout the early Middle Ages and where feudalism never took hold, there was also a tradition of schools controlled by the laity. The center of medical studies in Salerno and the law faculty of Bologna had been in secular hands since the 10th century.

A number of factors help to explain the rapid rise of formal education institutions in the 12th century. First, the increasing complexity of urban life created a demand for an educated class who could join the ranks of administrators and bureaucrats. Urban schools were not simply interested in providing basic literacy. They were designed to produce an educated class who could give support to the socioeconomic structures of society. Those who completed the arts curriculum of a 12th–century cathedral school (like the one at Chartres) could find ready employment in either the civil or ecclesiastical bureaucracy as lawyers, clerks, or administrators.

There were also intellectual and cultural reasons for the rise of the universities. In the period from 1150 to 1250 came a wholesale discovery and publication of texts from the ancient world. Principal among these were lost books by Aristotle that came to the West

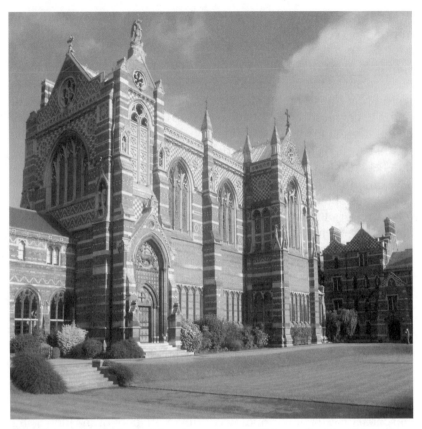

The University of Oxford has become one of the most prestigious centers of European learning.

through Muslim sources in Spain. Aristotle's writings covered a vast range of subjects ranging from meteorology and physics to logic and philosophy. Furthermore, with a closer relationship between Christian and Arabic scholars, a large amount of scientific and mathematical material was coming into Europe. There was also a renaissance of legal studies centered primarily at Bologna, the one intellectual center that could nearly rival Paris. Finally, there was a new tool being refined by such scholars as Peter Abelard and Peter Lombard: dialectics. Theologians and philosophers began to apply the principles of logic to the study of philosophy and theology. Abelard's book *Sic et Non* (1121) put together conflicting opinions concerning theological matters with contradictory passages from the Bible and the Church Fathers and then attempted to mediate and reconcile the apparent divergences. This method was later refined and stylized into the method which was to become *scholasticism,* so called because it was the philosophical method of the schools, the communities of scholars at the nascent universities.

The University of Paris

The most famous and representative university to emerge in the Middle Ages was the University of Paris. The eminence of Paris rested mainly on the fame of the teachers who came there to teach. At this state of educational development, the teacher really was the school. Students in the 12th century flocked from all over Europe to frequent the lectures of teachers like William of Champeaux (1070–1121) and, later, his formal student and vehement critic, Peter Abelard (1079–1142). Besides these famous individual teachers Paris also had some established centers of learning that enjoyed a vast reputation. There was a cathedral school attached to the cathedral of Notre Dame, a theological center associated with the canons of the church of Saint Victor, and a school of arts maintained at the ancient monastery of Sainte Geneviève.

Although it is difficult to assign precise dates, it is safe to say that the university at Paris developed in the final quarter of the 12th and early part of the 13th centuries. Its development began with the masters (*magistri,* teachers) of the city forming a corporation after the manner of the guilds. At this time the word universitas simply meant a guild or corporation. The masters formed the universitas in Paris in order to exercise some "quality control" over the teaching profession and the students entrusted to their care. At Bologna the reverse was true. The students formed the universitas in order to hire the teachers with the best qualifications and according to the most advantageous financial terms.

The universitas soon acquired a certain status in law with a corporate right to borrow money, to sue (and be sued), and to issue official documents. As a legal body it could issue stipulations for the conduct of both masters and students. When a student finished the course of studies and passed his examinations, the universitas would grant him a teaching certificate that enabled him to enter the ranks of the masters: He was a master of arts (our modern degree has its origin in that designation). After graduation a student could go on to specialized training in law, theology, or medicine. The completion of this specialized training entitled one to be called *doctor* (from the Latin *doctus,* learned) in his particular field. The modern notion that a professional person (doctor, lawyer, and the like) should be university-trained is an idea derived directly from the usages of the medieval university.

Since the Carolingian period—indeed, earlier—the core of education was the arts curriculum. In the late 12th century in Paris the arts began to be looked on as a prelude to the study of theology. This inevitably caused a degree of tension between the arts faculty and the theology masters. This tension resulted in 1210 in a split, with the masters and students of arts moving their faculty to the Left Bank of the Seine, where they settled in the area intersected by the rue du Fouarre (Straw Street—so named because the students sat on straw during lectures). That part of the Left Bank has traditionally been a student haunt. The name Latin Quarter reminds us of the old language that was once the only tongue used at the university.

By the end of the 12th century Paris was the intellectual center of Europe. Students came from all over Europe to study there. We do not have reliable statistics about their number, but an estimate of five to eight thousand students would not be far from the mark for the early 13th century. The students were organized into *nationes* by their place of national origin. By 1294 there were four recognized *nationes* in Paris: the French, the Picard, the Norman, and the Anglo-German. Student support came from families, pious benefactors, church stipends, or civic grants to underwrite an education. Certain generous patrons provided funds for hospices for scholars, the most famous of which was that underwritten by Robert de Sorbon in 1258 for graduate students in theology; his hospice was the forerunner of the Sorbonne in Paris.

Student Life

By our standards, student life in the 13th century was harsh. Food and lodging were primitive, heating scarce, artificial lighting nonexistent, and income sporadic. The daily schedule was rigorous, made more so by the shortage of books and writing material. An "ideal" student's day, as sketched out in a late medieval pamphlet for student use, now seems rather grim:

A Student's Day at the University of Paris

4:00 A.M.	Rise
5:00–6:00	Arts lectures
6:00	Mass and breakfast
8:00–10:00	Lectures
11:00–12:00	Disputations before the noon meal
1:00–3:00 P.M.	"Repetitions"—study of morning lectures with tutors
3:00–5:00	Cursory lectures (generalized lectures on special topics) or disputations
6:00	Supper
7:00–9:00	Study and repetitions
9:00	Bed

The masters' lectures consisted of detailed commentaries on certain books the master intended to cover in a given term. Since books were expensive, emphasis was put on note taking and copying so that the student might build up his own collection of books. Examinations were oral, before a panel of masters. Students were also expected to participate in formal debates (called disputations) as part of their training.

Geoffrey Chaucer provides us an unforgettable, albeit idealized, portrait of the medieval student (the clerk or cleric—many of the students were members of the minor clerical orders of the church) in his Prologue to the *Canterbury Tales:*

> A clerk from Oxford was with us also,
> Who'd turned to getting knowledge, long ago.
> As meagre was his horse as is a rake,
> Nor he himself too fat, I'll undertake,
> But he looked hollow and went soberly.
> Right threadbare was his overcoat; for he
> Had got him yet no churchly benefice,
> Nor was so worldly as to gain office.
> For he would rather have at his bed's head
> Some twenty books, all bound in black and red,
> Of Aristotle and his philosophy
> Than rich robes, fiddle, or gay psaltery.
> Yet, and for all he was philosopher,
> He had but little gold within his coffer;
> But all that he might borrow from a friend
> On books and learning he would swiftly spend,
> And then he'd pray right busily for the souls
> Of those who gave him wherewithal for schools.
> Of study took he utmost care and heed.
> Not one word spoke he more than was his need;
> And that was said in fullest reverence
> And short and quick and full of high good sense.
> Pregnant of moral virtue was his speech;
> And gladly would he learn and gladly teach.

Chaucer's portrait of the lean, pious, poor, zealous student was highly idealized to create a type. We get probably a far more realistic picture of what students were actually doing and thinking about from the considerable amount of popular poetry that comes from the student culture of the medieval period. This poetry depicts a student life we are all familiar with: a poetry of wine, women, song, sharp satires at the expense of pompous professors or poor accommodations, and the occasional episodes of cruelty that most individuals are capable of only when banded into groups.

The student subculture had also invented a mythical Saint Golias, who was the patron saint of wandering scholars. Verses (called Goliardic verse) were written in honor of the "saint." The poems that have come down to us are a far cry from the sober commentaries on Aristotle's *Metaphysics* that we usually associate with the medieval scholar.

One of the more interesting collections of these medieval lyrics was discovered in a Bavarian monastery in the early 19th century. The songs in this collection were written in Latin, Old French, and German and seem to date from the late 12th and the 13th centuries. Their subject range was wide but, given the nature of such songs, predictable. There were drinking songs, laments over the loss of love or the trials of fate, hymns in honor of nature, salutes to the end of winter and the coming of spring, and cheerfully obscene songs of exuberant sexuality. The lyrics reveal a shift of emotions ranging from the happiness of love to the despair of disappointment just as the allusions range from classical learning to medieval piety. One famous song, for example, praises the beautiful powerful virgin in language that echoes the piety of the church. The last line reveals, however, that the poem salutes not Mary but generous Venus.

In 1935 and 1936 the German composer Carl Orff set a number of these poems to music under the title *Carmina Burana*. His brilliantly lively blending of heavy percussion, snatches of ecclesiastical chant, strong choral voices, and vibrant rhythms have made this work a modern concert favorite. The listener gets a good sense of the vibrancy of these medieval lyrics by the use of the modern setting. Since the precise character of student music has not come down to us, Orff's new setting of these lyrics is a fine beginning for learning about the musicality of this popular poetry from the medieval university.

Did women study at the university? By and large they did not. Medieval customs sheltered women in a manner we find hard to imagine. Women were educated either privately (Heloise[1] was tutored by her uncle in Paris when she met Abelard) or within the cloister of the convent. Furthermore, most of university life was tied to the church. The masters were clerics (except at Bologna) and most students depended on ecclesiastical pensions (benefices) to support them. There are exceptions to this rule. There seem to have been women in universities in both Italy and Germany, but they were the exception. At Salerno, famous for its faculty of medicine, there may have been woman physicians who were attached to the faculty. We do know that by the 14th century the university was licensing women physicians. There is also a tradition that Bologna had a woman professor of law who, according to the story, was so beautiful that she lectured from behind a screen so as not to dazzle her students! It is well to remember that the universities were very conservative and traditional institutions. It was not until this century, for example, that provisions were made for women's colleges at Oxford that enjoyed the full privileges of university life. The discrimination against women at the university level was something, for example, that moved the bitter complaints of the English novelist, Virginia Woolf, as late as the 1930s.

1. Abelard's beloved and intellect in her own right.

Conflicting Philosophies: Humanism and Scholasticism

Dom. David Knowles

According to Dom. David Knowles, humanism flourished during the twelfth-century Renaissance. The humanists became intimately connected to the classical texts from Greece and Rome that they studied. Knowles argues that they revered the authors of the ancient past, and looked to them for guidance on how to think and live. Perhaps most significantly, humanists celebrated the classical mode of expression by imitating it, which resulted in some of the clearest and most beautiful Latin writings in history. A third trait of twelfth-century humanism was its emphasis on personal emotion. Knowles contends that the philosophy that ultimately prevailed was scholasticism, however. Those who followed this tradition viewed the ideas presented in the ancient texts in a detached, intellectual manner, without thought to the style in which they were written or the author who wrote them down. To these scholars, the ideas of the ancient writers alone were important. Dom. David Knowles was Regius Professor of Modern History at Cambridge University. He wrote a four-volume work entitled *The Monastic Order in England and The Religious Orders in England* in which he documented the history of the religious life in England from the tenth to the seventeenth century.

Excerpted from "The Humanism of the Twelfth Century," by Dom. David Knowles, *Studies,* an Irish Quarterly Review (Talbot Press, Dublin, Ireland), 1941. Reprinted with permission.

The two centuries that follow the [first] millennium, which have been so closely studied by the historians of politics, economics and art, have perhaps not yet yielded up all their secrets in the realm of cultural life. It is only too easy to regard the medieval period as a prelude and preparation for the modern world, and to consider the history of Western civilization as that of an ordered progress towards the material and intellectual perfection of man; within the medieval centuries themselves it is equally inviting to discover a steady and straightforward evolution from barbarism to enlightenment. Yet even in constitutional, legal and economic history where such a view is least misleading, the conception of an ordered and unhalting progress, familiar to Victorian writers, must receive modification in more than one respect; in the history of intellectual development and the changes of religious sentiment any idea of an unfaltering advance is wholly false.

This, perhaps, is particularly true in respect of the first great flowering of culture in Western Europe which began shortly after the year 1000. This age, save for its artistic life, had until recently been unduly neglected by historians of thought. The great moral and intellectual leaders—Anselm, Abelard and Bernard, and their lesser contemporaries such as Peter the Venerable or John of Salisbury—were indeed familiar figures, but they had been treated only in isolation; and even during the first half of the twentieth century, when the various schools of medieval philosophy and theology have at last attracted something of the attention they deserve, there has been a tendency to regard the eleventh and twelfth centuries as but a dawning, a prelude, to the thirteenth, the 'greatest of centuries', which opened with [Pope] Innocent III and St Francis [of Assisi], which saw the earliest and purest masterpieces of Gothic architecture spring into being at Chartres, at Paris, at Salisbury and at Westminster, which embraced all the glories of scholastic theology, and which closed upon the year in which Dante, waking in the hillside forest, passed in imagination through the realms beyond the grave. In consequence, even those who, like the late Professor [Charles] Haskins, have done most to extend our knowledge of the twelfth century or who, like Denifle and Ehrle and Mandonnet and Grabmann, have studied the growth of the universities, the origins of scholasticism and the prehistory of the friars—even these, when treating of earlier years, have given their attention to the seeds that were still to bear fruit rather than to the ripe ears of the summer's harvest. Yet to a careful observer the latter half of the twelfth century appears as a decline as well as a dawn, and as he looks back over the brilliant creative achievement of the hundred years between 1050 and 1150 and notes its deep and sympathetic humanism, which anticipated to an extraordinary degree much that is considered typical of the age of the

Medici and of Erasmus, he becomes sensible of a very real change and declension between 1150 and 1200 which helped to make the culture of the thirteenth century, for all its intense speculative force and abiding power, less universal, less appealing and, in a word, less humane than what had gone before.

It is the purpose of these pages to direct attention to the earlier years, to the brilliant and original creative energies of the late eleventh century, and to the wide and sympathetic humanism which between 1050 and 1150 made its appearance for the first time in Western Europe. This first great re-birth—the proto-Renaissance as it has sometimes been called by historians of art and architecture— took place earlier than is generally supposed; the movement reached maturity between 1070 and 1130; it changed and declined in the fifty years between the death of St Bernard and the pontificate of Inno- cent III, and the intellectual atmosphere of the thirteenth century which followed, though it was in some ways more rare, more brac- ing and more subtle, lacked much of the kindly warmth and fragrant geniality of the past. The culture of the schools was, in fact—to drop the language of metaphor—without many of the elements that make a society fully humane, and that the preceding age had possessed for a time and subsequently lost. . . .

The three notes of the new humanism, which set the great men of the eleventh and twelfth centuries apart from those who had gone be- fore and those who came after, may be put out as: first, a wide liter- ary culture; next, a great and what in the realm of religious sentiment would be called a personal devotion to certain figures of the ancient world; and, finally, a high value set upon the individual, personal emotions, and upon the sharing of experiences and opinions within a small circle of friends.

Since the ideas and emotions thus shared were often of a religious or, at least, of a philosophical character, and since the writers were in every case men who wrote little or nothing that could be called pure po- etry or secular literature, the fundamental humanism of their outlook has been overlooked or, at best, has been recognized only in those who, like John of Salisbury or Hildebert of Lavardin, were classical scholars of an eminence that would attract notice in any age. In one celebrated case, indeed, it has been obscured by the persistent attempts that have been made to romanticize the past in a totally unhistorical fashion. Nev- ertheless, the men of the early twelfth century, if they are regarded with attention and sympathy, show themselves as possessed of a rare deli- cacy of perception and warmth of feeling. It is to the sixteenth century, not to the thirteenth, that one looks for the spiritual kin of Anselm, of John of Salisbury, and of Héloïse.

The hall-mark of the revival, and the accomplishment that was most widely possessed by all whom it affected, was a capability of self-expression based on a sound training in grammar and a long and often loving study of the foremost Latin writers. The great ecclesiastics, one and all, who flourished between 1030 and 1180, could express themselves not only in fluent, correct and often elaborate language, but also in phrases and sentences of true dignity and eloquence. Peter Damian, John of Fécamp, Anselm, Abelard, Bernard, William of Malmesbury, Peter the Venerable, John of Salisbury—all these, and a hundred others, were masters of a flexible style and a wide vocabulary; they can be read with ease and pleasure; they are capable of giving adequate expression to their ideas and emotions, and do not fail to do so. Indeed, a student of the period comes to take this for granted—just as, in the use of contemporary manuscripts, he takes for granted the uniform, clear and beautiful script. Yet all this is in contrast alike to the age which had gone and to that which was to follow. Even the most learned men of the previous century, such as Abbo of Fleury, are narrow in the range of their ideas and awkward in their utterance; in England, among those who write Latin, the ideas are still less mature and the expression often laboured to the point of incomprehensibility. As for the century that came after, it may seem paradoxical to suggest that the great churchmen and thinkers of the age were inarticulate; yet those who have read in their entirety the correspondence of Adam Marsh, Robert Grosseteste and John Pecham, or who have endeavoured to pierce through to the personal experience and intimate characteristics of Albert the Great, Thomas Aquinas or Robert Kilwardby—to say nothing of the enigmatic Roger Bacon or Duns Scotus—will readily admit that in all the arts of language, in all manifestations of aesthetic feelings or personal emotions, in fine, in all the qualities of self-revealing intimacy, the great men of the thirteenth century are immeasurably poorer than their predecessors a hundred years before. And though the luminous and adequate expression of ideas and emotions does not of itself alone constitute a character which we call humanist—for neither Anselm nor Bernard, past masters of the craft of letters, are precisely humanists—yet the power of self-expression grounded upon, or at least reinforced by, a wide literary culture is a condition *sine qua non* of a humanist's growth.

The second trait of the humanism of the twelfth century was, it is suggested, a personal devotion to one or more of the great figures of the distant past. To look to the past as to an age wiser and more accomplished than the present, to imitate its masterpieces and hand on its doctrine, had been a common tendency in every country since the end of the Empire wherever any sort of enlightenment found scope. To rediscover and repeat the past had been the watchword of Charlemagne, as it was to be the watchword, differently understood, of Hildebrand, of the early fathers of Cîteaux and of the early promul-

gators of the newly revived civil and canon law. What was peculiar
to many of the humanists, and at the same time a striking anticipa-
tion of the sentiment of leading circles in the later Italian Renaissance, was a reverence for the precepts and a conscious endeavour
to imitate the lives of celebrated writers or characters of antiquity
considered as human beings or sages, rather than precisely as saints
or legislators. If we wish to see the more intimate aspects of this trait,
we cannot perhaps do better than consider the ways of thinking and
acting of three individuals, all endowed with eminent intellectual
gifts and exquisite emotional sensibilities and all eager to give expression to a part, at least, of their experience.

Abelard, Héloïse and Ailred of Rievaulx are among the comparatively few personalities of the early twelfth century whose lives and
words will continue to attract and move the minds of men throughout
the ages. All three are, though in very different ways, essentially of
their own period and remote from ours in the circumstances of their
lives and in the cast of their thought. The problems, the catastrophe
and the fate of Abelard and Héloïse are, quite as much as the austere
monastic life of Ailred, typical of the twelfth century and remote from
the experience of the twentieth. All three, on the other hand, by reason of their intense sensibility to emotions shared in some degree by
all civilized mankind, and by reason also of a vivid power of self-
expression, are not only of an age but for all time. With neither of the
characteristics just mentioned are we concerned here, however, but
with a third: the peculiar cast, that is, given to their thoughts and emotions by the humanistic training which they had undergone.

This appears, as has been said, most clearly in the reverence and
devotion with which they regarded certain great figures of antiquity.
With Abelard and Héloïse it is Cicero, Seneca, Lucan and St Jerome
who are principally revered; with Ailred it is Cicero (at least in
youth) and St Augustine. That in the case of all three the influence
has a strong religious colour and that its primary object is a saint (for
St Jerome is the exemplar to whom both Abelard and Héloïse turn
most readily) does not affect its peculiar character. . . .

The third trait common to Abelard, Héloïse and Ailred, though
again issuing in very different courses of action, is the importance
which all attached to their personal emotions. With Abelard the cri-
sis came comparatively late in life, when he was near his fortieth
year. Previously, we may suppose, the vivid interests and brilliant
successes of his intellectual life had kept all else suppressed; for the
deterioration of character, due to wealth and fame, to which he attributed his fall, may supply a moral explanation, but does not of itself reveal the psychological background of the drama. In any case,
his passion ran a not unusual course, though the genius of the man
and the tragical *dénouement* of his love affair with Héloïse have to

some extent sublimated it in the eyes of posterity.[1] From frank sensuality he rose to a deeper, if still wholly selfish, emotion; self-centred as he was, he must give his every mood expression (for in this, as in much else, he resembled a Newman or a Cicero), and the most acute dialectician of the schools, the successful rival of William of Champeaux and Anselm of Laon, became a singer of love lyrics which by their words and melody carried the name of Héloïse beyond the barriers of land and sea. All have perished, but when we read the hymns which Abelard wrote in a still later phase, we are not disposed to accuse of partiality the judgement passed upon his earlier verses by the one who was the theme of their praise.

Abelard's love for Héloïse long remained selfish; the sacrifices which it entailed were, as he himself pointed out somewhat coldly, the unwilled consequences and punishments of his fault, not a willing gift of self-surrender. Only when he had become a monk and a priest and was, partially at least, 'converted' to the religious life, did his affection for Héloïse show itself in actions inspired by a genuine and selfless devotion. Indeed, it is by reason of the care shown by this strange ex-abbot for his wife who still more strangely found herself abbess, rather than by the earlier phases of his emotional drama, that Abelard stands among the humanists, in contrast to the more conventional religious sentiments of his day.

Héloïse, on the other hand, at once greater and not so great as her lover, gave all in a very real sense from the beginning. With her, motives of the intellectual order meant nothing, and those of the spiritual order little more. Héloïse in truth, so far as her own deepest utterances go, has nothing of the Christian in her. What renders her unique and gives her nobility and even sublimity is the combination of exceptional mental power and unshakable resolve with the most complete and voluntary self-sacrifice—not, indeed, the surrender of her own will and life to God or to any ethical demand, but the surrender of herself in totality to another. Clinging to this sacrifice with an intensity worthy of a heroine of Scandinavian legend—and indeed the blood of the pagan North may well have flowed in her veins—she found her model not in any saint of the Christian or even of the Hebrew centuries, but in the haughty and despairing women of ancient Rome, as they were depicted by the Stoic poet. . . .

The familiarity of all educated men of the age with the masterpieces of Latin literature has often been remarked upon. The mention of Héloïse touches upon another aspect of this renaissance: the share, that is, of women in the higher culture of the day. Héloïse, indeed, was something of a prodigy, but nowhere is there any suggestion that her uncle, Fulbert, was acting in an eccentric or even in an

---

1. Abelard's relationship with Héloïse was strongly disapproved of, especially by her uncle. When she became pregnant, Abelard fled to a monastery and Héloïse to a convent.

unconventional manner when he decided to give his niece a perfect education in letters. Nor did she stand wholly alone. It may not be easy to point to individual *bas bleus* in Paris or even in the convents of France in general, but in England there was no lack of them. The daughter of Margaret of Scotland, the future Queen Maud, was given a thorough literary education at Romsey; Shaftesbury, a little later, sheltered Marie de France, and Muriel of Wilton was not the only other poetess in England, as is shown by the numerous copies of Latin verses attached by the convents of women to the bead-rolls of exalted personages. These cloistered elegists, however, scarcely differ in kind from their sisters who, four hundred years before, had corresponded with St Boniface; Héloïse, alike in her single-minded enthusiasm, in her real literary powers, and in her devoted, even pedantic reverence for her classical models, is a true predecessor of Camilla Rucellai, Margaret Roper and Lady Jane Grey; to her, as to these, Dorothea in George Eliot's novel *Middle March* would have looked with admiration.

Héloïse may well have outdistanced all rivals of her own sex. In deploring the lack of letters among men, however, Peter the Venerable, in his celebrated letter to the widowed abbess, is using the language of exaggeration, for no one acquainted with the literature of the age can be unaware of the wide familiarity shown by so many with Latin literature. Ailred of Rievaulx can assume a familiarity with Cicero's *De Amicitia* as a matter of course in a young Cistercian of his abbey; quotations from the poets are common in almost all the more elaborate chronicles and letters of the period; the greatest humanists, such as Hildebert of Lavardin, Abelard and John of Salisbury, quote aptly and copiously from a very wide range of Latin poetry. Rarely, perhaps, are the poets quoted solely on account of the intrinsic beauty of their words; Abelard, however, and John of Salisbury often give evidence of their appreciation of the purely poetic. For most the favourite authors are the rhetoricians and satirists of the Silver Age and the learned, artificial poets of the later Gallo-Roman culture. Though Virgil has pride of place, it may be suggested that even he may appear rhetorical to a superficial and unintuitive mind; Horace, significantly enough, is often quoted from the *Satires* and *Epistles*, rarely from the *Odes*—their beauty, it may be, was too sophisticated and too exquisite to be appreciated, their urbanity too unfamiliar, and their pagan morality and religion too obvious. For similar reasons Tibullus and Propertius rarely occur, and scarcity of manuscripts is sufficient of itself to account for unfamiliarity with Lucretius and Catullus. Juvenal, on the other hand, Lucan and the difficult Persius were, relatively speaking, more familiar to the contemporaries of Abelard than to classical scholars of today.

Nothing, perhaps, shows both the reality and the extent of the training on classical models than the facility with which numbers were able to compose sets of perfectly correct Latin verses, and that not only in hexameters and elegiacs, but in the lyric metres used by Horace and Catullus. That the inhabitants of nunneries in Wessex should have been able to write passable elegiacs, and that it should have seemed natural to a monk when composing a saint's life to break without warning or apparent reason into alcaics, hendeca-syllabics and the still more elaborate iambic and trochaic metres, are phenomena of the late eleventh century to which it would be hard to find a parallel save in the late fifteenth or early sixteenth. That only a few—a Peter Damian, an Abelard, a Hildebert—should have at-tained real poetry in their compositions should be no occasion for wonder; the rest fail where the most felicitous verses of a Jebb, of a Calverley, and even of a Milton fail; the remarkable fact is that so many had achieved a mastery of the language and the metre without any aid from a Gradus or dictionary. Occasionally, indeed, the level of true poetry is attained, together with perfect felicity of vocabu-lary; Peter Damian's Sapphic hymns to St Benedict, like the earlier hymn to the Baptist, *Ut queant laxis*, are supreme in their kind, and it would be difficult for a scholar, familiar only with ancient Latin literature, to assign their composition to the eleventh rather than to the sixth or the sixteenth century. More often, however, the nearest approach to true poetry is made in the simpler accentual metres and the lyrics that verge upon the vernacular.

The decline of this humanism, like its rise, was comparatively rapid. The phase of sentiment we are considering touched its apogee between the rise of Hildebert of Lavardin and the central years of the literary life of John of Salisbury. With Peter of Blois the decline is beginning, and though in England there was something of a time-lag, the end was reached with Walter Map, Gerald of Wales and their circle; Gerald, indeed, lived on into another world and lamented the change. By the death of King John the transformation was complete. The great figures of the early thirteenth century, whether thinkers or administrators, are all but inarticulate when not in their schools or chanceries. It is from the class of the unlettered, from a Francis of Assisi or a Joinville, that the clearest utterances come, 'the earliest pipe of half-awakened birds', heralding another dawn in Europe. Lit-erary, philosophical, scholarly humanism was dead, and it is signif-icant that the supreme and balanced art, the Pheidian assurance and repose of the sculptures of Chartres, of Wells, of Amiens and of Rheims, was the expression of life as seen, not by a Leonardo or a Michelangelo, but by unlettered handicraftsmen living wholly in the present and wholly ignorant of the literature and culture of the past.

This is not to say that the new age owed no debt, paid no homage, to the past. In one sense the debt of no century had been heavier; for, as recent scholarship has shown, a larger and larger portion of the corpus of Aristotelian writings and numerous dialogues of Plato and Greek philosophers of the Empire were becoming familiar to the West, together with works of science, Greek and Arabian. St Thomas rests upon Aristotle, 'the Philosopher', more completely and unreservedly than does Abelard upon Augustine or Jerome or Seneca; and, as regards language, all metal is tested upon the touchstone of Cicero. Plato, Aristotle and Augustine, in their various ways, are not merely the foundations of the fabric of scholasticism; they are its *materia prima*, the very medium in which Aquinas works. Yet scholars of today who, when rightly demonstrating the traditional and wholly European character of medieval culture, emphasize the debt of the schoolmen to the ancients, may perhaps mislead those familiar only with modern history when they speak of the humanism, or of the classical tradition, of the great scholastics. The attitude of St Thomas towards the masters of the past differs by a whole heaven from that of Abelard and Ailred, as it does from that of Erasmus and More. The humanists, though living in times so very different from those of Greece and Rome, scrutinize the lives and emotions of the ancients, imitate their modes of expression and seek to reach the heart of their thought by long and sympathetic examination; the schoolmen revere the past no less deeply, but it is the external, visible fabric of thought, the purely intellectual, impersonal element that they absorb, and so far from submitting themselves to its moulding influence, they adapt it without hesitation to serve a wholly new system of philosophy, an utterly different *Weltanschauung*. To the schoolmen the personalities, the emotions, the external vicissitudes of the lives of Aristotle and Augustine meant nothing; the skeleton of their thought was all in all. To Ailred and to Héloïse, as to the contemporaries of Cosimo de' Medici, the joy and anguish of an Augustine or a Cornelia were a consolation and a light; they turned to them, and to the poets of the past, for guidance and sympathy. 'Then 'twas the Roman, now 'tis I.' So the humanists, but never the schoolmen, found strength in a community of feeling with those who, centuries before, had trodden the same path, and it is this consciousness of the unchanging mind of man that divides the culture of the first Renaissance from the more familiar culture of the later Middle Age.

Abelard the Intellectual

Jacques Le Goff

Jacques Le Goff is a specialist on the Middle Ages and is considered the eminent representative of "new history," a theoretical approach to studying history. According to Le Goff, Abelard—who lived from 1079 to 1142 during the development of the first universities—became the first professor. His scholarly work was controversial and generated an endless series of conflicts with notable scholars and theologians of his day. Le Goff maintains that Abelard first warred with the leading scholar in Paris at that time, William of Champeaux, and was so successful in his intellectual arguments that he won students over to his side. The young scholar also quarreled with the most respected theologian of his day, Anselm, whose ideas Abelard thought passe. His success in debating Anselm earned him even more student followers, according to Le Goff. When Abelard was thirty-nine, he met the intellectual Heloise. Abelard married Heloise in spite of the strong anti-marriage sentiments that existed due to the influence of the writers of chivalric romances who claimed that real love could only exist outside of marriage, which was usually loveless. Le Goff contends that the couple tried to hide their marriage from the outside world, but her father misread the situation, thought Abelard was dissolving the marriage, and had him castrated. According to Le Goff, Abelard's last intellectual conflict was with Bernard of Clairvaux, a monastic reformer and powerful churchman, who believed that Abelard's ideas about religion were dangerous. Bernard ordered all of the scholar's books to be burned, and Abelard took refuge in a monastery where he died in 1142.

Excerpted from *Intellectuals in the Middle Ages,* by Jacques Le Goff, translated by Teresa Lavender Fagan. Copyright © 1993 by Basil Blackwell. Reprinted with permission from Blackwell UK.

Although he was a goliard [a wandering student], Peter Abelard, the glory of the Parisian milieu, meant and contributed much more. He was the first great modern intellectual figure—within the limits of the term "modernity" in the twelfth century. Abelard was the first *professor.*

Intellectual Battles

To begin, Abelard's career, like the man, was remarkable. This Breton from the outskirts of Nantes, born in Le Pallet in 1079, belonged to the petty nobility, for whom life was becoming difficult with the advent of a monetary economy. Abelard gladly abandoned a military career to his brothers and devoted himself to his studies.

If Abelard gave up the weapons of a warrior, it was to engage in another type of battle. Always the fighter, he was to become, in the words of Paul Vignaux, "the knight of dialectics." Always in motion, he went wherever there was a battle to be waged. Always awakening new ideas, he brought enthralling discussions to life wherever he went.

Abelard's intellectual crusade inevitably led him to Paris. There he revealed another trait of his character: the need to destroy idols. His admitted self-confidence—*de me presumens,* he willingly said, which does not mean "to be too presuming," but rather, "being aware of my worth"—led him to attack the most illustrious of the Parisian masters [teachers], William of Champeaux. He provoked him, pushed him into a corner, won the students over to his own side. William forced him to leave. But it was too late to stifle that young talent. Abelard became a master. Students followed him to Melun, then to Corbeil, where he ran a school. But his body suddenly failed him, this man who lived only for knowledge; ill, he had to retire for a few years to Brittany.

Having recuperated he went to Paris to look for his old enemy William of Champeaux. There were new jousts; a shaken William modified his doctrine by taking the criticism of his young detractor into account. Abelard, far from being satisfied, intensified his attacks and went so far that he again had to retreat to Melun. But Williams's victory was in fact a defeat. All his students abandoned him. The defeated old master gave up teaching. Abelard triumphantly returned to Paris and settled in the very place where his old adversary had retreated: on Mount Ste Geneviève. The die was cast. Parisian intellectual culture would no longer have the Île de la Cité as its center, but would forever have Mount Ste Geneviève on the left bank: this time a man had established the destiny of a quarter.

But Abelard suffered in not having an adversary at his level. As a logician, he was irritated, moreover, at seeing theologians placed above everyone else. He made an oath: he, too, would be a theologian. He returned to his studies and hurried off to Laon to work with Anselm, the most illustrious theologian of the time. The glory of Anselm did not last long in the presence of the iconoclastic passion of the impetuous antitraditionalist:

> I therefore approached the old man who owed his reputation more to his advanced age than to his talent or his culture. All those who approached him to have his advice on a subject about which they were uncertain left him even more uncertain. He was admirable in the eyes of his hearers, but of no account in the sight of questioners. His fluency of words was admirable, but in a sense they were contemptible and devoid of reason. When he kindled a fire he filled his house with smoke, rather than lighted it with a blaze. His tree, in full life, was conspicuous from afar to all beholders, but by those who stood near and diligently examined the same it was found to be barren. To this tree therefore, when I had come that I might gather fruit from it, I understood that it was the fig-tree which the Lord cursed, or that old oak to which Lucan compares Pompey, saying—
>
> > There stands the shadow of mighty name,
> > Like to a tall oak in a fruitful field.[1]
>
> Edified, I did not waste my time at his school.

Abelard was challenged to make good his promise. He took up the gauntlet. He was told that even if he had great knowledge of philosophy, he knew little of theology. Abelard's reply was that the same method could be used for both. His inexperience was pointed out. "I replied that it was not my custom to have recourse to tradition to teach, but rather to the resources of my mind." He then improvised a commentary on the prophesies of Ezekiel [Hebrew prophet] which delighted his listeners. People scurried for the notes taken at this lecture to have them copied. A growing audience implored him to continue his commentary. He returned to Paris to do so.

Abelard and Heloise

Abelard continued his rise to glory—which was abruptly interrupted in 1118 by his adventures with Heloise. We know the details of this adventure from Abelard's extraordinary autobiography *Historia Calamitatum*—"The History of My Troubles"—those premature *Confessions*.

It all began like Cholderlos de Laclos' novel, *Dangerous Liaisons*. Abelard was not a rake. But middle-aged lust attacked this intellectual who, at the age of thirty-nine, knew love only through the books of Ovid and the songs he had composed—in true goliard spirit, but not through experience. He was at the height of his glory and pride.

---

1. Roger Lloyd, *Peter Abelard: The Orthodox Rebel* (London: Latimer House, 1947), p. 49–50.— TRANS.

He confessed as much: "I believed there was only myself, the only philosopher in the world." Heloise was a conquest to add to those of his intelligence. And it was at first an affair of the head as much as of the flesh. He learned of the niece of a colleague, the Canon Fulbert; she was seventeen, pretty, and so cultivated that her scholarship was already famous throughout France. She was the woman he was meant to have. He would not have tolerated an idiot, but he was pleased that Heloise was also very pretty. It was a question of taste and prestige. He coolly devised a plan which succeeded beyond his greatest hopes. The canon entrusted the young Heloise to Abelard's care as a pupil, proud to be able to give her such a master. When they discussed his salary Abelard easily convinced the thrifty Fulbert to accept payment in kind: room and board. The devil was keeping watch. There were fireworks between the master and the pupil: first, intellectual exchanges, then, soon after, carnal exchanges. Abelard abandoned his teaching, his work—he was possessed. The affair continued and deepened. A love was born which would never end. It would resist all difficulties, then tragedy.

The first difficulty came when they were caught in the act. Abelard had to leave the home of his deceived host. The lovers met elsewhere. At first hidden, their relationship was soon flaunted. They believed they were above all scandal.

Next, Heloise became pregnant. Abelard took advantage of Fulbert's absence to take his lover, disguised as a nun, to his sister's home in Brittany. There Heloise gave birth to a son whom they called Astralabe (the danger of being the child of a couple of intellectuals . . .).

The third difficulty was the issue of marriage. Abelard, with a heavy heart, would have made amends to Fulbert for his actions by offering to marry Heloise. In his admirable study on the famous couple, Etienne Gilson has shown that Abelard's repugnance was not due to his being a clerk. As an unordained priest he was canonically allowed to have a wife. But Abelard feared that as a married man he would see his academic career hindered, and would become the laughing stock of the scholarly world.

An Anti-Marriage Current

In the twelfth century, there was in fact a very strong antimarriage current. At the same time that women were being liberated, were no longer considered the property of men or as baby-making machines, when the question of whether women had souls was no longer being asked—this was the age of Marian expansion in the West [cult of the Virgin Mary]—marriage was the object of disdain, both in noble circles—courtly love, carnal or spiritual, existed only outside marriage; it was embodied in Tristan and Isolde, Lancelot and Guinevere [lovers from Arthurian legend]—as well as in scholarly circles, where a complete theory of natural love, later found in the *Roman de la Rose* in the following century, was being developed.

There was a strong female presence, therefore. And Heloise's appearance beside Abelard, while it accompanied the movement supported by the goliards, which demanded the pleasures of the flesh for clerks as well as priests, strongly highlighted an aspect of the new face of the intellectual in the twelfth century. His humanism demanded that he be fully a man. He rejected anything that might appear to be a diminution of his self. He needed a woman by his side to be complete. With the freedom of their vocabulary, the goliards stressed, with the support of citations from the two Testaments, that men and women were endowed with organs whose use should not be made light of. Disregarding the memory of so many lewd and dubious jokes, we should think of that climate and psychology, to better grasp the significance of the tragedy which was to occur, and to better understand the feelings of Abelard.

Heloise was the first to express her feelings. In a surprising letter she begs Abelard to reject the notion of marriage. She evokes the image of the couple of poor intellectuals which they would form:

> You could not give your attention at the same time to a wife and to philosophy. What concord is there between pupils and serving-maids, desks and cradles, books or tablets and distaves, styles or pens and spindles? Who, either, intent upon sacred or philosophic meditations can endure the wailing of children, the lullabies of the nurses soothing them, the tumultuous mob of the household, male as well as female? Who, moreover, will have strength to tolerate the foul and incessant squalor of babes? The rich, you will say, can, whose palaces or ample abodes contain retreats, of which their opulence does not feel the cost nor is it tormented by daily worries. But the condition of philosophers is not, I say, as that of the rich, nor do those who seek wealth or involve themselves in secular cares devote themselves to divine or philosophic duties.[2]

Moreover, there were authorities to support this position and condemn the marriage of the sage. One might cite Theophrastus or rather St Jerome, who repeated his arguments in *Adversus Jovinianum,* which was so popular in the twelfth century. And, joining the Ancient to the Church Father, there was Cicero [Roman statesman] who, after rejecting Terentia, refused the sister of his friend Hirtius.

And yet Abelard rejected Heloise's sacrifice. The wedding was decided, but remained a secret. Fulbert, whom they wished to appease, was notified, and even attended the nuptial benediction.

But the intentions of the various actors in this drama were not the same. Abelard, with his conscience at peace, wanted to resume his

---

2. Cited in *The Letters of Abelard and Heloise,* translated from the Latin by C.K. Scott Moncrieff (New York: Alfred A. Knopf, 1942), pp. 16–17.—TRANS.

work with Heloise remaining in the shadows. And Fulbert wanted to announce the marriage, make public the satisfaction he had obtained, and undoubtedly weaken the credibility of Abelard, whom he had never pardoned.

Abelard, in distress, conceived of a strategy. Heloise would go into retreat in the convent of Argenteuil, where he had her wear a novice's habit. That would put an end to the stories. In that disguise, Heloise, who had no other will than that of Abelard, waited for the rumors to cease. They had not counted on Fulbert, for he thought he had been tricked. He believed that Abelard had gotten rid of Heloise by having her enter a convent, and that the marriage had been dissolved. One night he led an angry mob to Abelard's house where a crowd gathered, Abelard was mutilated, and the next morning there was a huge scandal.

Abelard went to hide his shame at the royal abbey of Saint-Denis. Remembering what was said above, one can understand the extent of his despair. Could a eunuch still be a man?

We will abandon Heloise here, as she no longer plays a role in the present work. Yet we know how the two lovers, from one cloister to another, continued to exchange the essence of their souls until death did them part.

New Battles

His intellectual passion cured Abelard. With his wounds bandaged he once again found his fighting spirit. The ignorant and slovenly monks weighed heavily on him. With his arrogant attitude Abelard weighed equally heavily on the monks, whose solitude was all the more troubled by the many disciples who came to implore the master to resume his teaching again. He wrote his first treatise on theology for them. Its success did not make everyone happy. In 1112 a conventicle[3] in the guise of a council assembled in Soissons to judge it. In a tumultuous atmosphere—to impress the council his enemies had stirred up the mob who threatened to lynch Abelard—in spite of the efforts of the bishop of Chartres who demanded additional information, the book was burned and Abelard was sentenced to end his days in a monastery.

He returned to Saint-Denis, where his quarrels with the monks became increasingly heated. He inflamed them by showing that the famous pages by Hilduin on the founder of the abbey were only so much nonsense, and that the first bishop of Paris had nothing to do with Denis of Athens (a.k.a. Dionysius the Areopagite], the Areopagite whom St Paul had converted. The following year he fled the monastery and finally found refuge with the bishop of Troyes. He

---

3. Conventicle here has a negative connotation: "an assembly or meeting regarded as having a sinister purpose."—TRANS.

was given some land, near Nogent-sur-Seine, settled there as a recluse, and built a little oratory to the Trinity. He had forgotten nothing; the condemned book was dedicated to the Trinity.

But his disciples soon discovered his refuge and there was a stampede toward solitude. A scholarly village of tents and huts rose up. The oratory, enlarged and rebuilt out of stone, was dedicated to the Paraclete, which was a provocative innovation. Only Abelard's teachings could make these ersatz country folk forget the satisfactions of the city. They sadly recalled that "in the city students enjoy all the conveniences they need."

Abelard's peace did not last long. Two "new apostles," he said, were organizing a conspiracy against him. They were St Norbert, the founder of the Prémontré, and St Bernard, the reformer of Cîteaux. He was persecuted so harshly that he dreamt of fleeing to the East:

> God knows, I fell into such a state of despair that I thought of quitting the realm of Christendom and going over to the heathen [to go to the Saracens, as is specified in Jean de Meung's translation], there to live a quiet Christian life amongst the enemies of Christ at the cost of what tribute was asked. I told myself they would receive me more kindly for having no suspicion that I was a Christian on account of the charges against me.[4]

He was spared that extreme solution—the first temptation of the Western intellectual who despairs of the world in which he lives.

He was elected abbot of a Breton monastery, but there were new confrontations. Abelard felt he was living among barbarians. Only Low Breton [the language of Lower Brittany] was spoken there. The monks were unimaginably vulgar. He attempted to refine them. They tried to poison him. He fled from there in 1132.

Abelard appeared once again on Mount Ste Geneviève in 1136. He resumed teaching with more students than ever before. Arnold of Brescia, banished from Italy for fomenting unrest in the towns, took refuge in Paris, joined up with Abelard, and brought his poor disciples, who begged for a living to listen to his teaching. Ever since his book was burned in Soissons, Abelard never ceased to write. It was only in 1140, however, that his enemies again began attacking his works. His ties with the Roman proscript must have been the greatest incitement to their hostility. It is understandable that the alliance of town dialectics and the democratic communal movement would appear significant to his adversaries.

St. Bernard and Abelard

Leading the movement against Abelard was St Bernard. According to the apt expression of Père Chenu, the abbot of Cîteaux "was in

---

4. *The Letters of Abelard and Heloise,* translated with an introduction by Betty Radice (Harmondsworth: Penguin, 1974), p. 93–4.—TRANS.

another realm of Christendom." That rural man, who remained a medieval and foremost a soldier, was ill-suited to understand the town intelligentsia. He saw only one course of action against the heretic or the infidel: brute force. The champion of the armed Crusade, he did not believe in an intellectual crusade. When Peter the Venerable asked him to read the translation of the Koran in order to reply to Mohammed in writing, Bernard did not respond. In the solitude of the cloisters he delved into mystical meditation—which he raised to the greatest heights—to find what he needed to return to the world as an administrator of justice. That apostle of the reclusive life was always prepared to fight against innovations he deemed dangerous. During the last years of his life he essentially governed western Christian Europe, dictating his orders to the pope, approving military orders, dreaming of creating a Western cavalry, the militia of Christ; he was a great inquisitor before his time.

A clash with Abelard was inevitable. It was St Bernard's second in command, William of Saint-Thierry, who led the attack. In a letter to St Bernard, William denounced the "new theologian," and encouraged his illustrious friend to pursue him. St Bernard went to Paris, tried to lure Abelard's students away (with the little success so far as we know), and became convinced of the seriousness of the evil Abelard was spreading. A meeting between the two men resolved nothing. One of Abelard's disciples suggested they debate in Sens before an assembly of theologians and bishops. The master undertook once again to uproot Abelard's followers. In secret St Bernard entirely changed the character of the gathering. He transformed the audience into a council, and his adversary into the accused. The night before the opening debate St Bernard assembled the bishops and gave them a complete file showing Abelard as a dangerous heretic. The next day Abelard could only impugn the competence of the assembly and make an appeal to the pope. The bishops communicated a very mitigated condemnation to Rome. Alarmed, St Bernard quickly regrouped. His secretary gave the cardinals, who showed him complete devotion, letters which extracted a condemnation of Abelard out of the pope, and Abelard's books were burned at St Peter's. Abelard learned of this *en route,* and took refuge at Cluny. This time he was broken. Peter the Venerable, who welcomed him with infinite charity, arranged his reconciliation with St Bernard, persuaded Rome to lift his excommunication, and sent him to the monastery of St-Marcel, in Chalon-sur-Saône, where he died on April 21, 1142. The great abbot of Cluny had sent him written absolution, and in a final gesture of exquisite delicacy, had it sent to Heloise, who was then the abbess of the Paraclete.

The Letters of Abelard and Heloise

Peter Abelard and Heloise

Abelard and Heloise were a pair of lovers living in the twelfth century who found their relationship devastated by events greater than themselves. Abelard became a preeminent professor in France whose original ideas gained him many enemies. Heloise became Abelard's student, and the two fell in love. Their relationship was troubled from the beginning, however. Abelard and Heloise enjoyed an intense sexual relationship, the knowledge of which quickly spread, harming Abelard's reputation and resulting in pregnancy for Heloise. Heloise did not want to get married because she feared such a commitment would jeopardize Abelard's career. However, Abelard decided that they should marry in order to appease Heloise's uncle. The uncle was determined to have his revenge, however, and had Abelard brutally castrated. During this upheaval, Abelard ordered Heloise to take refuge at a convent. When Abelard recovered, he too joined in the service of the church, but his enemies continued to persecute him. Many years went by without Heloise hearing from her beloved, so she finally wrote a letter to him. In this passionate letter, she upbraids him for his indifference to her needs and his unwillingness to recognize the sacrifice she made when becoming a nun for his sake. Abelard's letter in return shows his refusal to talk about her personal heartbreak. Rather, he addresses her as from an abbot to an abbess, and begs her and the other nuns to pray for his safekeeping. Many letters followed these, but the lovers never resumed their affair, and each died in service to the church.

Letter I. Heloise to Abelard

To her master, or rather her father, husband, or rather brother; his handmaid, or rather his daughter, wife, or rather sister; to Abelard, Heloise.

Not long ago, my beloved, by chance someone brought me the letter of consolation you had sent to a friend. I saw at once from the superscription that it was yours, and was all the more eager to read it since the writer is so dear to my heart. I hoped for renewal of strength, at least from the writer's words which would picture for me the reality I have lost. But nearly every line of this letter was filled, I remember, with gall and wormwood, as it told the pitiful story of our entry into religion and the cross of unending suffering which you, my only love, continue to bear.

Abelard's Troubles

In that letter you did indeed carry out the promise you made your friend at the beginning, that he would think his own troubles insignificant or nothing, in comparison with your own. First you revealed the persecution you suffered from your teachers, then the supreme treachery of the mutilation of your person, and then described the abominable jealousy and violent attacks of your fellow-students, Alberic of Rheims and Lotulf of Lombardy. You did not gloss over what at their instigation was done to your distinguished theological work or what amounted to a prison sentence passed on yourself. Then you went on to the plotting against you by your abbot and false brethren, the serious slanders from those two pseudo-apostles, spread against you by the same rivals, and the scandal stirred up among many people because you had acted contrary to custom in naming your oratory after the Paraclete.[1] You went on to the incessant, intolerable persecutions which you still endure at the hands of that cruel tyrant and the evil monks you call your sons, and so brought your sad story to an end.

No one, I think, could read or hear it dry-eyed; my own sorrows are renewed by the detail in which you have told it, and redoubled because you say your perils are still increasing. All of us here[2] are driven to despair of your life, and every day we await in fear and trembling the final word of your death. And so in the name of Christ, who is still giving you some protection for his service, we beseech

1. The Holy Ghost 2. The convent at the Paraclete.

you to write as often as you think fit to us who are his handmaids and yours, with news of the perils in which you are still storm-tossed. We are all that are left you, so at least you should let us share your sorrow or your joy.

It is always some consolation in sorrow to feel that it is shared, and any burden laid on several is carried more lightly or removed. And if this storm has quietened down for a while, you must be all the more prompt to send us a letter which will be the more gladly received. But whatever you write about will bring us no small relief in the mere proof that you have us in mind. Letters from absent friends are welcome indeed, as Seneca[3] himself shows us by his own example when he writes these words in a passage of a letter to his friend Lucilius:

> Thank you for writing to me often, the one way in which you can make your presence felt, for I never have a letter from you without the immediate feeling that we are together. If pictures of absent friends give us pleasure, renewing our memories and relieving the pain of separation even if they cheat us with empty comfort, how much more welcome is a letter which comes to us in the very handwriting of an absent friend.

Thank God that here at least is a way of restoring your presence to us which no malice can prevent, nor any obstacle hinder; then do not, I beseech you, allow any negligence to hold you back.

Abelard's Tie with the Convent

You wrote your friend a long letter of consolation, prompted no doubt by his misfortunes, but really telling of your own. The detailed account you gave of these may have been intended for his comfort, but it also greatly increased our own feeling of desolation; in your desire to heal his wounds you have dealt us fresh wounds of grief as well as re-opening the old. I beg you, then, as you set about tending the wounds which others have dealt, heal the wounds you have yourself inflicted. You have done your duty to a friend and comrade, discharged your debt to friendship and comradeship, but it is a greater debt which binds you in obligation to us[4] who can properly be called not friends so much as dearest friends, not comrades but daughters, or any other conceivable name more tender and holy. How great the debt by which you have bound yourself to us needs neither proof nor witness, were it in any doubt; if the whole world kept silent, the facts themselves would cry out. For you after God are the sole founder of this place, the sole builder of this oratory, the sole creator of this community. You have built nothing here upon another man's foundation. Everything here is your own creation. This was a wilderness open to wild beasts and brigands, a place which had known no home

3. Roman statesman who lived from 4 B.C. to 65 A.D. 4. The nuns at the convent.

nor habitation of men. In the very lairs of wild beasts and lurking-places of robbers, where the name of God was never heard, you built a sanctuary to God and dedicated a shrine in the name of the Holy Spirit. To build it you drew nothing from the riches of kings and princes, though their wealth was great and could have been yours for the asking: whatever was done, the credit was to be yours alone. Clerks and scholars came flocking here, eager for your teaching, and ministered to all your needs; and even those who had lived on the benefices of the Church and knew only how to receive offerings, not to make them, whose hands were held out to take but not to give, became pressing in their lavish offers of assistance.

And so it is yours, truly your own, this new plantation for God's purpose, but it is sown with plants which are still very tender and need watering if they are to thrive. Through its feminine nature this plantation would be weak and frail even if it were not new; and so it needs a more careful and regular cultivation, according to the words of the Apostle: 'I planted the seed and Apollos watered it; but God made it grow.' The Apostle through the doctrine that he preached had planted and established in the faith the Corinthians, to whom he was writing. Afterwards the Apostle's own disciple, Apollos, had watered them with his holy exhortations and so God's grace bestowed on them growth in the virtues. You cultivate a vineyard of another's vines which you did not plant yourself and which has now turned to bitterness against you, so that often your advice brings no result and your holy words are uttered in vain. You devote your care to another's vineyard; think what you owe to your own. You teach and admonish rebels to no purpose, and in vain you throw the pearls of your divine eloquence to the pigs. While you spend so much on the stubborn, consider what you owe to the obedient; you are so generous to your enemies but should reflect on how you are indebted to your daughters. Apart from everything else, consider the close tie by which you have bound yourself to me, and repay the debt you owe a whole community of women dedicated to God by discharging it the more dutifully to her who is yours alone.

Abelard's Debt to Heloise

Your superior wisdom knows better than our humble learning of the many serious treatises which the holy Fathers compiled for the instruction or exhortation or even the consolation of holy women, and of the care with which these were composed. And so in the precarious early days of our conversion long ago I was not a little surprised and troubled by your forgetfulness, when neither reverence for God nor our mutual love nor the example of the holy Fathers made you think of trying to comfort me, wavering and exhausted as I was by prolonged grief, either by word when I was with you or by letter

when we had parted.[5] Yet you must know that you are bound to me
by an obligation which is all the greater for the further close tie of
the marriage sacrament uniting us, and are the deeper in my debt because of the love I have always borne you, as everyone knows, a love
which is beyond all bounds.

You know, beloved, as the whole world knows, how much I have
lost in you, how at one wretched stroke of fortune that supreme act
of flagrant treachery robbed me of my very self in robbing me of
you; and how my sorrow for my loss is nothing compared with what
I feel for the manner in which I lost you. Surely the greater the cause
for grief the greater the need for the help of consolation, and this no
one can bring but you; you are the sole cause of my sorrow, and you
alone can grant me the grace of consolation. You alone have the
power to make me sad, to bring me happiness or comfort; you alone
have so great a debt to repay me, particularly now when I have carried out all your orders so implicitly that when I was powerless to
oppose you in anything, I found strength at your command to destroy myself. I did more, strange to say—my love rose to such
heights of madness that it robbed itself of what it most desired beyond hope of recovery, when immediately at your bidding I changed
my clothing along with my mind, in order to prove you the sole pos-
sessor of my body and my will alike. God knows I never sought anything in you except yourself; I wanted simply you, nothing of yours.
I looked for no marriage-bond, no marriage portion, and it was not
my own pleasures and wishes I sought to gratify, as you well know,
but yours. The name of wife may seem more sacred or more binding, but sweeter for me will always be the word mistress, or, if you
will permit me, that of concubine or whore. I believed that the more
I humbled myself on your account, the more gratitude I should win
from you, and also the less damage I should do to the brightness of
your reputation.

The Problems with Marriage

You yourself on your own account did not altogether forget this in
the letter of consolation I have spoken of which you wrote to a
friend;[6] there you thought fit to set out some of the reasons I gave in
trying to dissuade you from binding us together in an ill-starred marriage. But you kept silent about most of my arguments for preferring love to wedlock and freedom to chains. God is my witness that

5. This sentence, often mistranslated as if it refers to the present and so suggesting that Abelard
has never visited nor written to her at the Paraclete, his been used as evidence that the letters are
a forgery because it contradicts what Abelard says in the *Historia calamitatum* (p. 98). But the
tense *(movit)* is past, translated here as 'I was troubled,' and Heloise must be referring to his failure to help her by word before they separated and by letter after she had entered the convent.
6. This suggests that Heloise believed the *Historia calamitatum* to be a genuine letter to a real
person, and not an example of a conventional epistolary genre, unless she is writing ironically.

if Augustus, Emperor of the whole world, thought fit to honour me with marriage and conferred all the earth on me to possess for ever, it would be dearer and more honourable to me to be called not his Empress but your whore.

For a man's worth does not rest on his wealth or power; these depend on fortune, but worth on his merits. And a woman should realize that if she marries a rich man more readily than a poor one, and desires her husband more for his possessions than for himself, she is offering herself for sale. Certainly any woman who comes to marry through desires of this kind deserves wages, not gratitude, for clearly her mind is on the man's property, not himself, and she would be ready to prostitute herself to a richer man, if she could. This is evident from the argument put forward in the dialogue of Aeschines Socraticus[7] by the learned Aspasia to Xenophon and his wife. When she had expounded it in an effort to bring about a reconcifiation between them, she ended with these words: 'Unless you come to believe that there is no better man nor worthier woman on earth you will always still be looking for what you judge the best thing of all—to be the husband of the best of wives and the wife of the best of husbands.'

These are saintly words which are more than philosophic; indeed, they deserve the name of wisdom, not philosophy. It is a holy error and a blessed delusion between man and wife, when perfect love can keep the ties of marriage unbroken not so much through bodily continence as chastity of spirit. But what error permitted other women, plain truth permitted me, and what they thought of their husbands, the world in general believed, or rather, knew to be true of yourself; so that my love for you was the more genuine for being further removed from error. What king or philosopher could match your fame? What district, town or village did not long to see you? When you appeared in public, who did not hurry to catch a glimpse of you, or crane his neck and strain his eyes to follow your departure? Every wife, every young girl desired you in absence and was on fire in your presence; queens and great ladies envied me my joys and my bed.

You had besides, I admit, two special gifts whereby to win at once the heart of any woman—your gifts for composing verse and song, in which we know other philosophers have rarely been successful. This was for you no more than a diversion, a recreation from the labours of your philosophic work, but you left many love-songs and verses which won wide popularity for the charm of their words and tunes and kept your name continually on everyone's lips.[8]

---

7. Aeschines Socraticus, a pupil of Socrates, wrote several dialogues of which fragments survive. This is however no proof that Heloise knew Greek, as the passage was well known in the Middle Ages from Cicero's translation of it in *De inventione*, 1.31. 8. None of Abelard's secular verse survives.

The beauty of the airs ensured that even the unlettered did not forget you; more than anything this made women sigh for love of you. And as most of these songs told of our love, they soon made me widely known and roused the envy of many women against me. For your manhood was adorned by every grace of mind and body, and among the women who envied me then, could there be one now who does not feel compelled by my misfortune to sympathize with my loss of such joys? Who is there who was once my enemy, whether man or woman, who is not moved now by the compassion which is my due? Wholly guilty though I am, I am also, as you know, wholly innocent. It is not the deed but the intention of the doer which makes the crime, and justice should weigh not what was done but the spirit in which it is done.[9] What my intention towards you has always been, you alone who have known it can judge. I submit all to your scrutiny, yield to your testimony in all things.

Abelard's Neglect

Tell me one thing, if you can. Why, after our entry into religion, which was your decision alone, have I been so neglected and forgotten by you that I have neither a word from you when you are here to give me strength nor the consolation of a letter in absence?[10] Tell me, I say, if you can—or I will tell you what I think and indeed the world suspects. It was desire, not affection which bound you to me, the flame of lust rather than love. So when the end came to what you desired, any show of feeling you used to make went with it. This is not merely my own opinion, beloved, it is everyone's. There is nothing personal or private about it; it is the general view which is widely held. I only wish that it *were* mine alone, and that the love you professed could find someone to defend it and so comfort me in my grief for a while. I wish I could think of some explanation which would excuse you and somehow cover up the way you hold me cheap.

I beg you then to listen to what I ask—you will see that it is a small favour which you can easily grant. While I am denied your presence, give me at least through your words—of which you have enough and to spare—some sweet semblance of yourself. It is no use my hoping for generosity in deeds if you are grudging in words. Up to now I had thought I deserved much of you, seeing that I carried out everything for your sake and continue up to the present moment in complete obedi-

9. This is the 'ethic of pure intention' strongly held by Heloise and Abelard and set out in his *Ethica* or *Scito te ipsum (Know yourself)*: our actions must be judged good or bad solely through the spirit in which they are performed and not by their effects. The deed itself is neither good nor bad.
10. This is not to be taken as contradicting Abelard's statement . . . that he often visited the Paraclete, and had invited Heloise and her nuns to go there (either by letter or interview). Her complaint is that he never writes her a personal letter nor offers her help in her personal problems. In Letter 4, p. 145, he refers to her 'old perpetual complaint' to him, but he evidently will not be drawn into discussion. . . .

ence to you. It was not any sense of vocation which brought me as a young girl to accept the austerities of the cloister, but your bidding alone, and if I deserve no gratitude from you, you may judge for yourself how my labours are in vain. I can expect no reward for this from God, for it is certain that I have done nothing as yet for love of him. When you hurried towards God I followed you, indeed, I went first to take the veil—perhaps you were thinking how Lot's wife turned back[11] when you made me put on the religious habit and take my vows before you gave yourself to God. Your lack of trust in me over this one thing, I confess, overwhelmed me with grief and shame. I would have had no hesitation, God knows, in following you or going ahead at your bidding to the flames of Hell.[12] My heart was not in me but with you, and now, even more, if it is not with you it is nowhere; truly, without you it cannot exist. See that it fares well with you, I beg, as it will if it finds you kind, if you give grace in return for grace, small for great, words for deeds. If only your love had less confidence in me, my dear, so that you would be more concerned on my behalf! But as it is, the more I have made you feel secure in me, the more I have to bear with your neglect.

Remember, I implore you, what I have done, and think how much you owe me. While I enjoyed with you the pleasures of the flesh, many were uncertain whether I was prompted by love or lust; but now the end is proof of the beginning. I have finally denied myself every pleasure in obedience to your will, kept nothing for myself except to prove that now, even more, I am yours. Consider then your injustice, if when I deserve more you give me less, or rather, nothing at all, especially when it is a small thing I ask of you and one you could so easily grant. And so, in the name of God to whom you have dedicated yourself, I beg you to restore your presence to me in the way you can—by writing me some word of comfort, so that in this at least I may find increased strength and readiness to serve God. When in the past you sought me out for sinful pleasures your letters came to me thick and fast, and your many songs put your Heloise on everyone's lips, so that every street and house echoed with my name. Is it not far better now to summon me to God than it was then to satisfy out lust? I beg you, think what you owe me, give ear to my pleas, and I will finish a long letter with a brief ending: farewell, my only love.

Letter 2. Abelard to Heloise

To Heloise, his dearly beloved sister in Christ, Abelard her brother in Christ.

If since our conversion from the world to God I have not yet written you any word of comfort or advice, it must not be attributed to

11. Lot was Abraham's nephew, whose wife turned into a pillar of salt when she looked back as they fled from Sodom. 12. The Latin is *Vulcania loca,* Vulcan's regions, or Tartarus, and illustrates how Heloise's natural manner of expressing herself is classical.

indifference on my part but to your own good sense, in which I have always had such confidence that I did not think anything was needed; God's grace has bestowed on you all essentials to enable you to instruct the erring, comfort the weak and encourage the fainthearted, both by word and example, as, indeed, you have been doing since you first held the office of prioress under your abbess. So if you still watch over your daughters as carefully as you did previously over your sisters, it is sufficient to make me believe that any teaching or exhortation from me would now be wholly superfluous. If, on the other hand, in your humility you think differently, and you feel that you have need of my instruction and writings in matters pertaining to God, write to me what you want, so that I may answer as God permits me. Meanwhile thanks be to God who has filled all your hearts with anxiety for my desperate, unceasing perils, and made you share in my affliction; may divine mercy protect me through the support of your prayers and quickly crush Satan beneath our feet. To this end in particular, I hasten to send the psalter you earnestly begged from me,[13] my sister once dear in the world and now dearest in Christ, so that you may offer a perpetual sacrifice of prayers to the Lord for our many great aberrations, and for the dangers which daily threaten me.

The Power of Prayer

We have indeed many examples as evidence of the high position in the eyes of God and his saints which has been won by the prayers of the faithful, especially those of women on behalf of their dear ones and of wives for their husbands. The Apostle observes this closely when he bids us pray continually. We read that the Lord said to Moses 'Let me alone, to vent my anger upon them,' and to Jeremiah 'Therefore offer no prayer for these people nor stand in my path.' By these words the Lord himself makes it clear that the prayers of the devout set a kind of bridle on his wrath and check it from raging against sinners as fully as they deserve; just as a man who is willingly moved by his sense of justice to take vengeance can be turned aside by the entreaties of his friends and forcibly restrained, as it were, against his will. Thus when the Lord says to one who is praying or about to pray, 'Let me alone and do not stand in my path,' he forbids prayers to be offered to him on behalf of the impious; yet the just man prays though the Lord forbids, obtains his requests and alters the sentence of the angry judge. And so the passage

13. *Psalterium.* Heloise's letter does not mention this, but the request could have been made in person at the time when Abelard was still visiting the Paraclete: the tense *(requisisti)* suggests it was not very recent *(requiris* would be more natural for a request just received). Possibly the bearer of the letter was told to ask for it. Muckle *(Mediaeval Studies,* Vol. XV, pp. 58–9) suggests that the word refers not to a psalter, or Book of Psalms, which the convent would surely already have, but to a 'Chant', that is, the arrangement of versicles and responses at the end of this letter which are to be used in the prayers on his behalf.

about Moses continues: 'And the Lord repented and spared his people the evil with which he had threatened them.' Elsewhere it is written about the universal works of God, 'He spoke, and it was.' But in this passage it is also recorded that he had said the people deserved affliction, but he had been prevented by the power of prayer from carrying out his words.

Consider then the great power of prayer, if we pray as we are bidden, seeing that the prophet won by prayer what he was forbidden to pray for, and turned God aside from his declared intention. And another prophet says to God: 'In thy wrath remember mercy.' The lords of the earth should listen and take note, for they are found obstinate rather than just in the execution of the justice they have decreed and pronounced; they blush to appear lax if they are merciful, and untruthful if they change a pronouncement or do not carry out a decision which lacked foresight, even if they can emend their words by their actions. Such men could properly be compared with Jephtha, who made a foolish vow and in carrying it out even more foolishly, killed his only daughter. But he who desires to be a 'member of his body' says with the Psalmist 'I will sing of mercy and justice unto thee, O Lord.' 'Mercy,' it is written, 'exalts judgement,' in accordance with the threat elsewhere in the Scriptures: 'In that judgement there will be no mercy for the man who has shown no mercy.' The Psalmist himself considered this carefully when at the entreaty of the wife of Nabal the Carmelite, as an act of mercy he broke the oath he had justly sworn concerning her husband and the destruction of his house. Thus he set prayer above justice, and the man's wrongdoing was wiped out by the entreaties of his wife.

Here you have an example, sister, and an assurance how much your prayers for me may prevail on God, if this woman's did so much for her husband, seeing that God who is our father loves his children more than David did a suppliant woman. David was indeed considered a pious and merciful man, but God is piety and mercy itself. And the woman whose entreaties David heard then was an ordinary lay person, in no way bound to God by the profession of holy devotion; whereas if you alone are not enough to win in answer to your prayer, the holy convent of widows and virgins which is with you will succeed where you cannot by yourself. For when the Truth says to the disciples, 'When two or three have met together in my name, I am there among them,' and again, 'If two of you agree about any request you have to make, it shall be granted by my Father,' we can all see how the communal prayer of a holy congregation must prevail upon God. If, as the apostle James says, 'A good man's prayer is powerful and effective,' what should we hope for from the large numbers of a holy congregation? You know, dearest sister, from the thirty–eighth homily of St Gregory how much support the prayers of his fellow brethren quickly brought a brother, although he was unwilling and resisted. The depths of his misery, the fear of peril which tormented his unhappy soul, the utter despair and weariness of life which made him try to call his brethren from their prayers—all the details set out there cannot have escaped your understanding.

Women's Prayers Are Most Powerful

May this example give you and your convent of holy sisters greater confidence in prayer, so that I may be preserved alive for you all, through him, from whom, as Paul bears witness, women have even received back their dead raised to life. For if you turn the pages of the Old and New Testaments you will find that the greatest miracles of resurrection were shown only, or mostly, to women, and were performed for them or on them. The Old Testament records two instances of men raised from the dead at the entreaties of their mothers, by Elijah and his disciple Elisha. The Gospel, it is true, has three instances only of the dead being raised by the Lord but, as they were shown to women only, they provide factual confirmation of the Apostle's words I quoted above: 'Women received back their dead raised to life.' It was to a widow at the gate of the city of Nain that the Lord restored her son, moved by compassion for her, and he also raised Lazarus his own friend at the entreaty of his sisters Mary and Martha. And when he granted this same favour to the daughter of the ruler of the synagogue at her father's petition, again 'women received back their dead raised to life', for in being brought back to life she received her own body from death just as those other women received the bodies of their dead.

Now these resurrections were performed with only a few interceding; and so the multiplied prayers of your shared devotion should easily win the preservation of my own life. The more God is pleased by the abstinence and continence which women have dedicated to him, the more willing he will be to grant their prayers. Moreover, it may well be that the majority of those raised from the dead were not of the faith, for we do not read that the widow mentioned above whose son was raised without her asking was a believer. But in our case we are bound together by the integrity of our faith and united in our profession of the same religious life.

Heloise Must Pray for Abelard

Let me now pass from the holy convent of your community, where so many virgins and widows are dedicated to continual service of the Lord, and come to you alone, you whose sanctity must surely have the greatest influence in the eyes of God, and who are bound to do everything possible on my behalf, especially now when I am in the toils of such adversity. Always remember then in your prayers him who is especially yours; watch and pray the more confidently as you recognize your cause is just, and so more acceptable to him to whom you pray. Listen, I beg you, with the ear of your heart to what you have so often heard with your bodily ear. In the book of Proverbs it is written that 'A capable wife is her husband's crown,' and again, 'Find a wife and you find a good thing; so you will earn the favour of the Lord;' yet again, 'Home and wealth may come down from ancestors; but an intelligent wife is a gift from the Lord.' In Ecclesiasticus too it says that 'A good wife makes a happy husband,' and a little later, 'A good wife means a good life.' And we have it on the Apostle's authority that 'the unbelieving husband now belongs to God through his wife'. A special instance of this was granted by God's grace in our own country of France, when Clovis the king was converted to the Christian faith more by the prayers of his wife than by the preaching of holy men;[14] his entire kingdom was then placed under divine law so that humbler men should be encouraged by the example of their betters to persevere in prayer. Indeed, such perseverance is warmly recommended to us in a parable of the Lord which says: 'If the man perseveres in his knocking, though he will not provide for him out of friendship, the very shamelessness of the request will make him get up and give him all he needs.' It was certainly by what I might call this shamelessness in prayer that Moses (as I said above) softened the harshness of divine justice and changed its sentence.

You know, beloved, the warmth of charity your convent once used to show me in their prayers at the times I could be with you. At the conclusion of each of the Hours every day they would offer this special prayer to the Lord on my behalf; after the proper response and versicle were pronounced and sung they added prayers and a collect, as follows:

RESPONSE: Forsake me not, O Lord: Keep not far from me, my God.

VERSICLE: Make haste, O Lord, to help me.

PRAYER: Save thy servant, O my God, whose hope is in thee; Lord hear my prayer, and let my cry for help reach thee.

(LET US PRAY) O God, who through thy servant hast been pleased to gather together thy handmaidens in thy name, we beseech thee to grant both to him and to us that we persevere in thy will. Through our Lord, etc.

But now that I am not with you, there is all the more need for the support of your prayers, the more I am gripped by fear of greater peril. And so I ask of you in entreaty, and entreat you in asking, par-

---

14. Clovis (481–511), founder of the Merovingian House of France, was converted to Christianity after his victory over the Alamanni in 496; his wife Clotild, a princess of Burgundy, was already a Catholic and had long begged him to renounce his pagan ways. The story was well known from Gregory of Tours, *History of the Franks*, II. 29–31.

ticularly now that I am absent from you, to show me how truly your charity extends to the absent by adding this form of special prayer at the conclusion of each hour:

RESPONSE: O Lord, Father and Ruler of my life, do not desert me, lest I fail before my adversaries and my enemy gloats over me.

VERSICLE: Grasp shield and buckler and rise up to help me, lest my enemy gloats.

PRAYER: Save thy servant, O my God, whose hope is in thee. Send him help, O Lord, from thy holy place, and watch over him from Zion. Be a tower of strength to him, O Lord, in the face of his enemy. Lord hear my prayer, and let my cry for help reach thee.

(LET US PRAY) O God who through thy servant hast been pleased to gather together thy handmaidens in thy name, we beseech thee to protect him in all adversity and restore him in safety to thy handmaidens. Through our Lord, etc.

A Final Resting Place

But if the Lord shall deliver me into the hands of my enemies so that they overcome and kill me, or by whatever chance I enter upon the way of all flesh while absent from you, wherever my body may lie, buried or unburied, I beg you to have it brought to your burial-ground, where our daughters, or rather, our sisters in Christ may see my tomb more often and thereby be encouraged to pour out their prayers more fully to the Lord on my behalf. There is no place, I think, so safe and salutary for a soul grieving for its sins and desolated by its transgressions than that which is specially consecrated to the true Paraclete, the Comforter, and which is particularly designated by his name. Not do I believe that there is any place more fitting for Christian burial among the faithful than one amongst women dedicated to Christ. Women were concerned for the tomb of our Lord Jesus Christ, they came ahead and followed after, bringing precious ointments, keeping close watch around this tomb, weeping for the death of the Bridegroom, as it is written: 'The women sitting at the tomb wept and lamented for the Lord.' And there they were first reassured about his resurrection by the appearance of an angel and the words he spoke to them; later on they were found worthy both to taste the joy of his resurrection when he twice appeared to them, and also to touch him with their hands.

Finally, I ask this of you above all else: at present you are over-anxious about the danger to my body, but then your chief concern must be for the salvation of my soul, and you must show the dead man how much you loved the living by the special support of prayers chosen for him.

Live, fare you well, yourself and your sisters with you, Live, but I pray, in Christ be mindful of me.

John of Salisbury and Christian Humanism

Marjorie Chibnall

According to Marjorie Chibnall, John of Salisbury is the central figure of English learning in the twelfth century. He is recognized as the leading humanist of his day because he defended the value of the individual and supported his arguments using classical texts. John's humanism was also characterized by his Christian belief that learning should inform moral conduct and that the church was the ultimate authority in worldly affairs. As a humble and principled man, John wrote carefully, often advising his contemporaries about their political and personal conduct in delicately crafted letters. John also wrote larger works for a broader audience that have been hailed in later centuries as carrying on the living tradition of humanism. In his *Metalogicon,* the scholar defended the liberal arts against those who believed that learning was only useful if it led to a career. He argued against another prevailing belief in his day—that cold logic alone could reveal truth—in *Policraticus* in which he defended Christian humanism as a conduit to higher understanding. Marjorie Chibnall is a professor of history at Cambridge University and is considered to be one of the world's leading historians.

John of Salisbury belongs to that group of scholars and statesmen, like St Anselm[1] and Hugh of St Victor,[2] whose character and motives have never given rise to controversy. The few extant judgments of his contemporaries have been confirmed by later historians. The churchman who was to Benedict of Peterborough 'a man of much learning, great eloquence and profound wisdom . . . firmly established in the fear and love of God', and who in the conventional eulogy of the Chartres necrology was 'a man of profound religion, distinguished in every kind of learning', is still recognisable as 'the central figure of English learning', or the man of 'deep yet sober piety and quiet humour . . . convinced that the highest function of knowledge is to be an instrument of the good life'. Yet perhaps because of this unanimity of opinion the man himself is not easily painted in living colours. The characters of such men as Abailard[3] and St Thomas of Canterbury[4] emerge all the more clearly from the criticism or appraisement directed at them from every angle by men who knew them. John of Salisbury is known principally through his own writings, which are the works of the most accomplished Latin stylist of the twelfth century, produced in the active, mature years of his life, between thirty and fifty. Consequently it will always be easier to know the scholar than to know the man.

Scholar and Friend

The only glimpse of his early life is given in his *Policraticus,* where he tells how he was sent for instruction to a priest who practised magic in secret, and who tried to persuade his pupils to assist him in crystal-gazing. With the practical common sense that was to be with him all his life, John refused to see anything but the familiar objects, and so succeeded in being shut out of the room whenever his instructor was practising his unholy arts. Thereafter he can be seen more clearly as a student in Paris and Chartres,[5] steadily deepening his knowledge and widening the circle of his friends and correspondents. There can be no doubt of his talent for making and keeping friends. It was during his student years that he formed what was to become a lifelong friendship with Peter of Celle, a young man of noble birth from the region of Provins in Champagne, who may for a time have been John's pupil and certainly was one of the first to find employment for him. Peter, unlike John, took monastic vows and became abbot successively of Montier la Celle and St Rémi of Rheims; he was the friend to whom John most frequently turned for

---

1. Archbishop of Canterbury in the period from 1093 to 1109. 2. Twelfth-century scholar and theologian. 3. French philosopher and theologian of the twelfth century who came into frequent conflict with other scholars and theologians. 4. English Roman Catholic martyr who came into conflict with King Henry II over the power of the church and was assassinated. 5. Centers of learning in the twelfth century.

counsel, who continually encouraged him in his writing and offered him a refuge in his abbey of St Rémi, when in 1164 he was forced into exile. But if Peter was his 'dearest friend and master' there were many others who could be counted amongst his friends: the scholars Gilbert de la Porrée, who had taught him at Chartres, John Sarrazin, famous for his translations from the Greek, and William Brito of Canterbury; amongst ecclesiastical statesmen Nicholas Breakspear, later Pope Adrian IV, archbishop Theobald, Gerard Pucelle, bishop of Coventry, and St Thomas of Canterbury, and many others. When he made enemies it was rather through his principles than his personality; and his friends paid him the surest tribute of respect by their readiness to take criticism from him. The traits of character that emerge in his writings are sanity and moderation, tolerance and readiness to compromise wherever possible, but in the last resort inflexibility of principle. His gentle humour at the expense of others went with a clear perception of his own limitations, and perhaps the most characteristic picture of him is given in his last conversation with archbishop Thomas [Becket], as recorded in one anonymous chronicle: Thomas, returning from a stormy interview with Reginald FitzUrse and the other knights, had told his own clerks that he was ready to undergo death for the sake of God and of justice, at which John remonstrated, '*We* are sinners and not yet prepared to die: I see no-one here save you who is anxious to die for dying's sake'.

Much has been written on his scholarship. Although he studied at Paris as well as Chartres and followed his grounding in the seven liberal arts by attending lectures on theology, he remains above all the finest product of the school of Chartres in its heyday under Bernard and Thierry [teachers at Chartres]. As a result of his studies in grammar John became a master of the Latin language and a leading humanist of his day, for he more than any of his contemporaries was soaked in the literary tradition of ancient Rome. He might aptly have quoted the familiar dictum of Hugh of St Victor, 'Learn everything: it will all come in useful somewhere'. But whereas Hugh used his accumulated knowledge to build up a scheme of study in which every aspect of the works of God might be used to learn something of the Creator's will, and his *Didascalion* embraces the whole of twelfth-century learning, John was most deeply concerned with human conduct and used classical literature as a storehouse of moral examples. Men who had never read the Latin classics were, to him, illiterate, even though they could read and write. Even the classical poets who wrote fables in which vice triumphed were not to be shunned as dangerous: they described vice, but did not praise it, and after all, as John observed, 'it is all the easier to avoid evil if you clearly recognise it for what it is'. 'I myself', he declared in one place, 'wholeheartedly agree with those who maintain that a man cannot be regarded as literate unless he is widely read', though he adds characteristically that a man cannot be wise without virtue, and reading alone will be to little purpose without the illumination of divine grace. He has recently been compared to St Jerome[6] for his 'latinity', his acceptance of the Latin classics as part of a living tradition without compromising his Christian morality.

Christian Humanism

This Christian, Latin humanism is the keynote of his works. Needless to say he knew as much Greek thought as was the common heritage of educated men in his day; that is, strands of the metaphysical speculations of Plato, in part reshaped by Plotinus, and all the logical works of Aristotle, including the recently translated books of the 'new logic' that were just coming into circulation in the West. John himself relied completely on translations: he was no Greek scholar, though he picked up a few Greek words . . . to convey conceptions where Latin was inadequate, and gave Greek sounding names, *Policraticus* and *Metalogicon,* to his two major works. Of all his writings there is no doubt that his *Policraticus* was the most influential. In part a satire on court life, in part a work of political thought, it embodied a great deal of his learning and practical wisdom. Characteristically, it was a work of morality intended to influence the conduct of his contemporaries in high places, not least King Henry II himself and his chancellor, Thomas Becket. Consequently censures and unwelcome advice had to be presented in the most palatable form that John's experience could devise. He could not conceal his belief in the ultimate authority of the ecclesiastical power, but he could stress the virtues of a Christian prince and his unassailable authority within the state. Whilst much has been made of John's discussion of tyrannicide, it must be understood that to John only a usurper was to be regarded as a tyrant, and a properly constituted ruler—even an unjust one—must be obeyed. Where his views on the moral duties of a prince might seem too new or extreme John took care to veil them in the decent authority of classical tradition, and even invented a treatise, the *Institutio Trajani,* attributed by him to Plutarch, to convey views that have recently been shown to be those of his master, Robert Pullen. Although the structure of the *Policraticus* was artificial and somewhat tortuous, there is clarity and consistency in the thought which made the work widely read in John's own day and throughout the Middle Ages. It became deservedly popular in the fourteenth century amongst the humanistic legists of south Italy, who reacted against the arid technicalities of legal studies just as John had turned critically away from the logic-chopping of many professional masters in his time. Indeed

---

6. Latin scholar who lived from 340 to 420 AD.

they may be said to carry on the living tradition of humanism as John had interpreted it, and it is a tribute to the independent value of the *Policraticus* that legists such as Lucas de Penna always cited it as though Policraticus was the name of a person and they were ignorant of the real author. This is the more striking since the value of most of John's other writings lies rather in the individual point of view they express than in their furtherance of a growing tradition of thought. Even in the *Metalogicon,* where he defended the liberal arts against the attacks of utilitarian careerists, to whom knowledge was worthless if it did not directly lead to a lucrative profession, his statement of his own philosophical conceptions was to have little influence on the history of philosophy. In part this may have been because the impact of the metaphysical and scientific works of Aristotle was shortly to transform philosophical speculation in western Europe. More important perhaps was the fact that to John learning and conduct were intimately connected. His studies were a training for his later career as an ecclesiastical statesman; when he wrote it was rather to influence the conduct of others in a particular situation than to make an abstract contribution to scholarship. For this reason he is outstanding as a letter-writer; and it may be added to his lasting credit that he himself never shrank from the course of action he urged as just even when it involved him in 'the pains of exile and the perils of proscription'. But the popularity of his *Policraticus* also shows that he had direct influence on the development of a type of humanism that was essentially Christian.

In Defense of Eloquence

John of Salisbury

John of Salisbury (1115 to 1180) was the central figure of English learning during the twelfth century. He wrote eloquent letters to his contemporaries as well as longer works intended for a wider audience. In *Metalogicon*, from which this excerpt was taken, John defends the study of grammar, rhetoric, and particularly logic, which younger scholars were beginning to embrace. John argues that eloquence—the faculty to express exactly what one's mind wants to say—is the conduit for attaining wealth, winning favor, and earning fame. He argues that humans should aspire to be eloquent since the human facility with language is what sets them apart from other beasts. Nature alone does not provide one with eloquence, however. John argues that one must cultivate eloquence through the study of grammar and rhetoric.

Book I, Chapter 7: Praise of Eloquence.

The foolish flock of Cornificians caws away[1] (in a language all their own), evidencing that they have contemned every rule of speech. For, as they themselves inform us, they cannot simultaneously take care to make sense and also to worry about the troublesome agreement of [verb] tenses and [noun, pronoun and adjective] cases. We refrain from comment. The sect may still perceive the truth, even while it is lying, but this condition surely cannot endure.

1. *Cornicatur,* above, chap. 5.

Excerpted from *Metalogicon of John of Salisbury,* translated by Daniel D. McGarry. Reprinted with permission from Peter Smith Publishing, Inc.

A man who is a liar in word and spirit will come to believe the false-hood he peddles. According to the Cornificians, "Rules of eloquence are superfluous, and the possession or lack of eloquence is depen-dent on nature." What could be farther from the truth? What is elo-quence but the faculty of appropriate and effective verbal expres-sion?[2] As such, it brings to light and in a way publishes what would otherwise be hidden in the inner recesses of man's consciousness.[3] Not everyone who speaks, nor even one who says what he wants to in some fashion, is eloquent. He alone is eloquent who fittingly and efficaciously[4] expresses himself as he intends. This appropriate ef-fectiveness[5] postulates a faculty (so called from facility), to follow our wont of imitating the concern of the Stoics about the etymolo-gies of words as a key to easier understanding of their meanings. One who can with facility and adequacy verbally express his men-tal perceptions is eloquent. The faculty of doing this is appropriately called "eloquence." For myself, I am at a loss to see how anything could be more generally useful: more helpful in acquiring wealth, more reliable for winning favor, more suited for gaining fame, than is eloquence. Nothing, or at least hardly anything, is to be preferred to this [precious] gift of nature and grace.

Virtue and wisdom, which perhaps . . . differ in name rather than in substance, rank first among desiderata, but eloquence comes sec-ond. Third is health, and after this, in fourth place, the good will of one's associates and an abundance of goods, to provide the material instruments of action. The moralist lists things to be desired in this order, and aptly epitomizes the sequence:

> What more could a fond nurse wish for her sweet charge,
> Than that he be wise and eloquent,
> And that friends, fame, health, good fare,
> And a never failing purse be his without stint?[6]

If man is superior to other living beings in dignity because of his powers of speech and reason, what is more universally efficacious and more likely to win distinction, than to surpass one's fellows, who possess the same human nature, and are members of the same human race, in those sole respects wherein man surpasses other be-ings? Moreover, while eloquence both illumines and adorns men of whatever age, it especially becomes the young. For youth is in a way to attract favor so that it may make good the potentialities of its nat-ural talent.[7] Who are the most prosperous and wealthy among our fellow citizens? Who the most powerful and successful in all their

2. Literally: "of fittingly saying what our mind wants to express"; cf. Cicero, *De Orat.*, i, 6, § 21, *passim.* 3. Literally: "the heart," as the supposed seat of consciousness. 4. *commode,* fittingly, ap-propriately, and effectively. 5. *commoditas,* fitness, appropriate effectiveness, easy adequacy. 6. Horace, *Ep.*, i, 4, 8–11. 7. Or: For youth attracts favor and so makes good its claim to intellectual distinction.

enterprises? Is it not the eloquent? As Cicero observes "Nothing is so unlikely that words cannot lend an air of probability; nothing is so repulsive and rude that speech cannot polish it and somehow render it attractive, as though it had been remade for the better."[8] He who despises such a great boon [as eloquence] is clearly in error; while he who appreciates, or rather pretends to appreciate it, without actually cultivating it, is grossly negligent and on the brink of insanity.

Book I, Chapter 8: The Necessity of Helping Nature by Use and Exercise.

The Cornificians argue that nature herself gratuitously grants eloquence to anyone who ever comes to possess it, whereas she arbitrarily and irrevocably refuses and denies it to those fated never to become eloquent. They conclude that efforts to acquire eloquence are useless or superfluous. Why, therefore, oh most learned Cornificians, do you not understand[9] all languages? Why do you not at least know Hebrew, which, as we are told, mother nature gave to our first parents and preserved for mankind until human unity was rent by impiety, and the pride which presumed to mount to heaven by physical strength and the construction of a tower, rather than by virtue, was leveled in a babbling chaos of tongues?[10] Why do not the Cornificians speak this language, which is more natural than the others, having been, so to speak, taught by nature herself? Nature is, according to some (although it is not easy to explain this definition)[11] "a certain genitive[12] force, implanted in all things, whereby they can act or be the recipients of action."[13] It is called "genitive," both because everything obtains a nature as a result of being brought into existence, and because this nature is for each being its principle of existence. Everything derives its suitability for this or for that form its composition. This is true whether a thing is composed of what are known as parts; or its composition consists in a union of matter and form, as with simple things that do not admit of an assemblage of parts; or its manner of composition is a consequence solely of the decree of the divine goodness. The latter [the divine decree] is verily "first nature," according to Plato, who, as Victorinus and many others attest, asserted that the divine will is the surest nature of all things, since created nature flows from this fountain, and the activities of all things can ultimately be traced back to God.[14] We exclude, of course, corruption and sin, whereby nature degenerates from its

---

8. Cicero, *Paradox.*, praef., § 3. 9. *peritiam . . . habetis*, have a practical knowledge or mastery of. 10. Cf. Augustine, *De C.D.*, xvi, II. 11. Cf. Cicero, *De Inv.*, i, 24, § 34; and Victorinus, *loc. cit.* 12. *genitiua*, genitive, innate or inborn; also dynamic, begetting or originating. 13. *facere uel pati*. 14. Victorinus, *In Lib. I de Inv.* (Cicero, *Opp.*, ed. Orell., V, 70).

original state. That force which is originally implanted in each and every thing and constitutes the source of its activities or aptitudes is a nature, but a created one. I believe that other definitions [of nature] found among authors generally refer to created nature. Even that "master artisan, fire," which produces visible effects in an invisible way,[15] is created; although some, begging leave of Aristotle"[16] and Chalcidius,[17] doubt that it is a nature.[18] I further believe that the principle of movement as such[19] traces back to God, and that Aristotle would not deny this. I am sure that Boethius would agree, since he does not deny that what can act or be acted upon is created [nature].[20] But the specific differences that provide forms for every thing either come from Him by Whom all things have been made, or they are nothing at all. There are also other descriptions of nature, but anything else that is postulated by a Platonist must be either nothing at all, or a work of God.[21] For the present, however, let us use the first definition, which seems best suited for our purpose. We will grant that the genitive force originally implanted in things is powerful and effective. But, certainly, just as it can be canceled or hindered by defects, so it can, on the other hand, be restored or helped by aids. It is not uncommon to hear children, in their prattle, remark that one lacks the use of a given natural ability which he otherwise possesses. An animal that naturally has leg locomotion is sometimes crippled, whereas one who is by nature two-footed, often lacks either or both of his feet. Care is accordingly not superfluous. Rather, it assists nature, and makes easier something that is already possible in one way or another. Socrates, we are told,[22] was naturally wanton[23] and overly susceptible to women[24] (to use history's own word).[25] But he subdued and controlled his passionate nature, which he corrected by philosophy and the exercise of virtue. They say that Scaurus Rufus was far from naturally bright, but that by assiduously employing his meager natural talents, he became so accomplished that he even called Cicero himself "a barbarian."[26] If [more] examples were adduced, it would everywhere be apparent that, even where nature is sluggish, it is not unreasonable to apply oneself, and that even though natural endowment might have been more effective in a given case, diligence is not futile as though it were wasted.

---

15. Cf. *ibid.* 16. See Boethius, *Contra Eut. et Nest.*, chap. i (ed. Peiper, p. 190). 17. Cf. Chalcidius, *Comm. in Tim. Plat.*, §§ 23, 323. 18. *naturam*, a nature, or simply nature (in general). 19. *principium motus secundum se;* cf. Boethius, *loc. cit.* 20. Boethius, *op. cit.* (ed. Peiper, p. 189). 21. *aut de numero rerum tollendum est aut diuinis operibus ascribendum,* literally: is either to be separated from the number of things or ascribed to the divine works. 22. Cf. Cicero, *De Fato*, 5, § 10. 23. *petulcus,* inclined to butt with the horns, wanton. 24. *muliebrosus* (from *mulier*), overly affectionate toward women, or lascivious regarding women. 25. Namely, to quote the very word used in the story itself. 26. *Allobroga,* literally: An Allobrogian, a member of a warlike people of Gaul; a barbarian. Cf. Juvenal, *Sat.*, vii, 213, though Juvenal here has "that Rufus, whom they have so often called 'the Allobrogian Cicero.'"

Although frequently nature is a dominant factor, and has greater proclivity in one or in another person,[27] still, just as natural ability easily deteriorates when neglected, so it is strengthened by cultivation and care.

> The question is raised whether a poem[28] is due to nature or art;
> But I neither see what study can do in the absence of natural talent,
> Nor what natural talent can accomplish without cultivation,
> So much does one demand[29] the assistance of the other, and so closely
> do they coöperate.[30]

Although the gifts of nature are definitely helpful, they are never or rarely so effective that they are fully realized without study. Nothing is so strong and robust that it cannot be enfebled by neglect,[31] nothing so well constructed that it cannot be razed. On the other hand, diligent application can build up and preserve the lowest degree of natural talent. If nature is propitious, it should be industriously cultivated, rather than neglected, so that its fruits may be readily harvested. On the other hand, if nature is unbenign, it should still be nursed even more carefully, so that, with the aid of virtue, it may more happily and gloriously grow strong.

---

27. This may mean either: "in one or the other respect," or "in one or the other person." 28. *carmen*, song, poem. 29. *poscit* should be substituted here for *possit* in the Webb edition. Cf. MSS C, B, A, as well as the text of Horace. 30. Horace, *A.P.*, II, 408–411. 31. *diligentia* in the Migne and Webb editions is evidently a mistake for *negligentia;* cf. MSS C, B, A.

Human Intellect Is Limited

Moses Maimonides

Moses Maimonides lived from 1135 to 1204. He was born in Spain during a time when Arabs ruled most of the country, but warring factions created danger and instability in Spain that forced Maimonides to move to northern Africa. He became a physician to Saladin, the Egyptian military leader who conquered the Christians during the Third Crusade. In the following excerpt, Maimonides argues that the human mind—like human senses—has only a limited ability to perceive. He delineates four reasons why humans can't know everything: human arrogance, the complexity of the subject, the mind's inability to comprehend, and habit and training. Although many things lie outside human understanding, people continue to fight over these things as though they comprehend them. Maimonides argues that such arrogance leads to weakness and imperfection. He maintains that it is best to humbly admit doubt and accept as a possibility that which cannot be disproved.

Chapter XXXI

Know that for the human mind there are certain objects of perception which are within the scope of its nature and capacity; on the other hand, there are, amongst things which actually exist, certain objects which the mind can in no way and by no means grasp: the gates of perception are closed against it. Further, there are things of which the mind understands one part, but remains ignorant of the other; and when man is able to comprehend certain things, it

Excerpted from "On the Limits of Man's Intellect," by Moses Maimonides (written in the Twelfth Century).

does not follow that he must be able to comprehend everything. This also applies to the senses: they are able to perceive things, but not at every distance; and all other powers of the body are limited in a similar way. A man can, e.g., carry two kikkar, but he cannot carry ten kikkar. How individuals of the same species surpass each other in these sensations and in other bodily faculties is universally known, but there is a limit to them, and their power cannot extend to every distance or to every degree.

All this is applicable to the intellectual faculties of man. There is a considerable difference between one person and another as regards these faculties, as is well known to philosophers. While one man can discover a certain thing by himself, another is never able to understand it, even if taught by means of all possible expressions and metaphors, and during a long period; his mind can in no way grasp it, his capacity is insufficient for it. This distinction is not unlimited. A boundary is undoubtedly set to the human mind which it cannot pass. There are things (beyond that boundary) which are acknowledged to be inaccessible to human understanding, and man does not show any desire to comprehend them, being aware that such knowledge is impossible, and that there are no means of overcoming the difficulty; e.g., we do not know the number of stars in heaven, whether the number is even or odd; we do not know the number of animals, minerals, or plants, and the like. There are other things, however, which man very much desires to know, and strenuous efforts to examine and to investigate them have been made by thinkers of all classes, and at all times. They differ and disagree, and constantly raise new doubts with regard to them, because their minds are bent on comprehending such things, that is to say, they are moved by desire; and every one of them believes that he has discovered the way leading to a true knowledge of the thing, although human reason is entirely unable to demonstrate the fact by convincing evidence.—For a proposition which can be proved by evidence is not subject to dispute, denial, or rejection; none but the ignorant would contradict it, and such contradiction is called "denial of a demonstrated proof." Thus you find men who deny the spherical form of the earth, or the circular form of the line in which the stars move, and the like; such men are not considered in this treatise. This confusion prevails mostly in metaphysical subjects, less in problems relating to physics, and is entirely absent from the exact sciences. Alexander Aphrodisius said that there are three causes which prevent men from discovering the exact truth: first, arrogance and vainglory; secondly, the subtlety, depth, and difficulty of any subject which is being examined; thirdly, ignorance and want of capacity to comprehend what might be comprehended. These causes are enumerated by Alexander. At the present time there is a fourth cause not mentioned by him, because it did not then prevail, namely, habit and training. We naturally like what we have been accustomed to, and are attracted towards it. This may be observed amongst villagers; though they rarely enjoy the benefit of a douche or bath, and have few enjoyments, and pass a life of privation, they dislike town life and do not desire its pleasures, preferring the inferior things to which they are accustomed, to the better things to which they are strangers; it would give them no satisfaction to live in palaces, to be clothed in silk, and to indulge in baths, ointments, and perfumes.

The same is the case with those opinions of man to which he has been accustomed from his youth; he likes them, defends them, and shuns the opposite views. This is likewise one of the causes which prevent men from finding truth, and which make them cling to their habitual opinions. Such is, e.g., the case with the vulgar notions with respect to the corporeality of God, and many other metaphysical questions, as we shall explain. It is the result of long familiarity with passages of the Bible, which they are accustomed to respect and to receive as true, and the literal sense of which implies the corporeality of God and other false notions; in truth, however, these words were employed as figures and metaphors for reasons to be mentioned below. Do not imagine that what we have said of the insufficiency of our understanding and of its limited extent is an assertion founded only on the Bible; for philosophers likewise assert the same, and perfectly understand it, without having regard to any religion or opinion. It is a fact which is only doubted by those who ignore things fully proved. This chapter is intended as an introduction to the next.

Chapter XXXII

You must consider, when reading this treatise, that mental perception, because connected with matter, is subject to conditions similar to those to which physical perception is subject. That is to say, if your eye looks around, you can perceive all that is within the range of your vision; if, however, you overstrain your eye, exerting it too much by attempting to see an object which is too distant for your eye, or to examine writings or engravings too small for your sight, and forcing it to obtain a correct perception of them, you will not only weaken your sight with regard to that special object, but also for those things which you otherwise are able to perceive: your eye will have become too weak to perceive what you were able to see before you exerted yourself and exceeded the limits of your vision.

The same is the case with the speculative faculties of one who devotes himself to the study of any science. If a person studies too much and exhausts his reflective powers, he will be confused, and will not be able to apprehend even that which had been within the power of his apprehension. For the powers of the body are all alike in this respect.

The mental perceptions are not exempt from a similar condition. If you admit the doubt, and do not persuade yourself to believe that there is a proof for things which cannot be demonstrated, or to try at once to reject and positively to deny an assertion the opposite of which has never been proved, or attempt to perceive things which are beyond your perception, then you have attained the highest degree of human perfection, then you are like R. Akibha,[1] who "in peace entered [the study of these theological problems], and came out in peace." If, on the other hand, you attempt to exceed the limit of your intellectual power, or at once to reject things as impossible which have never been proved to be impossible, or which are in fact possible, though their possibility be very remote, then you will be like Elisha Aher;[2] you will not only fail to become perfect, but you will become exceedingly imperfect. Ideas founded on mere imagination will prevail over you, you will incline toward defects, and toward base and degraded habits, on account of the confusion which troubles the mind, and of the dimness of its light, just as weakness of sight causes invalids to see many kinds of unreal images, especially when they have looked for a long time at dazzling or at very minute objects.

Respecting this it has been said, "Hast thou found honey? eat so much as is sufficient for thee, lest thou be filled therewith, and vomit it" (Prov. xxv. 16). Our Sages also applied this verse to Elisha Aher.

How excellent is this simile! In comparing knowledge to food, the author of Proverbs mentions the sweetest food, namely, honey, which has the further property of irritating the stomach, and of causing sickness. He thus fully describes the nature of knowledge. Though great, excellent, noble and perfect, it is injurious if not kept within bounds or not guarded properly; it is like honey which gives nourishment and is pleasant, when eaten in moderation, but is totally thrown away when eaten immoderately. Therefore, it is not said "lest thou be filled and loathe it," but "lest thou vomit it." The same idea is expressed in the words, "It is not good to eat much honey" (Prov. xxv. 27); and in the words, "Neither make thyself over-wise; why shouldst thou destroy thyself?" (Eccles. vii. 16); comp. "Keep thy foot when thou goest to the house of God" (ibid. v. I). The same subject is alluded to in the words of David, "Neither do I exercise myself in great matters, or in things too high for me" (Ps. cxxxi. 2), and in the sayings of our Sages: "Do not inquire into things which are too difficult for thee, do not search what is hidden from thee; study what you are allowed to study, and do not occupy thyself with mysteries." They meant to say, Let thy mind only attempt things

---

1. **R. Akibha** Aqiva' Ben Yosef (c.40–135 A.D.), Palestinian scholar. 2. **Elisha Aher** Elisha ben Vayah, (known as Aher, the other) flourished in the second century A.D. He was a Palestinian scholar who doubted the unity of God.

which are within human perception; for the study of things which lie beyond man's comprehension is extremely injurious, as has been already stated. This lesson is also contained in the Talmudical passage, which begins, "He who considers four things," etc., and concludes, "He who does not regard the honour of his Creator"; here also is given the advice which we have already mentioned, viz., that man should not rashly engage in speculation with false conceptions, and when he is in doubt about anything, or unable to find a proof for the object of his inquiry, he must not at once abandon, reject and deny it; he must modestly keep back, and from regard to the honour of his Creator, hesitate [from uttering an opinion] and pause. This has already been explained.

It was not the object of the Prophets and our Sages in these utterances to close the gate of investigation entirely, and to prevent the mind from comprehending what is within its reach, as is imagined by simple and idle people, whom it suits better to put forth their ignorance and incapacity as wisdom and perfection, and to regard the distinction and wisdom of others as irreligion and imperfection, thus taking darkness for light and light for darkness. The whole object of the Prophets and the Sages was to declare that a limit is set to human reason where it must halt. Do not criticise the words used in this chapter and in others in reference to the mind, for we only intended to give some idea of the subject in view, not to describe the essence of the intellect; for other chapters have been dedicated to this subject.

Vertical Cathedrals: The Rise of Gothic Architecture

Russell Chamberlin

Russell Chamberlin is the author of several books on Europe including *Florence and Tuscany*. According to Chamberlin, Gothic architecture developed out of earlier Romanesque and Norman designs. Early Romanesque churches were built with rounded arches which needed massive columns for support; the support systems for these cathedrals provided little space for windows, so Romanesque churches tended to be heavy and dark. By contrast, the pointed arches of the Gothic cathedrals were supported by graceful buttresses, which made it possible to achieve great height without large columns. As a result, Gothic churches tended to have numerous stained-glass windows that illuminated the interior of the church and made the display of religious artifacts possible. Chamberlin argues that the idea for the pointed arch was originally developed by the Arabs and was transported to Europe during the Holy Crusades.

S ome time before the year 1130 a French monk, Honorius of Autun, set down carefully and precisely what could be called a manual of symbolism. Every part of a great church, no matter how humble or how exalted that part, had a dual role: the physical function it was created to perform, and the symbolism it was meant to express. Beginning with the church itself, Honorius pointed out that it was set on stone foundations, even as the Church itself was founded on the sure rock of Christ. He then takes the reader on a kind of conducted tour explaining as he goes. The windows are to be seen as the learned Fathers of the Church: just as the glass keeps out cold but lets in light, so the Fathers keep out heresy and let in the divine light of the Church's teaching. The numerous columns of the building are to be seen as bishops supporting the organization; the very tiles on the roof, protecting the building from rain, are typecast as Christian soldiers protecting the faith. The pavements underfoot are the ordinary people themselves; the relics of saints preserved in the altar are the treasures of wisdom hidden in Christ. The great bell of the building is the Church speaking to her people, while the cock that crowns all, glittering high up on the steeple, stands as symbol for the priest calling the faithful to mass, even as the cock awakens sleepers in the morning. Every part of the cathedral, every action within it, is directed to a single end *ad majorem Dei gloriam*—to the greater glory of God.

Romanesque Origins

Honorius inevitably touches on the dominant ground-plan of the building—the cruciform, in memory of the cross of Christ. Yet this was a relatively new development, for throughout the formative years of the Church it had been the Roman basilica, the ordinary law court of a Roman town, that inspired the ground-plan. The darkness of the Dark Ages has been rendered less impenetrable in recent years. Archaeologists and archivists alike have succeeded in throwing light over much of its course to show that, during the centuries-long period between the final extinction of the Roman empire and the appearance of nation states, though Europe had lost social cohesion, it had not slumped back into savagery. Art, sure index to a society's mind, shows an admittedly confused but immensely vigorous period whose vitalities were dispersed through many channels. Gradually, these channels found their way into one great stream, the Romanesque—that massive style of building which took its plan from the basilica but whose elevation perfectly expressed its time. Raoul Glaber's glittering white sanctuaries were as much castles as temples: Europe was still an embattled, fragmented society groping for unity through the universal Church.

Throughout the twelfth century Romanesque, that most suprahuman of religious styles, dominated. It was perhaps more truly international than the succeeding 'Gothic', even though its regional styles could vary from the mosaic-encrusted blaze of Venice's San

Marco, to the dark, gloomy strength of Durham. It was not a style influenced by humanism.[1] While the low doorway, enormous pillars and lack of windows were doubtless the result of architectural need, the decorations clearly reflected the philosophy. The elongated figures sculptured on the portals, with their remote, austere faces, inspire awe rather than affection. In His portrayal, Christ appears as Creator and as Judge: the Child is yet to come. In all its ramifications, from engineering to illumination, in stone, brick, vellum or glass, Romanesque art is the working-out of a theology more Oriental than Occidental.

The Arrival of Gothic

The internationalism of Romanesque was essentially an expression of that great international institution, the monastery, which created it, but the cathedral came to express itself in 'Gothic'. This all-embracing term is of comparatively recent date. The Italian artist, Raphael, used it pejoratively in the sixteenth century, contrasting this 'barbaric' style with the sophistication of Greece and Rome. The term passed into England, still in the contemptuous mode, via Sir Henry Worton. Evelyn followed him and the great authority of Christopher Wren established it firmly, still as an expression of contempt. But then, beginning with Horace Walpole,[2] there began a reaction in its favour. The reaction obscured its essential nature as thoroughly as did the contemptuous assessments of the Renaissance, and culminated in the 'Gothic' of Victorian England when psalters were illuminated by chromo-lithography and produced on steam presses. Even as late as 1888 the great Ninth Edition of the *Encyclopaedia Britannica* was uncertain as to what term to use for the architecture, deciding at last, though hesitantly, on the non-committal phrase 'Pointed Architecture'.

Architectural Classification Systems

Meanwhile, in 1835, an architectural historian called Thomas Rickman, in a laudable attempt to bring some order into a confused subject, created a classification which has put the whole subject into a kind of straitjacket or bed of Procrustes.[3] Discussing the admittedly botched attempts at repairing the ancient churches and cathedrals by builders who were ignorant 'of every real principle of English architecture' he proposed the following:

> English architecture may be divided into four distinct periods of styles which may be named: first, the Norman style; second, the Early English style; third, the Decorated style and fourth, the Perpendicular style.

1. Humanism is a philosophy that is concerned with human beings, rather than with theology. 2. English man of letters living from 1717 to 1797. 3. A Greek giant who stretched or shortened captives to fit in one of his iron beds.

Rickman's useful piece of shorthand became, in time, a tyranny whereby every guidebook felt it necessary to classify the described building as 'Norman', 'EE', 'Dec' or Perp'. The sheer naïvety of trying to find one label for a building whose construction covered perhaps centuries is summed up by Pevsner's comment on York Minster: 'Between about 1230 and 1475 every stage is represented so much so that the following description [of the Minster] has to be chronological by parts'. If a cathedral or great church could be photographed by some speeded-up camera, as is done to show some aspect of natural history, then the viewer would see it growing virtually organically, forms melting one into the other over the centuries. The fact that Rickman's classification ends with 'Perp', that is, around the 1550s, with nothing whatsoever to say about the intervening three centuries, much less the period extending down to our time, shows the severe limitation of this pedantic wish to cram a living, ever-changing structure into a pigeonhole.

Nevertheless, Rickman's classification was of value for it brought to the attention of his contemporaries the fact that ecclesiastical architecture, like all other intellectual activities, had its changing fashions and that those fashions reflected something of the contemporary world. It did this partly through the limitations imposed by that world, for example the fact that the Norman structures were massive because their builders had not yet learned the sciences of stress, and partly by the psychological bent of that world, as for example the richly flowing forms of the style Rickman called Decorated.

The Norman Style

A capital of a column in the Norman crypt at Canterbury shows an extraordinary monster, a moustached winged creature holding a fish in its right hand, a figure more familiar in Byzantine than in European art. The carving hints at the mystery of the people we lump together under the title of 'Norman', and the blend of Oriental, Byzantine and Western European influences in their art is a summary of that people's achievement. The 'Norman Conquest' which, for the British, marks an epoch in their history was but one of several conquests. By the year 1098 the Normans were settled in the Middle East, at Antioch, throughout southern Italy and Sicily, as well as Normandy and England. But scattered though they were and influenced by such widely differing climates—so that William II, king of Sicily, has himself portrayed as a Byzantine emperor, while William I king of England is a home-spun Norman—despite these cultural differences, they were one race. In the words of the historian Charles Homer Haskins:

> They did their work pre-eminently not as a people apart, but as a group
> of leaders and energisers, the little leaven that leaveneth the whole lump.
> Wherever they went, they showed a marvellous power of initiative and

assimilation: if the initiative is more evident in England, the assimilation is more manifest in Sicily.

Scattered though they might have been, they retained their identity as 'Normans', so that the manifold influences flowed into one channel, in architecture producing that astonishing style called simply 'Norman'. It is a style which, at first glance, seems simply an expression of brutal strength, a style which the landscape historian Richard Muir likens accurately enough to the Nazi or the Stalinist. But it is one, too, with sudden extraordinary grace notes, such as the cool elegance of the nave of Norwich cathedral.

The Pointed Arch

It was at Durham that, in the early decades of the twelfth century, some innovating mason took a step which, though simple in appearance, was to transform the whole world of architecture. Instead of making a curved arch, he sharpened the angle and brought into being the 'pointed arch'.

Romanesque builders had overcome the limitations of the barrel vault, which formed their round, shallow arches, by developing the cross vault. The substitution of panels of lighter masonry in the four triangular panels of the cross vault was a natural development, and the entire weight of the vault thus rested on ribs. But these, in their turn, still required massive, almost windowless walls to support them. The builders were still governed by the idea of orders rising one upon the other in order to achieve height—massive, enduring but still essentially earthy, the abiding characteristic of Norman work. The pointed arch, by contrast, took the weight of the vault straight down, to be supported by buttresses. It was as though sections had been cut out of the wall and placed at right angles to it, eliminating the appearance of solidity so that the building seems to be soaring up weightless. The walls could now be pierced with more, and larger windows, flooding the interior with light which meant, in turn, that internal decorations could be far richer and more detailed.

The unknown mason in Durham was certainly not working in the dark. The pointed arch was one of the gifts of those Crusaders which, though utterly failing in their objective, were to alter the history of Europe by transmitting to it the genius of the Arabs. Certainly the idea of the pointed arch, travelling from the Middle East, had rooted itself in France in time for it to be adopted by Abbot Suger, the energetic, innovative man who, between 1132 and 1144, rebuilt the royal abbey of St Denis in the exciting new style. And here is a certain, if rare, instance of a cleric being truly the builder, for Suger recorded every detail of the work and its difficulties and triumphs in a vivid account that has an almost boyish excitement about it. He ran into difficulty with the construction of the towering new arches and breathlessly tells of the night of storm when it seemed that the work would come tumbling down. But the Arab mathematicians were vindicated, and the new arch stood the test though its mortar was still far from set.

After Durham the new style stood its fullest testing when William of Sens built the choir at Canterbury. Then, in 1175, the foundations were laid for the first purely English Gothic cathedral, the exquisite little cathedral church of St Andrew in Wells. Though one of the smaller of English cathedrals it dominated its host city, for even in the twentieth century Wells has a population of only 8,000 or so and the area covered by the cathedral and its ancillary buildings is about equivalent to the historic heart of the city itself. Bishop Reginald de Bohun is credited with the design of the building, and whether it was truly his work, or the inspired work of some unknown master mason, the plans were so detailed and fully developed that, though its construction extended over eighty-five years, and was not completed until 1260, the entire building is in one harmonious style. Much of this would be to the credit of the master mason, Adam Lock, whose powerful head is sculpted on the north wall of the nave. He died in 1229 and it is therefore chronologically possible that he was indeed the original architect. The difference between Durham cathedral and Wells is the difference between two cultures: Durham overawes, Wells enchants with an atmosphere almost of gaiety, a delightful introduction of the style which would be known as Early English.

Asia

The twelfth century was a time of important transitions in government and culture. New rulers, methods of government, and artistic movements took hold in Asia, particularly in China, Japan, and among the Mongol clans.

From its inception, the Sung dynasty was a time of important changes in Chinese society. Chao K'aung-yin and his brother founded the dynasty in 960 and reunited China after more than five decades of war and anarchy. Divided into two eras, the first era was Northern Sung, because the dynasty was first established in north China. From the start of the dynasty's establishment until 1127, the northern provinces were frequently under attack by foreign invaders. The most successful of these invaders were the Jurchen, a people from Manchuria that, in attacks between 1114 and 1126, conquered northern China and overthrew the Northern Sung. Following the Jurchen conquest, the Sung empire shrank to the southern portion of China, with the Yangtze Valley as its northern border. This led to the second era of the Sung dynasty—Southern Sung, which ran from 1127 until the Mongols completed their conquest of China in 1279.

The Sung era is noted especially for its art, literature, and philosophy. According to Woodbridge Bingham, Hilary Conroy, and Frank W. Iklé, the authors of *A History of Asia, Volume I: Formation of Civilizations, from Antiquity to 1600,* the Sung period was a pivotal time. They write: "During the Sung, Chinese society and culture as a whole crystallized into forms which were to last to modern times." Though the eleventh century had its fair share of great artists who captured in poetry and paintings vibrant images of mountains and other landscapes, Sung culture began to truly bloom in 1100, when the emperor Hui-tsung was crowned. The emperor was a connoisseur of art and a skilled painter of birds and flowers. Although his reign ended in 1126, upon the fall of northern China to the Jurchen, south China remained a place conducive to artists and scholars. Scholarship and philosophy also flourished in the twelfth century, as the traditional form of Confucianism began to include the influences of Buddhism and Taoism. The scholar Chu Hsi, according to Bingham, Conroy, and Iklé, created "a Sung school of Confucianism, which was to remain a powerful influence in China in succeeding centuries." The spread of high-quality printing made the writings of Chu Hsi and others easy to disseminate.

The key event in twelfth-century Japan was the shift of power from the emperor and powerful families to the military. The most powerful of these families were the Fujiwara, who wielded great control throughout much of the Heian period (784 to 1156). Through marriages to the emperors' daughters and various machinations, the Fujiwara clan essentially ruled Japan until 1160. But that year, the power in Japan began to shift toward the military classes, culminating in 1185 in the establishment of the Kamakura government, founded by the Minamoto Yoritomo. Yoritomo centralized the Japanese feudal system, leading to a warrior class that would dominate Japan for the next seven centuries. Central to this system were the samurai—warriors who received land and position in exchange for loyalty to and protection of their daimyos (feudal landowners). At the bottom of the feudal ladder was the *bonge* (commoners) class. The Kamakura government further strengthened the military class by placing the greatest power in the hands of feudal military dictators called shoguns.

Finally, the Mongols were a largely disunited people until the mid-1100s. Prior to that time, they lived a primitive existence as nomads, traveling throughout the year in search of viable places to hunt and to feed their flocks. Unfortunately, little is known of these years, because the Mongols were illiterate and did not provide a written history until after the death of Chingis (or Genghis) Khan. It was Chingis's father, Yesügei, who helped unify the Mongol clan and adjoining clans. Upon his father's death, Chingis—then known as Temüjin—continued the work of uniting the clans. Temüjin made great strides during the twelfth century in transforming the Mongols into a powerful people, although he would not achieve his greatest power until the early 1200s, when the Mongolian Empire stretched to include northern China, Korea, Manchuria, and India.

In the following chapter, the authors explore key historical developments in China, Japan, and among the Mongols.

The Rise of China as a Sea Power

Jung-Pang Lo

Jung-Pang Lo explains how a variety of geographic, economic, and social factors led to the rise of China as a sea power in the twelfth century. Lo follows China's continued naval importance into the seventeenth century, though focusing much of his attention on the early growth of the Chinese navy. The northwest portion of China was impoverished, due largely to poor agricultural conditions, and often faced foreign attacks. Consequently, residents began to migrate toward the southeast coast. Because the geography of the coastal regions is not conducive to agriculture, its residents had to find other types of work. Many people turned to commerce and industry. These industries began to outgrow the domestic market, so their proprietors took to the seas for further expansion. The government followed their people's interest in the sea, which led to the development of Chinese navies and naval expeditions. The growth of the coastal economy was a boon to the government coffers, Lo notes, as foreign trade flourished in the twelfth century. Lastly, the attitude of the Chinese people changed during this period. They became more willing to explore new ideas and travel to new lands. Lo was a professor at the University of California at Davis and a founder of that university's Asian American studies program.

If the domination of the sea and the employment of naval strength as an instrument of national policy characterizes a sea power, then China during the late Sung [960 A.D. to 1279 A.D.], Yüan [1279 A.D.

Excerpted from "The Emergence of China as a Sea Power During the Late Sung and Early Yuan Periods," by Jung-Pang Lo, *Far Eastern Quarterly,* August 1955. Reprinted with permission from *Far Eastern Quarterly.*

to 1368 A.D.] and early Ming period [1368 A.D. to 1644 A.D.] would qualify. Why was it that China emerged as a sea power at this particular period and not at an earlier or later time? To seek an answer, we must take a broad view of sea power. Mere possession of a navy does not, *ipso facto,* make sea power. Sea power is the culmination and the physical expression of a set of geographical and sociological conditions which Admiral [Alfred T.] Mahan called the "elements of sea power."[1] The maritime expansion of China from the twelfth to the fifteenth century was the result of a fortuitous combination of these conditions.

Geography and Social Development

Geographical environment is one of the basic determining factors of social development. The long coastline of China, large sections of which, as in Shantung, Chekiang, Fukien and Kwangtung, are endowed with harbors and timber-clad mountains, and the adjoining seas enclosed by an island fringe, provide the physiographical conditions which favor and promote maritime activities. But the territorial vastness of China and her cohesion with the continent of Eurasia exercise so profound an influence that for long centuries the attention of the Chinese was occupied with internal problems and the defense of their land frontier on the north and northwest, the directions from which danger had historically threatened. During the ancient period, the hub of China was the inland provinces of Shensi and Honan, which became not only the political and strategic, but also the economic, cultural and population center of the country. The diffusion of population was toward the marginal areas around the heartland, and cultural and commercial relations were primarily carried on over caravan routes with countries of the west. The preoccupation with internal affairs and, to a lesser extent, with the affairs of the northwest frontier was again evident during the Ch'ing period.

The prosperity of China's northwestern provinces depended, however, on a number of factors, chief of which were temperate climate, abundant rainfall and fertile soil. During the medieval period, the climate and geology of the entire region underwent a gradual and profound change. The winters became more severe and the atmosphere drier, rainfall diminished in amount but increased in intensity, the streams became shallower and more saline, and erosion ate steadily into the farmlands. The Cheng-kuo Canal and the Pai Canal, which in Han times [202 B.C.E. to 9 C.E., 25 C.E. to 220 C.E.] irrigated two million *mou* of land in the Wei River Valley, site of the capitals of successive dynasties of the past, by the Northern Sung period wa-

1. From Alfred T. Mahan's book, *The Influence of Sea Power upon History, 1660–1783.*

tered only a hundred thousand *mou*, or five per cent of the former area. As the soil declined in productivity, the struggle to eke out a living began to absorb more and more of the energy of the people.

Coeval with the impoverishment of the Northwest was the prodigious advance of the coastal region of Southeast China as this became the economic center of the nation. In the salubrity of its climate, in the productivity of its soil, and in the potential wealth of its rivers, lakes and mountains, the Southeast far surpasses the Northwest. From the fourth century, when the Northwest was beginning to decline, the progressive peopling of the Southeast and its comparatively peaceful environment led to the extensive development of its resources. The construction of irrigation works was but one example of the efforts of the people of Southeast China to improve the conditions of their already bountiful land. The economy of Southeast China developed to such an extent that by 1119, for example, over seventy per cent of the money and goods (*ch'ien-wu*) sent to the court as tribute came from the lower Yangtze Valley.

For a long time, Chinese rulers, cherishing a sentimental attachment for the ancient centers of China's civilization and motivated by strategic considerations, continued to locate their capitals in Shensi or Honan, and they built an elaborate system of waterways to transport supplies from the Southeast to the civilian population in the capital and to the troops on the northwest frontier. But with the progressive desiccation of the Northwest and the frequent wars, these waterways, like the irrigation canals, suffered from shortage of water, damage and lack of repair. Without a continuous supply of food it was impossible to maintain large garrisons and the weakening of the frontier defenses tempted the border peoples to invade.

Foreign Invasions

On one hand, the absence of effective resistance and the attraction of the riches of China; on the other, their own economic distress and population pressure, the appearance of capable leaders and the consolidation of tribal organization were some of the many forces that agitated the nomads and impelled them to erupt periodically in massive tidal waves. The invasions of border peoples have not only had a profound and far-reaching effect on the history and culture of China but also served as a negative factor in turning the attention of the Chinese people to the sea.

The establishment by foreign conquerors of strong militaristic states in Northwest China sealed off Chinese contact with Central Asia, thus obliging the Chinese to carry on cultural and commercial intercourse abroad by sea. This shift in orientation is illustrated by a spot check in the section on foreign countries in the *Sung hui-yao kao* (*Draft of Sung institutes*). Before the fall of K'ai-feng in 1127, thirty-five per cent of the tribute-with-trade missions came to China by land and sixty-five per cent by sea. After this date all came by sea. The dislodgment of the Chinese from North China also destroyed much of their attachment for Shensi and Honan as sites for their capital. From 1127 on, their capitals were located near the seacoast.

The invasions from outside, coming at times when China was racked by civil strife, aggravated the economic distress and intensi-fied the migration of the people. This happened from the fourth to sixth centuries and, on a greater scale, from the tenth to thirteenth centuries. During these times the slow drift of the population became a swift stream. The magnitude of the unrest may be seen from the fact that the census takers had to divide the population into two classes, "settled" and "transient," and that during the Sung period, as the census of 1080 showed, one-third of the population (mostly from North China) was listed as transient.

Migration Toward the Coast

Instead of spreading more or less evenly into the southern provinces or, as in the eighth century, streaming into Szechwan, from the tenth to thirteenth centuries the people poured into Southeast China as if they were shoved by a gigantic force from the Northwest. This re-sulted in an abnormal swelling of the coastal population. The six seaboard provinces, with but a tenth of the area of the nation, had, during the Sung and Ming periods, half of the total population, a proportion higher than any in the pre-Sung or post-Ming periods. But if we examine the Yüan census of 1330, taking into account its imperfections and omissions, we find that two-thirds of the tax-paying population resided in the coastal regions.

With the exception of Kiangsu, the coastal provinces are hilly and cannot support a dense population by agriculture alone. Large num-bers of people moved into urban areas to find other means of liveli-hood and the result was the growth of cities. Hangchow, which boasted a population of nearly two million, was but one of the many teeming cities that rose along the southeastern coast. Urbanization led to the development of commerce and industry which, outgrow-ing the domestic market, sought to expand abroad. The more ven-turesome spirits sailed out to sea, some to support themselves by fishing or even by piracy and smuggling in nearby waters, others to trade or to colonize distant lands.

The movement of the people into the cities or out to sea was ac-celerated not only by civil disturbances but also by natural disasters. According to one investigator, the frequency of floods and droughts increased sharply in the Sung period. . . .

Thus, as the tilting of a table sends articles on the surface sliding to one side and off the edge, so social turmoil and climatic disturbances caused a shifting of the population to the coastal provinces and out to sea. Governments and rulers felt the impact of social and economic forces and were drawn along by the strong currents of popular feeling to turn their attention to the sea. In the creation of the Southern Sung navy under Kao-tsung (1127–1162), the overseas campaigns of Qubilai Qan, and the naval expeditions sent out by Emperor Yung-lo, the aims and ambition of the rulers and the policies of their governments merely supplemented the tendency of the people.

An Increase in Commerce and Trade

The contraction of the Sung empire and the disruption of normal economic activities, as a result of the inroads of northern peoples on one hand and the rise of money economy and industry on the other, led to another change in Chinese society. This was the participation of the government in monopolistic enterprises and commerce, a practice which the scholar-official class of China was supposed to regard with disdain. But during the Sung period, not only did foreign trade flourish under private management, not only did officials and members of the court hold shares in shipping and manufacturing companies, but the government itself operated monopolies in domestic trade and various productive enterprises. As a result, half of the government's revenue came in the form of returns from monopolies and excise taxes and as much as twenty per cent of the cash income of the state came from maritime trade, as was true during the first years of Kao-tsung's reign. Even the Emperor declared: "The profits from maritime commerce are very great. If properly managed they can be millions [of strings of cash]. Is it not better than taxing the people?"

Under government patronage, Chinese merchants sailed their ships to Southeast Asia and India and succeeded in wresting from their Moslem rivals the monopoly of the freight and passenger business. The merchants not only contributed funds and imported military supplies but also furnished ships and seamen to the Sung navy. Three hundred and thirty-eight huge merchantmen took part in the war of 1161, notably in the battles on the Yangtze. . . .

Maritime commerce and naval wars spurred the development of technology and the expansion of geographical knowledge. They encouraged the opening of ports and dredging of harbors, they advanced the art of navigation by such means as the mariner's compass and star and sea charts, and they furthered the publication of treatises on tides and currents and maps of foreign countries. Most remarkable was the achievement in naval architecture, for it was by the construction of larger and more seaworthy ships that the Chinese were able to capture the shipping business from the Arabs whose vessels at this time were still flimsy craft lashed together with ropes. The ships of the Chinese, by contrast, were ocean liners boasting

staterooms, wineshops, and the service of negro stewards. All were
sturdily built, with watertight bulkheads, and the larger ones had
lifeboats in tow. . . .

Investigations and Adventures

A factor which significantly influenced the technological progress
and economic development of the Sung, Yüan and early Ming periods was the mental attitude of the people. The jolt of environmental
changes loosened the grip of tradition on the men's minds. Not content with classical learning alone, the Chinese of this period displayed a measure of scientific spirit by their inclination to investigate and to experiment, their disposition for noting and sharing their
discoveries, and their aptitude for improvisation and invention. Instead of insisting on their own intellectual superiority, they readily
accepted the contributions of the Arabs and Hindus in the fields of
astronomy, geography and navigation. Instead of opposing foreign
trade as unnecessary, they fostered commerce with nations abroad
and tried, though unsuccessfully, to import goods needed by and of
value to China.

Another manifestation of the broadened outlook of the Chinese
of this period was their embarkation on colonial undertakings and
voyages of discovery. The spirit of adventure among the Chinese,
we are told, is repressed by their attachment to the family and the
ideals of filial piety. But wars and unrest shattered family ties and,
together with economic stress and population pressure, set in motion the first large-scale emigration by sea and the establishment of
the first permanent Chinese settlements in Southeast Asia. "The people depended upon the sea and commerce for their livelihood," states
the *Gazetteer of Fukien*. "They would leave their parents, wives and
children without a thought to dwell among the barbarians."

The stories of adventure and descriptions of foreign lands current
in the literature of the times stirred not only the masses but also
many men of the scholar-official class. There was, for example, Mo
Chi who, as director of the National Academy (*Kuo-tzu chien*) during the reign of Kao-tsung, may be supposed a staunch Confucian-
ist. But when out of office, he would charter ships and sail out to sea
both for the thrill of sailing and to satisfy his curiosity. Once he
sailed to the "Northern Ocean" (*Pei-yang*) and when his crew became fearful and mutinous, be drew his sword and compelled them
to sail on.

Government Policy

The maritime interest of the officials was reflected in the policy of
the government. One of the major policy debates in the Southern
Sung court took place between those who advocated a counter-

offensive to recover North China and those who favored defense to hold and consolidate South China. A counter-offensive would necessitate the employment of land forces, especially cavalry, in which the Southern Sung army was weak. So the policy adopted was that of defense and the physiography of Southeast China dictated the use of naval forces. Chang I, president of the Board of Revenue, in one of three memorials on naval preparedness he submitted in 1131, called the sea and the Yangtze River the new Great Wall of China, the warships the watch-towers, and the firearms the new weapons of defense.

Propaganda was used in support of the naval program. A political pamphlet published in 1131 stated: "Our defenses today are the [Yangtze] River and the sea, so our weakness in mounted troops is no cause for concern. But a navy is of value. . . . To use our navy is to employ out strong weapon to strike at the enemy's weakness." Emperor Hsiao-tsung (1163–1189), converted to the naval program, remarked, "The navy is our strong arm and we cannot afford to neglect it."

As the Yüan inherited the Sung navy so the Ming inherited the Yüan navy. Thus the spirit and tradition of the Sung navy were carried on by the two succeeding dynasties. From a defensive arm the navy developed into an instrument of aggression and political domination, and from the East China Sea the naval power of the Chinese advanced to the South China Sea and into the Indian Ocean.

Broadly speaking, the maritime expansion of China during the late Sung, Yüan and early Ming periods was the cumulative result of changing sociological conditions arising from climatic and geological disturbances, political unrest, and the pressure of alien invaders from the Northwest. The movement of the population to the coastal regions and out to sea, the orientation of the nation towards the Southeast, the interest of the people, even the scholar-official class, in maritime affairs and technological development, and the attention which the government paid to commerce and to the development of a navy, all illustrate the inconstancy of social characteristics commonly attributed to the Chinese and the inconclusiveness of general statements made about them. Social characteristics change under the compelling forces of nature and general statements blur our view of the facts and dynamics of historical change. We cannot discern the zigzags in the course of the historical and cultural development of a people like the Chinese if we remain so close to the ground that we become preoccupied with what Professor Harry Elmer Barnes calls "the episodical aspects of conventional historiography," but we can see them quite clearly if we stand upon an eminence where we can survey the wide sweep of each epoch of Chinese history.

Confucianism in Twelfth-Century China

James T.C. Liu

James T.C. Liu presents an overview of Confucianism in China during the Sung dynasty. One of the schools of Confucian thought is Neo-Confucianism, whose followers adhere to the teachings of eleventh-century philosopher Ch'eng I. They sought, in varying degrees, to reform the traditional Confucian views of government and society. Those views centered on a hierarchical system that included the emperor as superior to all with a stringent class system ranked below. Although many scholars have regarded Neo-Confucianism as the most important school of thought in China during the twelfth century, Liu believes this emphasis does not present a complete view of Chinese philosophy. Other Confucian schools during that century included the School of Mind, which de-emphasized the role of conduct and morality in Confucianism. Liu was the author and editor of other books on China, including *Change in Sung China: Innovation or Renovation?*, and a professor of East Asian studies at Princeton University in New Jersey.

Sung Confucianism[1] developed energetically in many directions; but because its vigorous intellectual contributions were additions

1. Sung was the dynasty that ruled China between 960 A.D. and 1279 A.D. Confucianism is a moral philosophy founded by Confucius in the sixth and fifth centuries B.C. In its traditional form, it focuses on human relationships and how people should treat each other. Taoism and Buddhism heavily influenced Sung Confucianism.

Excerpted, with editorial changes, from James T.C. Liu, *China Turning Inward: Intellectual-Political Changes in the Early Twelfth Century* (Cambridge, MA: Harvard University Council on East Asian Studies, 1988) pp. 43-51. Copyright © 1988 by the President and Fellows of Harvard College. Reprinted with permission from Harvard University Asia Center.

to an ancient heritage, it may generally be described as neo-traditional. Although many of its leaders were concerned with ethics and metaphysics, it was not confined to philosophy; nor was its philosophical output limited to one dominant school. An overview of Sung Confucian thought on government and education (*cheng-chiao*) should correct the mistaken impression that only one branch made contributions. Unfortunately, a host of both premodern sources and twentieth-century scholars—Chinese, Japanese, and Western—have conventionally given overwhelming and sometimes even exclusive attention to its prominent philosophical dimensions, particularly to the renowned Neo-Confucian school.

Masters of Confucianism

The term *Neo-Confucianism* was originally used in Western literature to designate the Chu Hsi school of thought. Since the middle of the present century, it has also been loosely applied to other Sung Confucians, in the broad sense that they were different from those of earlier periods. This has led to some confusion and needs to be clarified. Recent scholarship prefers to revert to the original, narrow usage. Neo-Confucianism refers exclusively to the Chu Hsi school or Li-hsueh, the School of Principles, and no one else. The present study identifies the moralistic conservatives, especially those who followed the teachings of Ch'eng I (1033–1107), as the forerunners of the Neo-Confucians. It characterizes the Neo-Confucians themselves as transcendental moralists, in recognition of their profound metaphysical system.

The special emphasis on Neo-Confucianism, which began with important historical sources, is not without reason; for Neo-Confucianism eventually became the state orthodoxy. The Sung dynastic history creates a special category for the "biographies of the True Way masters" (*Tao-hsueh chuan*), that is, biographies of the leading thinkers of the school. (Tao-hsueh, or the True Way school, was the name collectively applied to the forerunners of Neo-Confucianism, Chu Hsi himself, and his followers.) After the fall of the Ming empire, an apparently painful failure of the Confucian way, the loyalist Huang Tsung-hsi (1610–1695) started to compile a monumental work to uphold the intellectual contributions of the Sung Confucians. Entitled *Sung Yuan hsueh-an,* it is often translated as *Sung and Yuan Intellectual History.* Its literal translation is *Sung and Yuan Schools of Learning*; but a more informative rendering would be *The Sung and Yuan Confucian Schools of Learning,* for it virtually equated formal intellectual activity with Confucian learning. It did not include any Buddhists, literary figures, or intellectuals, working outside Confucianism. Instead, its author took Neo-Confucianism to be the mainstream of intellectual life and traced one school after another, listing masters and disciples, companions and friends, often with cross-references to show the collateral affiliations between one school and another. He relegated other thinkers and Confucian schools to brief summations at the very end of the book because by Ming times they were considered heterodox. Among these were Wang An-shih the reformer and Su Shih (1036–1101) from the Northern Sung; the School of the Mind (Hsin-hsueh), which was the chief rival of Neo-Confucianism; and a few intellectuals in the northern, Jurchen empire,[2] who were beyond the pale of Sung society. Huang did not finish this work, but its completion by an editor in the eighteenth century and its voluminous nineteenth-century supplement complied by two adherents kept strictly to the original approach.

A number of modern works on Sung thought continue to follow the same approach, limiting themselves to the mainstream, Neo-Confucian philosophy and paying much attention to the five masters of the Northern Sung whom the Neo-Confucians honored: Chou Tun-i (1017–1073), Shao Yung (1011–1077), Chang Tsai (1020–1077), Ch'eng Hao (1032–1085), and his brother Ch'eng I. Other works in this field, however, especially in the history of political thought, have revised the approach, considering it necessary to deal with many other thinkers, such as Sun Fu (992–1057) and Fan Chung-yen (989–1052), who both taught before the five Northern Sung masters; Ssu-Ma Kuang, a great historian-statesman; Lu Hsiang-shan (1139–1192), the founder of the School of the Mind and adversary of Chu Hsi; Ch'en Liang (1143–1194), a hawkish utilitarian theorist who argued against Chu Hsi; and Yeh Shih (1150–1223) who excelled in utilitarian studies of key institutions. The picture so revised in these books of modern scholars already indicates the rich variety of neo-traditional Confucianism other than Neo-Confucianism.

Classifying Sung Thinkers

These revised views, however, have not really redressed the balance. They retain an emphasis on Neo-Confucianism and simply add material that should not be omitted. Furthermore, they fall short of suggesting themes or devising schemes of analysis that would order the whole intellectual array. Without any pattern, the picture looks confused: the Neo-Confucians-plus-others does not hang together. The remedy is to place the various Sung thinkers and schools in an organized or meaningful pattern.

The suggested classification that follows is but one such possible pattern. Historical realities are so very complex that they do not lend themselves to a single classification system or reduction to one and

2. The Jurchen were a semi-nomadic people from Manchuria that conquered northern China, reigning from 1115 A.D. to 1234 A.D.

only one way of looking at them. On the contrary, a fully adequate treatment would be pluralistic. It would proceed to analyze reality from one viewpoint after another, shedding more light at each turn. A simple analogy is the way to look at a finely cut diamond: One does not look at it from a fixed angle only, but keeps turning it over and over again to see its shifting facets.

To accomplish a particular purpose, however, a single system has the advantage of clarity. The classification offered here is designed for the specific purpose of looking at various Sung ideas and developments in government and education, both of which were central to Confucianism. The intellectuals and schools of thought to be analyzed are those that played a part in the evolution of Sung Confucianism. When intellectuals are here separated into groups, the group labels are broad. They by no means specify exactly the characteristics of each individual in the group; they represent only clusters or trends. Nor are such groupings watertight or mutually exclusive; they merely help define the positions each group held in relation to others of their own time and to similar trends of thought across time.

The point of departure for this classification scheme is the received Confucian tradition that prevailed throughout the Sung dynasty. Although this was the beginning of neo-traditional China, it must be emphasized that there was hardly much *neo* about the majority of scholar-officials. They were conventional Confucians who abided by the long-established value system with relatively little thought of changing it. Their writings were legion but received scanty attention from later generations, for they contributed few original or creative ideas. This is to be expected. Like bureaucrats and members of the elite in other cultures, many Sung scholar-officials tended to be conservative and opposed to innovation. Nevertheless, a small but highly significant number of intellectuals, rising like sparkling tips above the submerged icebergs, refused to remain conventional. What they advocated were what they believed to be much needed changes in the establishment. And they justified their opinions by their innovative interpretations of the ancient classics.

Of course, these neo-traditional Confucians did not necessarily agree among themselves about what should be changed or how to make the changes. A simple yardstick that would clarify the diversity is the relative degree to which the intellectuals were critical of the established Confucian ways that prevailed in thought, government, and society. Some wanted to infuse them with new, idealistic enthusiasm in order to revitalize or re-energize them, but not necessarily to change them otherwise. Others wished to introduce some selective changes within the current system. Yet others with much stronger convictions, would go so far as to demand fundamental and even sweeping changes of the establishment. From this particular standpoint, the Neo-Confucian school, while they claimed to be orthodox and not innovative, and seemed conservative with reference to the eleventh-century Reform that had failed, were in a very real sense also reformers insofar as they desired to change on-going practices and the value system. No Neo-Confucian would ever admit that, for the word *reform* had a bad reputation in the Southern Sung. Nevertheless, from the standpoint of our classification, it is evident that both the earlier reformers and the Neo-Confucians shared something significant. Both groups wanted fundamental improvements. Both groups aimed to reconstruct existing ways in some thorough manner. They differed categorically and clashed diametrically mainly about what was to be reconstructed, in which direction, and how. . . .

Trends in Confucianism

The advocates of re-energizing ideals put emphasis on relatively simple principles, without elaborate theories. Sun Fu, for example, issued a "Confucian manifesto," attacking Buddhism and Taoism for ideas and practices that violated the precepts of Confucian society. Ssu-ma Kuang stressed personal conduct and values in social groups beginning with the family. History shows, he reasoned, that moral standards in government are of decisive importance. As the leading opponent of Wang An-shih's New Policies, he directed his basic objection to their deviations from traditional principles and to their demoralizing effects. Although he is invariably labeled as a conservative and did oppose the Reform and drastic changes, in fact, he himself sought *gradual* changes to improve the administrative quality of the government through the selection of upright officials. Su Shih, the multifarious genius, upheld the hope of promoting refined culture, without indoctrination, as the way to raise the level of enlightenment among scholar-officials and through their influence that of society in general.

As time went on, a fair number of neo-traditional intellectuals followed this line of thinking without necessarily making outstanding or very distinguished contributions. This was true of a forerunner in the Neo-Confucian school, Yang Shih (1053–1135), a disciple of both Ch'eng brothers, who was credited with being the key transmitter of their teaching to the Southern Sung. Lecturing briefly at the court of the restoring emperor Kao-tsung, he, too, gave more emphasis to uplifting moral standards and conduct than to philosophical formulations. In short, those who advocated re-energizing ideals tended to produce few elaborate theories or platforms.

The second cluster or trend consisted of the selective renovators, who believed in developing both theory and a feasible platform designed to make the old system work better. They tried to introduce significant changes, but not on a grand scale, so as not to upset the current situation. This approach applied to the diverse categories they engaged themselves in: state affairs, education, literature, study of the classics, and metaphysics. Fan Chung-yen expressed what may be called "the scholar's declaration of dedication," a statement still used today, that "a scholar should be the first to be concerned with the worries of the world and the last to enjoy its happiness." He was the leader of a short-lived Minor Reform of administrative affairs in 1043–1044. Ou-yang Hsiu, though an important participant in this Minor Reform, did not push hard for it. His greatest contribution was in developing a clear prose style and new interpretations in classical studies. Surprising though it may seem, the Ch'eng brothers and other philosophers, who were later honored as pioneering masters by the Neo-Confucian school, did not advocate in their time a thoroughgoing transformation of either the government or society. The significant changes they produced were in philosophy, their specialty and select area of emphasis. Theirs was a reform of ideas that developed profound dimensions in metaphysics and cosmology.

In a time of peace and prosperity, these Neo-Confucian forerunners could afford the luxury of philosophical speculation in quietness. Yet, sensing signs of possible troubles ahead, they went to the root of the matter and raised ultimate questions about life, the universe, and their meaning. These questions pertained to a field that had been previously dominated by Buddhism, though not quite monopolized by it. Now, the Confucian philosophers took them up and formulated refreshing, absorbing, and invigorating concepts, such as supreme principle, great ultimate, great harmony, human nature, and humanity. Even to those not convinced, these formulations appeared to be impressive, deep, and challenging. At least in metaphysics they did no less than build a strong, new foundation for Confucianism, making it much more profound than it had ever been. Nonetheless, they were not interested in an immediate social reconstruction.

Renovating Confucianism

The selective renovators, on the other hand, eagerly searched for and identified certain key elements in Confucianism that would, they believed, lead to the way of a stronger state and a better society. This approach reverberated in the Southern Sung. Ch'en Liang, the best known utilitarian "hawk," advocated in the mid twelfth century needed improvements in government affairs, with an insistent stress on his proposed reforms in the military system. His hope was to recover the North China plain from the Jurchen enemies. Ch'en Fuliang (1137–1203), another utilitarian thinker, realized the inseparable relationship between the military system and other parts of the government. He studied how to improve and change certain key institutions in a practical way. Later on, while citing the classics and simultaneously observing current conditions acutely, Yeh Shih proposed a number of excellent, original ideas to improve specific institutions.

Lu Chiu-yuan (better known as Hsiang-shan) was the founder of the School of the Mind, much admired at the same time but more so in subsequent centuries as the worthy adversary of the great philosopher Chu Hsi. Instead of concentrating on such areas as the military or institutions, he chose philosophy and developed deep dimensions of psychology. In place of the standard Confucian emphasis on conduct or morality, he focused on the concept of mind. Only better mind, he explained, would make better individuals and hence a better society. In this respect, he paralleled but did not agree with the Northern Sung Confucian forerunners.

The third major group, the advocates of fundamental improvements, wanted nothing less than to set the whole system right once and for all. With comprehensive and high-minded ideas, they tended to be insistent, uncompromising, and aggressive. The reformer Wang An-shih was like that; he overflowed with self-confidence. But he was not alone. The great founder of Neo-Confucianism, Chu Hsi himself, and his followers as well also had the boldness to call for a thorough reshaping of government and society. It may seem preposterous to group Chu Hsi and Wang An-shih together, yet it is often the case that adversaries at opposite poles tend to share characteristics. Wang wanted to make drastic institutional changes in intellectual, economic, and political areas, while the Neo-Confucians led by Chu demanded an equally thorough transformation of society through philosophical, moral, intellectual, and ultimately social and political improvements. In short, the Neo-Confucians aimed not only at a state orthodoxy but at the reorientation of everything. Although they claimed that their teaching constituted what had been the true way since antiquity, in reality it represented no less than a new way of thinking about the whole of society.

Chinese Rituals in the Twelfth Century

Chu Hsi, translated by Patricia Buckley Ebrey

Chu Hsi was one of the great Chinese philosophers of the twelfth century. In his work, *Family Rituals,* he describes common Chinese rituals, such as weddings and funerals. In this excerpt, Chu Hsi explains how to properly perform sacrificial rites. This translation is by Patricia Buckley Ebrey, a professor of East Asian languages and culture at the University of Illinois at Urbana-Champaign, and the editor or translator of eleven books on Chinese history and rituals.

T he content of this [article] is devoted to the regular forms of the daily courtesies of families, the ones that cannot be neglected for even one day.

The Offering Hall

This section originally was part of the chapter on sacrificial rites. Now I have purposely placed it here, making it the first subject, because its contents form the heart of "repaying one's roots and returning to the beginning," the essence of "honoring ancestors and respecting agnatic kin," the true means of preserving status responsibilities in the family, and the foundation for establishing a heritage and transmitting it to later generations. My arrangement will let the reader sense that what is placed first is the most important. This chapter provides the basis for understanding the fine points in the later chapters concerning movements and postures, for walking here and there, getting up and down, going in and out, and facing directions.

The ancient system of ancestral shrines (*miao*) does not appear in the classics. Moreover, there are elements of it not permitted to the lower ranks of today's gentlemen (*shih*) and commoners. Therefore, I have specially named the room the "offering hall" and extensively adapted customary rituals in formulating its procedures.

When a man of virtue (*chün-tzu*) plans to build a house, his first task is always to set up an offering hall to the east of the main room of his house.

In setting up the offering hall use a room three *chien* wide.[1] In front of the altars is the inner door and in front of it the two staircases, each with three steps. The one on the east is called the ceremonial stairs, the one on the west the western stairs. Depending on how much space is available, below the steps should be a covered area, large enough for all the family members to stand in rows. On the east there should be it closet for books, clothes, and sacrificial vessels inherited from the ancestors, and it spirit pantry.[2] Have the wall go around them and add an outer door, which should normally be kept bolted.

If the family is poor and its space cramped, set up it one-*chien*-wide offering hall, without the closet and pantry. As substitutes, cases may be put at the base of the east and west walls. In the western one store the inherited books and clothes and in the eastern one the sacrificial vessels.

The main room refers to the front hall. When space is limited [and there is no front hall], it is also acceptable to make the offering hall to the east of the reception room.

As a general rule, the house with the offering hall should remain in the possession of the descent-line heir[3] generation after generation, and not be subject to partition.

Here and throughout this book, in organizing the room, no matter which direction it actually faces, treat the front as south, the rear as north, the left as east, and the right as west.

How to Prepare Altars

Make four altars to hold the spirit tablets of the ancestors.

Inside the offering hall, near the north end, have a stand for the four altars. Inside each altar, put a table. In the case of a great line, or a lesser line that is heir to a great-great-grandfather, the great-great-grandfather

---

1. A *chien* was a unit used to measure the size of rooms, being the space between two pillars.
2. The commentator in the 1732 ed. said the spirit pantry held the dishes used for the spirits.
3. The descent-line heir (*tsung-tzu*) is the eldest son, generally in a line of eldest sons.

is furthest to the west, with the great-grandfather next to him, the grand-father next, and the father last. A lesser-line succeeding to a great-grandfather does not presume to sacrifice to a great-great-grandfather, and so leaves the westernmost of the altars empty. Likewise, a lesser-line heir to a grandfather does not presume to sacrifice to a great-grandfather, and so leaves the two western altars empty; and a lesser-line heir to a fa-ther does not presume to sacrifice to the grandfather, and so leaves the three western altars empty. If a great line has a gap in its generations, a western altar is also left empty, as in a lesser line.

The spirit tablets are all stored in a case and placed on the table, the front to the south. Hang a short curtain in front of each altar. In front of these altars, set up an incense table in the center of the room, with in-cense burners and incense boxes on it. Set up another, similar incense table in the space between the staircases.

Anyone who is not the eldest main-line son does not presume to sac-rifice to his father.[4] After a younger brother dies, his sons and grandsons, if they live with the eldest brother, will set up an offering hall for him in their private apartment, adding new altars each generation. When they leave and set up a separate residence, they will set up a full offering hall. If the younger son lives separately during his own lifetime, he can set up a study where he lives, on the model of an offering hall. After his death, his descendants can turn it into an offering hall.

On the format of spirit tablets, see the section on "preparing for the burial" in the chapter on funerals [4, 10].

Collateral relatives who died without descendants may have associ-ated offerings made to them there according to their generational se-niority.

Associate a great uncle and his wife with the great-great-grandfather. Associate and uncle and his wife with the great-grandfather. Associate one's wife, a brother, or a brother's wife with one's grandfather. Associ-ate one's son or nephew with one's father. All these tablets should face west. The tablet cases for them should be like the standard ones. If a nephew's father later sets up an offering hall, his tablet should be moved there.

Master Ch'eng [I] said that when children die so young that there is no mourning for them, no sacrifices are made either. When they die in early youth, sacrifices are performed only during the lifetime of their par-ents. When they die in middle youth, mourning continues through the lifetime of their fraternal nephews. When adults die without heirs, sacri-fices are made through the lifetime of their brothers' grandsons. These rules were all created on the basis of moral principles.

---

4. "Main-line" sons are sons of the legal wife. Thus, sons of concubines, even if older than sons of the wife, do not take charge of the sacrifices to their father. Nor do younger sons of the wife.

Sacrificial Fields

On first erecting an offering hall, calculate the size of the current fields and for each altar set aside one part in twenty as sacrificial fields. When "kinship is exhausted" for any ancestor, convert the specified land into grave fields. Later on, do the same for each regular or associated ancestor. The descent-line heir manages the property to supply the expenses of the sacrifices.

If earlier generations did not set aside any fields, then gather the descendants together at the grave site, calculate the size of their total land, and take a share. The descendants should write an agreement and inform the authorities. Neither mortgaging nor sale of the sacrificial fields is allowed.

Prepare sacrificial utensils.

Suitable numbers of benches, mats, armrests, tables, wash basins, braziers, and dishes for wine and food should be prepared and stored in the closet. They should be kept locked up and not used for other purposes. In the absence of a closet they may be kept in a case. Those that cannot be stored may be lined up along the inside of the outer gate.

Early each morning the presiding man enters the outer gate to look in.

The presiding man here is the descent-line heir who is in charge of the sacrifices of this hall. When he looks in the morning he wears the long garment, burns incense, and bows twice.

All comings and goings must be reported.

When the presiding man and presiding woman are about to go some place, before departing they enter the outer door of the offering hall and perform the "respectful look." They do the same on returning. After they return from staying away overnight, they burn incense and bow twice. When they will go far or will stay away more than ten days, before leaving they bow twice, burn incense, and report, "So and so is about to go to such a place and presumes to report it," then repeat the double bow. They do the same on their return, except they say, "Today A returned from such a place and presumes to appear here." If they are gone for a month, they open the inner doors, bow twice at the bottom of the stairs, then ascend the ceremonial staircase and burn incense. When their report is completed, they bow twice, go down, resume their earlier places, and bow twice again. Other family members do the same but do not open the inner door.

Here . . . the following conventions are followed. The presiding woman is the wife of the presiding man. Only the presiding man uses the ceremonial steps to go up and down; the presiding woman and other people, even seniors, use the western steps. For bowing, men bow two times and women four times, in either case called a double bow. This is also the practice when men and women bow to each other.

The Samurai Code of Honor

Eiko Ikegami

During eleventh- and twelfth-century Japan, the samurai became a distinct social group with a specific culture of honor. According to Eiko Ikegami, these men, who were both warriors and landed lords, believed deeply in military professionalism and courage. Samurai began to be seen as men of principle, garnering admiration from the nonsamurai. In contrast to earlier times, when samurai were caricatured as unsophisticated musclemen, Japanese literature in the twelfth-century depicted the samurai with greater respect. However, the samurai did not always hew to the values of their culture; violations of the rules for warfare were frequent and tolerated. Ikegami is a professor of sociology at the New School University in New York City.

In the eleventh and twelfth centuries, the samurai emerged as a clearly defined social category that combined two important roles: landed lord and warrior. During this formative period, they could not claim the rich and complex cultural resources of their historical descendants, but they already manifested a set of vivid and distinctive cultural characteristics. Having achieved a certain stability as a class of military landed lords, the samurai were no longer known only as "butchers" and "aliens" to society at large. Their connection to public offices and their settlement within an agricultural society made them more acceptable members of their surrounding culture.

With the political maturity of the samurai class in the late Heian period [794 A.D. to 1185 A.D.], the samurai's culture of honor also took a distinctive form. First, the samurai's sense of military pride generated a set of rules that exalted fighting as an expression of honor. Although simple physical strength and martial skills continued to be the basis of their sense of pride, certain rules and idioms served to express that strength. Second, the development of their unique master-follower relationship (vassalage) provided a new dimension within the samurai's culture of honor. The emerging political hierarchies and coalitions of samurai, related to the subsequent formation of the samurai government at Kamakura, constituted a community of honor. In this community, a warrior's honor was publicly evaluated and conferred. During this social process, from the late Heian through the Kamakura periods [1185 A.D. to 1333 A.D.], we observe the emergence of a sense of pride associated with being a samurai, of a collective samurai identity, manifesting the first signs of a distinctive cultural style.

The following story conveys the earliest and most admirable image of the behavior of honorable warriors found in *Konjaku monogatari*.[1] The narrative concerns two rival samurai, Minamoto no Mitsuru and Taira no Yoshifumi, who fight a duel for the sake of honor. The outline of the story runs as follows:

> The two samurai were competing in military skills. Each of them believed that he was stronger than the other, and finally they agreed to stage a formal battle in a large open field. The appointed day arrived; both samurai had mobilized about five to six hundred men who were fully determined to fight to the last drop of blood. Both troops lined up with their shields. Each side sent a soldier to exchange the declaration of war. A battle usually began with a volley of arrows after the envoys had returned to their troops. Right before the fray, however, Yoshifumi sent another messenger to Mitsuru, saying, "Today's combat will not be interesting if it ends with the shooting of our troops. Our only intention is the testing of our own military skills. Let us not fight in the company of our armies, but let us have a single combat between the two of us shooting with our best skill."
>
> Having accepted this offer at once, Mitsuru stepped out of the line of shields. Yoshifumi ordered his retainers not to assist him and went out to fight. While both troops of retainers stood watching, the two master warriors fought on their horses. The two samurai first spurred their horses while fixing arrows to their bowstrings. Each of them tried to allow the other to shoot first (showing their bravery). They spurred their horses and shot in passing again and again, but each of them was skillful enough to dodge the other's arrows. After a long fight, Yoshifumi said, "Both of us can shoot arrows precisely to their targets. We know each other's skills. We are not ancestral enemies. It is time to stop." Mit-

1. A collection of folklore translated as *Tales of Times Now Past*.

suru replied, "We have seen each other's skills. Let's stop. It was a good fight." Their retainers, watching the duel and afraid that their masters might be shot at any moment, were pleased when they heard their decision. After the fight, Yoshifumi and Mitsuru got along very well.

In the glorious, wide-open spaces of the Kanto plain, the duel of the two samurai leaders was prompted by a vigorous spirit of honor. The two samurai fought each other in front of their men because their sense of pride would not permit a less honorable course of action. The story suggests the rise of a chivalrous sentiment among the samurai, as well as the existence of some rules encouraging fighting as a way to prove one's honor. The detail concerning the two leaders' attempts to let each other shoot first is an example. The narrative also describes how, for the heralds who delivered official summons to battle, there was a consensus regarding honorable behavior and attitudes. After exchanging the declaration of war, the messengers should each return to their sides without urging their horses, thus showing that they had sufficient confidence to turn their backs to the opponent without moving in unseemly haste. In this collection of stories, the writer displays deep admiration and sympathy for a courageous, simple, straightforward samurai culture. This is one of the earliest literary examples suggesting that the samurai had developed some rules for combat based upon a strong sense of honor.

Literature About the Samurai

Of course, to use a collection of folklore as a source of historical inquiry requires caution. There is evidence that these two rival samurai were actual historical figures who lived in the eastern region of Japan around the mid-tenth century. Therefore, since the event presumably took place more than 150 years before *Konjaku monogatari* was written in the beginning of the twelfth century, it is difficult to take this story as a precise reflection of a historical event.

What we should note from this description, however, is its *symbolic* significance to the early twelfth century. As mentioned earlier, *Konjaku monogatari* appeared in the early twelfth century and was edited by an unknown person(s), who was either a priest or an aristocrat in Kyoto. We can only assume that the compiler heard the story just told, which was probably widely shared among his contemporaries, and considered it trustworthy insofar as it presented an ideal image of the honorable warrior. Samurai culture had apparently reached the stage where it could make a favorable impression on the nonsamurai editor of *Konjaku monogatari*. By contrast, earlier in the mid-Heian period, the samurai had not always looked respectable; indeed, court literature often caricatures the samurai as musclemen who were culturally unsophisticated and therefore inferior to the well-bred aristocracy.

Military Attitudes

In the meantime, some samurai, in particular those who lived in prosperity far from Kyoto, acquired a greater sense of confidence about their own military lifestyle. And their distinctive culture, based upon their identity as military specialists, sometimes made a good impression on the people in the capital city. Even though their manners were simple and unpolished, these samurai with their culture of honor appeared to be men of principle, at least compared with the crafty and underhanded courtier-politicians.

An important asset of the samurai culture was a distinct military achievement-oriented attitude, brought into late ancient Japan through the samurai's military professionalism. In contrast, the ancient Japanese state, centering around the emperor's court, did not fully adopt a meritocratic system of recruiting elites, as had its Chinese model. Instead, the higher governmental positions continued to be occupied by men born into the limited bloodlines of the aristocracy. Conversely, though samurai houses were also largely considered hereditary, the very nature of military professionalism, which required constant demonstration and improvement of military efficacy, prevented the samurai from taking their inherited positions for granted.

In general, *Konjaku monogatari* contains many descriptions of the lively atmosphere of the samurai's *yakata* (residence house), implicitly contrasting it with the bland, passive existence of the aristocracy in Kyoto. The samurai are usually described as uncomplicated, energetic, straightforward men who would risk their lives in order to keep their good name as warriors. For example, as *Konjaku monogatari* recounts, a mighty samurai, Taira no Koremochi, usually called Yogo, when on the verge of defeat by an unexpected attack did not run for the hills as his retainers advised him to do. Yogo said to them, "It would be the shame (*haji*) of my descendants," and sprang to his feet with determination. His unexpected courageous counterattack routed his enemies. Yogo thereafter increased his reputation and was renowned as the strongest samurai in the eastern region.

The leaders of the samurai bands realized that gaining the trust of capable samurai was crucial to their success, and that having a fearsome reputation was important for keeping the confidence of otherwise unruly warriors. Anyone who acquired the stigma of cowardice was at a serious disadvantage in this competition for power. Honor, conversely, was instrumental to success. Yogo's not attempting to escape from the enemy was an instinctively calculated action. If he had fled, he would have been more likely to survive, but he would have surrendered his reputation as the leader of his samurai band. Honorable men needed to be perpetually alert competitors on the field of honor in order not to damage their good names as warriors. This strong drive to keep one's good name was one of the most impressive aspects of the samurai culture in the eyes of nonsamurai observers.

Violations of Samurai Rules

The development of certain rules for fighting and the cultivation of a chivalrous spirit should not be overemphasized, however. This idealized image aside, the daily pursuit of honor in the twelfth century may not have been so assiduous as the foregoing stories imply. The war literature of the period also suggests that it was common for the samurai to violate rules of warfare when it suited their purpose.

The following famous episode from *Heike monogatari*[2] provides one such example. Two warriors were engaged in competition for the honor of being the first rider to charge at the Battle of the Uji River, a crucial battle between the Minamoto and Taira clans (riding first was usually considered one of the most daring and honorable actions in battle). The Minamoto troops commanded by Minamoto no Yoshitsune came to the Uji River. The bridges were pulled up and "angry white waves raced downstream." Two warriors of the *genji* troops, Kajiwara Genta Kagesue and Sasaki Shirō Takatsuna, galloped into the river, each resolving to be the first man across. Falling behind, Takatsuna called out to Kagesue:

> "This is the biggest river in the west. Your saddle girth looks loose; tighten it up!"
>
> Kagesue must have feared that the girth did indeed require tightening. He stiffened his legs in the stirrups to hold them away from Surumumi's belly, tossed the reins over the horse's mane, undid the girth, and tightened it. Meanwhile, Takatsuna galloped past him into the river. . . . [As he arrived at the opposite bank,] Takatsuna stood in his stirrups and announced his name in a mighty voice. "Sasaki Shirō Takatsuna, the fourth son of Sasaki Saburō Hideyoshi and a ninth-generation descendant of Emperor Uda, is the first man across the Uji River!"

Interestingly, the unknown author of *Heike monogatari* did not criticize Sasaki Shirō's behavior, even though he had cheated his competitor in order to gain the military merit of being the first rider in a charge. Indeed, this kind of violation of the rules of fair fighting was not uncommon among the samurai in the war literature of the period.

Breaking the rules of warfare in order to exalt one's name as a mighty warrior was often tolerated, because people at that time thought of killing and fighting as primal *musha no narai* (customs of the samurai), and exhibitions of one's manliness and superiority on the field were more important than chivalrous decency. Such con-

---

2. This is an anthology of war literature that translates as *Tales of Heike*.

duct was further legitimated by the development of samurai vassalage within the public domain. With the maturation of the samurai master-follower relationship, the warrior's self-interest regarding participation in battle—the expectation of economic rewards—was often camouflaged by the moral principles of trust associated with vassalage. The individual warrior took part in battle in order to fulfill his promise to the master that he would contribute his military might whenever called upon to do so. Thus, fighting courageously and achieving military merit became not simply a matter of self-interest but an element in the very foundation of the master-follower relationship.

Furthermore, as the samurai's political power increased, warfare was often conducted as a public cause; that is, the war was ordered by the imperial court, or later, following the establishment of the shogun's authority, directly by the shogun. If the higher authorities had taken responsibility for the war, and if the samurai's military action was seen as a contribution to the public good, the warrior's individual rule-breaking might be more easily tolerated.

An Example of Japanese Storytelling

Anonymous, translated by Marian Ury

Konjaku monogatari—translated into English as *Tales of Times Now Past*—is a collection of Japanese stories that is believed to have been compiled in approximately 1120 A.D. It is unknown who the compiler was or if there was more than one. The book consists of sixty-two stories that depict life in India, China, and Japan. The following story is about the bravery and leadership of a Japanese lieutenant. This edition of *Tales of Times Now Past* was edited by Marian Ury. Prior to her death in 1995, Ury had translated other works of Japanese literature, including *Poems of the Five Mountains: An Introduction to the Literature of the Zen Monasteries.*

A t a time now past, when the Lord of Uji was in his glory,[1] he had in attendance on him one night High Priest Myōson of Miidera.[2] No lamps were lit, and after a short time his lordship suddenly decided to send the High Priest on an errand—what exactly, one doesn't know, but he was to go and return again the same night. A

---

1. The Lord of Uji was Fujiwara Yorimichi (992–1074), son of the all-powerful Michinaga; the incident narrated here seems to have taken place some time between 1021 and 1028. 2. Myōson (the name is also read Myōzon): 971–1063. Miidera is another name for the Tendai temple Onjōji, in modern Ōtsu, east of Kyoto. Myōson was in attendance on the lord in order to perform the rituals that warded away illness.

horse was saddled for him in his lordship's stables, one that would not shy or bolt. "Who will accompany him?" inquired his lordship when the horse had been led out. Taira no Munetsune, lieutenant of the Left Division of the Outer Palace Guards, announced himself. "Excellent," said his lordship. "The Assistant High Priest must go to Miidera tonight," his lordship announced (at that time the High Priest was Assistant High Priest), "and return immediately. He is to be back before the night is over. You are responsible for his safety." Munetsune listened to the order. In the barracks he always kept bow and quiver in readiness, and he had a pair of straw sandals hidden under a mat. He retained only a single attendant, a base-born servant, so that people who saw him thought, "What a stingy mean fellow he is!" Upon receiving the order, then, he tucked up his trouser hems, groped about until he had found his sandals, put them on, strapped the quiver to his back, and went over to where the horse had been led out for Myosōn. He stationed himself beside it.

"Who are you?" asked the priest.

"Munetsune," he replied.

"We shall be going to Miidera," said the priest. "Why have you prepared yourself to go on foot? Have you no mount?"

"Even if I'm on foot I won't fall behind, never fear. Only make haste yourself," he said.

The priest thought this all very strange. Torchbearers were sent out ahead. The two had traveled seven or eight hundred yards when two men dressed in black and armed with bows and arrows came toward them on foot. The priest was frightened, but the two men fell to their knees the moment they saw Munetsune. "Your horse, sir," they said. They had led horses out; since it was night, the color of the horses could not be made out. The men were carrying riding shoes for Munetsune. Munetsune put these on over his straw sandals and mounted a horse. Now that there were two men, mounted and armed, accompanying, the priest felt easy in mind. They proceeded another two hundred yards, and from the side of the road there appeared two more bowmen dressed in black, who prostrated themselves just as before. Munetsune said not a word on either occasion. They mounted the horses they had led out and joined the escort. No doubt these too were Munetsune's retainers—but what a queer way he goes about his business! the priest thought. And then two hundred yards farther on two more men appeared and joined them in the same way. Again Munetsune said not a word; and the new companions said not a word. Whenever the party had gone a hundred yards and yet another hundred, two more men were added to their number, so that by the time they reached the banks of the Kamo River there were more than thirty. What a queer way he goes about his business! the High Priest thought, and thus they arrived at Miidera.

He attended to the affair he had been charged with and started back before midnight. Before him, behind him, surrounding him, rode Munetsune's retainers. He felt very much at ease. The escort rode in a body as far as the Kamo River banks. After they reentered the capital, though Munetsune said not a word, the men dropped off two at a time at the places from which they had emerged, so that when his lordship's mansion was only a hundred yards away there remained only the two companions who had appeared first. At the spot at which he had mounted his horse, Munetsune dismounted and took off the shoes he had put on, so that now he was dressed as he had been when he left. He walked away as the two men vanished into the shadows with his shoes and the horse. Accompanied only by his servant and wearing straw sandals, he went on foot through the gate of his lordship's mansion.

The High Priest was astounded at what he had witnessed. He thought it utterly uncanny, how horses and men performed as though rehearsed and instructed beforehand. "I'll tell his lordship about it at the first opportunity," he thought as he went into his presence. The lord had waited up for him. The priest reported on the discharge of his own commission; then he said, "Munetsune certainly goes about his business queerly," and related everything that had happened. "What splendid followers he has!" he added.

His lordship listened. "Surely he'll question me further," the priest thought, but—whatever the lord was thinking—he did not, and the priest's expectation was frustrated.

This Munetsune was the son of a warrior named Taira no Muneyori.[3] He was fierce and bold, and he shot especially large arrows unlike those used by ordinary marksmen. For that reason people called him the Large Arrow Lieutenant. So the tale's been told, and so it's been handed down.

---

3. Muneyori (d. 1011) was a popular subject of anecdote. The story immediately preceding the present one deals with a private war that he fought with another provincial warrior. He reappears in *Konjaku* 31:24 as the leader of a hired army in a brawl between two monasteries.

The Development of the Kamakura Government

Edwin O. Reischauer

The Japanese government underwent a significant change in the 1100s, as Edwin O. Reischauer explains. In 1185, twenty-five years after losing two wars to the Taira family, the Minamoto family defeated the Taira and established a government at the town of Kamakura. Although Japan still had emperors, the true power was in Kamakura, led by the Shogun Minamoto Yoritomo and his successors. Reischauer notes that although the Kamakura government had a fairly simple organization, it was an effective central government that was able to control all levels of Japanese society. Culture was influenced by Kamakura rule as well, with literature and art emphasizing the values of the warrior class. Before his death in 1990, Reischauer was a professor at Harvard University, the U.S. ambassador to Japan, and the author of many books on Asia, including *China: Tradition and Transformation* and *Japan: The Story of a Nation.*

The tenth and eleventh centuries saw many clashes and small wars between different groups of knights in the provinces. These contests are often described in histories as revolts against imperial authority, for one faction would resist domination by another faction which enjoyed the backing of the central government. The provin-

Excerpted from *Japan: Past and Present,* by Edwin O. Reischauer. Copyright © 1964 by Alfred A. Knopf, Inc. Reprinted with permission from Alfred A. Knopf, a division of Random House, Inc.

cial knights, however, for the most part showed little desire to assume the governmental prerogatives of the Kyoto court. They were content to leave the central government undisturbed as long as they themselves could continue to rule the peasants on their own estates and to organize their cliques for local defense without interference from the capital.

Fights Between Court Factions

The court aristocrats, rather than the knights themselves, eventually brought these provincial warriors onto the capital stage. The courtiers, lacking all knowledge of the arts of war themselves, would from time to time bring knights from their provincial estates to the capital to help protect their interests or to overawe their enemies. Sometimes the knights were used to defend the court from the great local monasteries, which often attempted to force their will upon the effete courtiers by a joint display of Buddhist relics and armed might drawn from the warriors of the monastery estates. At other times, the knights were brought in to settle, by a show of force or by actual conflict, factional disputes over the imperial succession and the headship of the Fujiwara family.[1]

In the middle of the twelfth century disputes of the latter type led to fairly large scale clashes between the two strongest warrior cliques of the time in support of two quarreling court factions. The warrior cliques centered around two great provincial families, the Taira and the Minamoto, both of whom claimed descent from cadet branches of the imperial family which, because of declining income, had been forced to seek their fortunes in the provinces. There they had merged with the local aristocrats and had risen to leadership among them because of their prestige as descendants of emperors.

As a result of two small wars in 1156 and 1160, one of the court factions won out over the other. A far more significant outcome was the sudden realization on the part of Taira Kiyomori, leader of the victorious Taira clique of warriors, that he and his band now formed the paramount military force in the land and that the emperor and his court were powerless in his hands. To the consternation of the courtiers, Kiyomori and his leading knights settled down in Kyoto and took over control of the court, Kiyomori taking for himself the title of Prime Minister and adopting the old Fujiwara trick of marrying his own daughter to the emperor and putting her son on the throne.

By settling in Kyoto and becoming in effect a new group of courtiers, Kiyomori and his henchmen weakened their hold over the knights of their clique who remained on their estates in the provinces and who tended to resent the position and pretensions of the court

---

1. The Fujiwara were a noble family that wielded great power over the Japanese emperor and court from the ninth to twelfth centuries A.D.

aristocracy. Meanwhile the remnants of the Minamoto family slowly recouped their fortune in their old family stronghold in eastern Japan. Eventually the Minamoto felt themselves strong enough again to challenge Taira supremacy, and in a bitterly fought war between 1180 and 1185 they completely crushed the Taira faction. The Taira leaders either were killed or committed suicide, and the new boy emperor who was the grandson of Kiyomori perished with his Taira relatives in the final battle of the war.

The Kamakura Government Is Established

Minamoto Yoritomo, the leader of the triumphant Minamoto faction, profiting from the mistakes of the Taira, left Kyoto and the court alone and settled down at the small seaside town of Kamakura, near the estates of his relatives and his partisans in the Kanto region of eastern Japan. In typically Japanese fashion, he decided to permit the emperors and Fujiwara to continue their sham civil government unmolested. He took for himself only the title of Shogun, a term perhaps best translated as "Generalissimo," and he rewarded his men not with government posts but with the more lucrative positions of estate managers in manors formerly controlled by members of the Taira faction. Although personally commanding the only strong military force in all Japan, Yoritomo was content to permit the continuation of the fiction that an emperor and his civil government ruled the land and that he himself was merely the commander of the emperor's army. Yoritomo and his band, however, constituted the only effective central government Japan possessed, and Kamakura became the true political capital of the land. Thus Japan's first military dictatorship was established.

The administration which Yoritomo and his successors set up at Kamakura was not in theory or in outward form a national government. It was merely a simple but efficient organization designed to control the relatively small band of knights that owed personal allegiance to the Minamoto. It was, in fact, nothing more than a "family" government, not of a single clan as had been customary in ancient times, but of a loose association of knights held together by bonds of family relationship or by long-standing ties of friendship and traditions of mutual support.

Under the Shogun, three small offices were created as the chief organs of this "family" government—an office to watch over and control the affairs of the individual knight members of the clique, an administrative board, and a final court of appeal, making legal decisions based upon the customary law which had gradually developed among the provincial warrior aristocrats during the preceding two centuries and which the Kamakura administration issued in codified form. The provincial organization of this government was even simpler than its central administration. It consisted only of the individual knights themselves, free to manage their individual estates as each saw best, but organized for mutual defense under a constable in each province.

The whole "family" government of the Minamoto may have been designed simply to control the private affairs of the clique and not to administer the nation as a whole, but by controlling the members of this group, who had now been spread throughout the whole land as the key class of estate managers and local knights, the government at Kamakura effectively controlled all classes of society throughout Japan. Its member knights ruled the peasants, who were serfs on their estates, and they also controlled the purse strings of the court aristocracy, which derived its income from these same estates. Although it maintained the fiction of being a private organization, the Kamakura regime had become the most effective central government Japan had yet known; and the people of all classes, realizing that Kamakura alone had the power to enforce its decisions, went there rather than to Kyoto for justice and looked to the Shogun's administration rather than to the emperor's court for leadership.

The End of Imperial Rule

An ambitious retired emperor in 1221 dared challenge this indirect and unannounced control of national life by Kamakura, but found himself overwhelmed by the Minamoto cohorts. The incident revealed conclusively that imperial rule was at an end. The imperial family and the noble families around it continued to receive their income from the estates they nominally owned, but as far as political realities were concerned, the emperor and his court had become anachronistic survivals of an earlier age, with no valid place in the political order of feudalism. Yet the prestige of the imperial line and its continuing religious functions kept alive the fiction of imperial rule during the following six centuries of feudalism, until new conditions made possible its reappearance as a significant element in the political life of the nation.

The Kamakura system centered around the Shogun, the leader of the clique, and in theory the only unifying force was the personal loyalty of each individual knight to the Shogun. In practice, however, the person of the Shogun soon became an unimportant factor, and the system proved to have amazing strength of itself.

Yoritomo, the first Shogun, jealously rid himself of his hero brother and other leading members of his family. After the death of Yoritomo factional strife among his descendants, fostered by his wife's relatives, who had the family name of Hojo, soon led to the elimination of his heirs. In 1219 an assassination ended the Minamoto line, and thereafter the Hojo, who in typical Japanese fashion contented themselves with the title of "Regent," ruled through a puppet Shogun, first chosen from the Fujiwara family and then from the imperial family.

Thus, one finds in thirteenth century Japan an emperor who was a mere puppet in the hands of a retired emperor and of a great court family, the Fujiwara, who together controlled a government which was in fact merely a sham government, completely dominated by the private government of the Shogun—who in turn was a puppet in the hands of a Hojo regent. The man behind the throne had become a series of men, each one in turn controlled by the man behind himself.

A Warrior-Influenced Culture

The rise of the provincial warrior class to a position of dominance produced a new culture as well as a new political system. The literature and art of the tenth and eleventh centuries had been an expression of the culture of the narrow court society under Fujiwara leadership. The new culture naturally inherited much from this glorious period, but the most significant and, in time, dominant elements in it came from the warrior class of the provinces.

The knight brought with him his own concepts and attitudes, which were in some respect similar to those of his counterpart in medieval Europe. In contrast to the effete courtier at Kyoto, he gloried in a life of warfare, in the Spartan virtues, and in the ascetic practices of self-discipline and physical and mental toughening. He made a cult of his sword, and this cult, revived in recent years, accounts for the extraordinary pride of the modern Japanese officer in his old-fashioned, long, curved sword. The warrior reemphasized personal loyalties and the importance of family ties, and his two outstanding virtues, Spartan indifference to suffering or death and a great capacity for unswerving personal loyalty, became characteristics of the Japanese people as a whole.

The warrior's tastes in literature produced a whole new type of prose writing—the heroic tale of warfare, quite different from the diaries and novels of the court ladies. These martial tales usually centered around the conflicts between the Taira and Minamoto factions, which became the central themes of much of later Japanese literature.

The successive triumphs of the Taira and Minamoto marked the commencement of 700 years of unbroken rule by warrior aristocrats. Small wonder that the impress of feudalism lies so heavily upon the nation and that the attitudes and ideals of the feudal warriors have sunk so deeply into the consciousness of the Japanese people. Accustomed for so long to rule by wearers of the sword, even in recent times the Japanese have looked instinctively to their military men for leadership and have been prone to assume that military men *per se* were always honest and sincere. Seven centuries of domination by the feudal military class has left patterns of thought and behavior which have not been easy to discard in recent times and which will not be easily erased even today.

The Rise of Genghis Khan

Daniel Cohen

Genghis (also known as Chingis) Khan is one of the most important figures of the twelfth and thirteenth centuries. Although he did not achieve his greatest power until the early 1200s, his rise as one of the most notable conquerors in world history began in the late twelfth century. Daniel Cohen details some of the key events in Khan's early life, as a boy and young adult named Temüjin. Between his birth in 1167 and his elevation to Khan in 1196, Temüjin overcame a variety of problems, notably the murder of his father, imprisonment, the kidnapping of his wife, and a break with his closest friend. He then achieved wide support from his clansmen and established a professional army. Cohen is a former editor for *Science Digest* and the author of over 100 books, including *The Black Death, 1347–1351* and *Human Nature—Animal Nature: The Biology of Human Behavior.*

A t about the beginning of the twelfth century we can start putting approximate dates to Mongol history. This was when Qaidu was acknowledged as the first of the Mongol khans. Khan is usually translated as king, but the early Mongol khans had very limited powers over the chiefs of other tribes. Individual clans and families turned to Qaidu for protection and leadership. Wandering horse bowmen joined Qaidu's force on the promise of food and plunder. Qaidu defeated many of the neighboring peoples and forced them to pay tribute to him. Gradually, the Mongols became a power to be reckoned with.

Excerpted from *Conquerors on Horseback* (Garden City, NY: Doubleday, 1970) by Daniel Cohen. Copyright © 1970 by Daniel Cohen. Reprinted with permission from the author and Henry Morrison, Inc., his agents.

Relations Between China and Mongolia

Northern China had recently been conquered by a barbarian people of Tunguz stock from Manchuria called the Jurchets. They ruled from Peking, and took the Chinese title of Kin or "Kings of Gold." A few generations after Qaidu, the Mongols had become powerful enough to attract the attention of the Kin state. The reigning Mongol khan, Qabul, was invited to Peking where, the story goes, he behaved like the barbarian he was. The Kin had lost their barbarian habits and had acquired a taste for Chinese manners and cultivation. They were astounded at the amount the Mongol could eat and even more astounded at the amount he could drink. Once, while particularly drunk, Qabul rushed forward and pulled the beard of the King of Gold. The Kin quickly sent their rambunctious guest back to Mongolia laden with gifts. Bribery was one way of keeping the northern barbarians friendly.

But the Kings of Gold, like the native Chinese before them, knew that the best way to handle the barbarians was by a policy of divide and conquer. The Chinese expression was "Use barbarians to control barbarians." To check Mongol power the Kin allied themselves with the Tatars, a people closely related to the Mongols who dwelt to the south and east of Mongol territory. Deep and ancient hatreds existed between Tatar and Mongol, and the Kin diplomats encouraged the blood feud.

The Tatars ambushed one of the Mongol khans and shipped him to Peking, where he was tortured to death. This khan died swearing vengeance against the Tatars and the Kings of Gold. But with Kin backing, Tatar power increased during the second half of the twelfth century. They became the most powerful tribe in the northeastern Gobi region, supplanting the Mongols.

The Arrival of Chingis Khan

One man, Chingis Khan, changed all of this. Fortunately, we know a good deal about the Mongol conqueror. We have to look at Attila through the eyes of his enemies, for the Huns never wrote their own history. But the Mongols did. In 1240, when many of the people who had actually served with the conqueror himself were still alive, Mongol historians compiled a document called the *Secret History of the Mongols*. The *Secret History* was what we might call today a classified state document. It was to be read only by the members of the imperial family, for it contained an account of the errors of the rulers as well as their successes.

The Mongols borrowed the practice of keeping a *Secret History* from the Chinese. The purpose was to allow rulers to contemplate how much their predecessors had owed to good fortune and to encourage them to be more humble. Most scholars believe that the *Secret History* is fairly accurate and much of what is known of Chingis Khan is based upon it.

By the end of the twelfth century the fortunes of the Mongols had fallen so low that Chingis Khan's father, Yesügei Baghutur, could not even claim the title of khan. He was merely a chief of the Kiyad tribe, a subdivision of the clan of Borjigid Mongols. Yesügei's uncle had been the last of the Mongol khans. Yesügei, however, was moderately successful. In 1167 he defeated the Tatars and captured one of their chiefs, Temüjin ("Ironworker"). To commemorate the occasion he named his eldest son, born that year, after the defeated Tatar, (There is much dispute over the exact year of Temüjin or Chingis Khan's birth, but 1167 is the date accepted by most historians.)

Years later while the Mongols were conquering Asia, Chingis Khan often left the conquest of civilized nations to his generals. He himself concentrated on what was really important—making allies out of the other nomadic tribes or exterminating them. If any single factor can account for Chingis Khan's fantastic success, it was his supreme mastery of the complex politics of the steppe. . . .

Temüjin's Childhood

Temüjin was about ten years old when his father was murdered by the Tatars. Yesügei had come across a group of Tatars who were holding a festival. Despite the deadly hatred between the tribes, the Tatars invited the Mongol leader to their feast and offered him a seat of honor. To refuse would have been an intolerable breach of the custom of the steppe. Yesügei momentarily forgot that poison could be as deadly as an arrow.

Yesügei had gathered a respectable following during his life. Now, upon his death, they deserted his family. The Mongols were divided into two major clans, the Borjigid and the Tayiji'ud. Yesügei was a Borjigid and since he left no grown sons to take his place the Tayiji'ud chiefs moved to assume command at his death. Yesügei's widow, the Lady Hö elün, was a woman of great strength and intelligence. (Mongol women often played an important role in the rough nomad society.) But no woman could hold the men of other clans. Soon Yesügei's camp was reduced to his two widows and their children. Temüjin, age ten, was the eldest. The family was almost without resources. Their meager flocks and what Yesügei's six sons could obtain from hunting and fishing were their only source of food. Often, they were reduced to eating rodents, or worse, berries and roots, food the Mongols detested. Without protectors they were exposed to all the natural dangers of the steppe and, to the numerous hereditary enemies of the Borjigids.

In addition, there was a feud within the family itself between the four sons of Hö elün and the two sons of Yesügei's second wife. One day Temüjin and one of his brothers killed their half brother. Hö elün was furious and accused them of being, "like the falcon that swoops on its own shadow. . . ." How could they kill their own brother, she asked, when, "the outrage the Tayiji'uds committed against us, you cannot even avenge it."

Gathering Power and Followers

Somehow, the family survived. The Tayiji'uds had expected them to starve, and when they did not, the Tayiji'ud chief, Tarqutay-Qiriltug decided to take action. He knew that Temüjin was growing up and would soon challenge him for leadership among the Mongols. In a surprise attack the Tayiji'uds captured Temüjin. Normally they would have killed him, but for some reason they did not. Later Tarqutay-Qiriltug said that some irresistible force held him back. Temüjin was put into a cangue, a large portable wooden frame the Chinese used to hold prisoners. But the young Mongol made a daring escape aided by a Tayiji'ud vassal who was impressed "by the fire in his glance and the radiance of his face."

Many stories tell of the hypnotic power of Temüjin's eyes. Sadly, we do not know how he really looked. All portraits of the conqueror were painted long after his death and are idealized. From bits of description it seems that when he was mature, Chingis Khan was tall, broadly built, and had an exceptionally long beard, for a Mongol,

Genghis Khan overcame many obstacles to become known as a fair and tolerant leader.

who usually have scanty beards. The descriptions also mention his "cat's eyes."

Shortly after Temüjin's escape a group of robbers made off with eight of the family's nine horses. Without horses the nomad was lost. Temüjin pursued the robbers on the remaining horse. During the chase he encountered a boy named Bo'orchu from another Mongol tribe and asked him if he had seen the stolen horses. Not only had Bo'orchu seen the horses but he gave Temüjin a fresh mount and immediately joined him in the chase without even bothering to tell his father where he had gone. According to Mongol history Bo'orchu's reason was, "the unwithstandable light of those falcon's eyes."

Thus Temüjin acquired his first *nükür*. This is a word that cannot be translated exactly. It means roughly "friend" or "comrade." But the two "friends" are not equal; the *nükür* was a man who freely decided to follow a particular leader. This new obligation outweighed all others including the ties of blood. That is the significance of Bo'orchu not even telling his own father he had gone with Temüjin. In years to come Chingis Khan was to make great use of the institution of *nükür*. By becoming *nükür* of the conqueror, many men who would otherwise have been enemies were converted to loyal followers.

Temüjin and Bo'orchu recovered the horses and from that point on the young Mongol lord's fortunes improved. He could now think of claiming the bride that had been promised him. Temüjin still had few followers and many enemies, but he was strong and resourceful. In the steppe, such a man could easily become a great chief in a few years. Börte's father was more than willing to honor his agreement.

The Kidnapping of Temüjin's Wife

Still, Temüjin's family had only nine horses. When they were attacked by another tribe, the Merkits, a Mongol people from the northern forests, the entire family could not get away. The priorities of who was to get a horse and who was to be abandoned give us a significant look into the family life of the Mongols. There was a horse for Temüjin, of course, and one for his mother Hö elün. His brothers, Qasar, Qachi'un, Temuge, and Belgute and his two *nükür* Bo'orchu and Jelme also got mounts. A riderless horse was needed in case of emergency. That took care of all the horses. Börte, Temüjin's new bride, along with Yesügei's second wife were left behind.

There was nothing cowardly or disloyal about this act in the morality of the steppe nomad. One could always get a new wife. Besides, Börte was not being condemned to death or to a life of slavery. She would simply be married off to a Merkit of appropriate rank. Lady Hö elün herself had originally been the wife of a Merkit chief. She had been abandoned by her husband when they were ambushed by Yesügei. When Yesügei attacked, Hö elün had given her Merkit husband her own horse. Her parting words to him were, "If you can get away alive, you will not want for maidens perched on wagon seats." The Mongols admired her wisdom.

Marriage among the Mongols was complicated, difficult, and not at all romantic. Various types of relatives, even distant ones, were forbidden by custom to marry one another. Other marriages were impossible because of clan feuds. Since the total number of Mongols was small, it was often hard for a suitable marriage to be arranged. Therefore, kidnapping was a common and accepted way of obtaining a wife. Common as it was, each abduction had to be revenged. With the capture of Börte the Merkits had avenged Yesügei's earlier capture of Hö elün.

To take revenge upon the Merkits, Temüjin needed allies. He called upon his father's old friend, Toghril, the khan of the Kereits, whom he had begun to address as "father." Temüjin also called upon Jamukha, chief of the Mongol tribe of the Jajirats. Temüjin and Jamukha had been friends when young and had sworn an oath to be "brothers" or *anda*. The oath of *anda* was a solemn and serious one, and was as binding as blood loyalty. Unlike the oath of *nükür* the *anda* oath implied that the two "brothers" were equal in rank.

A year passed before the forces of the three allies could gather for war upon the Merkits. When they did attack they were completely successful. Much Merkit wealth was taken and Börte was rescued. During her year of captivity, Börte had been married off to a Merkit chief and when Temüjin reclaimed her she was pregnant. Temüjin treated this casually. He never reproached Börte in any way. She remained his chief wife and most trusted advisor. Her first-born son, the child of a Merkit chief, was called Jochi or "the guest." Jochi was given the same position as Temüjin's own sons.

The Merkit males, down to small children, were slaughtered, and the women were taken off to be wives or concubines of the victorious Mongols and Kereits. The surviving Merkits fled into the forest and nursed their hatred of the Mongols. They would return to plague the Mongols again and again. No compromise was possible between these two closely related tribes and ultimately the Merkits had to be completely exterminated, before the Mongols could feel secure.

A Crucial Split

After the battle Toghril and his Kereits returned to their homeland. The two Mongol "brothers," Temüjin and Jamukha, renewed their friendship and their respective hordes traveled together for a year and a half. In all but name they had become the dual khans of the Mongols. Divided power, however, could not last long among the nomads.

The break between the two came in a very puzzling way. One day as they were riding along Jamukha said to Temüjin, "Let us camp near the hills and there will be tents for the horse herders. Let us camp near the stream and there will be food for the shepherds and the watchers of lambs." Temüjin did not know what this paradox meant. The horde could not camp in two places at once. He dropped back to the end of the line of march where the carts with the women were, to ask his mother about the riddle. Before she could answer Börte spoke up and said that Jamukha had always been untrustworthy and that they must break with him immediately. That very night Temüjin gathered his followers and continued to march while Jamukha and his followers camped. The two former friends had become the deadliest of enemies.

Obviously Jamukha's statement had great significance, but centuries of historians have been as puzzled by it as Temüjin was. The best guess today as to the meaning of the paradox is that Jamukha had presented Temüjin with an unsolvable problem of whether to favor the herders or horsemen among his followers—the shepherds or the warriors. Whatever Temüjin's answer, Jamukha would have opposed it, for he wished to force a split.

When the horde broke into two parts more men chose to follow Temüjin than Jamukha. As Temüjin's fortunes rose, many who had originally chosen Jamukha came over to Temüjin's camp. Among the new followers were some chiefs whom Temüjin had called upon in his days of troubles, but who had ignored him. If Temüjin felt any bitterness he concealed it. On the steppe a man was loyal to his family and those he was bound to by oath. Beyond that, loyalty was only paid to those who rewarded it. Temüjin was planning to change this system, but he was not yet strong enough.

Becoming a Khan

In 1196 Temüjin was "elevated" to the position of khan. He was the first Mongol khan in over a generation. The chiefs who had helped to elevate the new khan did not think they were choosing a master. The khan served only as a leader in war and in mass hunting expeditions. During peace the chiefs promised only to "keep faith" with the khan. He was to be first among equals—nothing more.

The young khan chose for himself the name Chingis. It is a Turkish word which means "a large body of water, the ocean." As far as the Mongols were concerned the earth was flat and the land was entirely surrounded by ocean. Thus the title Chingis Khan meant "the all-encompassing lord." It must have seemed a foolishly exaggerated title when first proclaimed on some remote grazing ground in the upper reaches of Mongolia.

One reason Temüjin triumphed so completely and easily in his power struggle with Jamukha was that he commanded traditional loyalties, for he was related to the royal line of the Mongols. Jamukha's connections to royalty were distant and doubtful. Yet there were other Mongol princes who had far stronger claims to the royal succession than Chingis Khan. The basic reason for his success was that he represented stability and moderation. Jamukha was a brilliant leader, but temperamental and, as Börte had observed, untrustworthy, even to his friends. While Chingis could be merciless when necessary, Jamukha was often pointlessly cruel. After one battle he had enemy prisoners thrown into boiling caldrons. This was an old Chinese torture and the Mongols, fierce as they were, saw no need for it.

In contrast, Chingis was tolerant and generous. He welcomed new followers liberally, even if they had once opposed him. When a man entered the service of the khan, he knew exactly where he stood. Throughout the *yurts* of the steppe the young khan began to get the reputation of a man who could feed his warriors and keep his camp in good order.

Subtly, but effectively, Chingis Khan began to change the social organization of the nomads. He created special units of soldiers, the Day Guards and the Night Guards. The apparent purpose of these units was to watch over the khan's tent both night and day. Their significance, however, was that membership in the guards was not based on tribe. Any warrior who proved himself brave and completely loyal to the khan could join these special units. Guard members outranked any officer of the regular tribal army. Chingis Khan was laying the groundwork for a professional army.

Temujin Slays His Brother

Anonymous, translated by Paul Kahn

Chinghis (or Chingis or Genghis) Khan, the Mongol who was one of the greatest conquerors in world history, died in 1227. Within a few decades of his death, a history of his life was written in Mongolian. It is believed that the book was intended to be read only by the royal family and perhaps other nobles. Although this book was written in the middle of the thirteenth century, the following excerpt details the murder of Begter by his half-brothers Temujin (the birth name of Chinghis Khan) and Khasar, an incident that most likely occurred around 1180. This edition of *The Secret History of the Mongols* is a verse translation by the poet Paul Kahn.

One day Temujin and Khasar,
along with their half-brothers Begter and Belgutei,
were sitting together on the riverbank
pulling a hook through the water
when they saw a shiny fish had been caught on it.
When they landed the fish
Begter and Belgutei took it away from Temujin and Khasar.
Temujin and Khasar ran back to their tent to complain to Mother Ujin:
"Begter and Belgutei took a fish from us,
a shiny fish that bit on our hook."
But even though Begter and Belgutei were only her stepsons
Mother Ujin replied:

Excerpted from *The Secret History of the Mongols: The Origin of Chinghis Khan* (Boston: Cheng & Tsui, 1998) by Anonymous, translated by Paul Kahn. Reprinted with permission from the publisher.

"Stop this!
How can brothers act this way with each other?
Now, when we've no one to fight beside us but our own shadows,
when there's nothing to whip our horses but their own tails,
how will we get our revenge on the Tayichigud brothers?
Why do you fight among yourselves like the five sons of Mother Alan?[1]
Don't be this way."
But Temujin and Khasar wouldn't listen to what she said.
They ignored her warning and answered instead:
"Besides that, yesterday they took a bird from us,
a lark we'd shot down with one of our own arrows.
And now they've stolen a fish.
How can we live with them?"
The two boys pushed aside the door of the tent and stalked out.
While Begter sat in a clearing watching the family's nine horses
   grazing,
Temujin hid himself in the grass and crept up from behind
while Khasar crept up from the front.
Then suddenly they sprang up,
drawing their arrows to shoot,
and Begter, seeing what they meant to do to him, said:
"How can you do this to me,
when our mouths are filled
with the bitterness of what the Tayichigud clan has done,
and we ask ourselves,
'How can we get our revenge on them?'
how can you treat me like some dirt in your eye,
like something that's keeping the food from your mouth?
How can you do this,
when there's no one to fight beside us but our shadows,
when there's nothing to whip our horses but their own tails,
how can you kill me?
But if you must
don't destroy the fire of my hearth.
Don't kill my brother Belgutei too!"
Then Begter sat down before them,
crossing his legs,
and waited to see what they'd do to him.
At close range both Temujin and Khasar shot arrows into him,
striking him down in the front and the back,
and then left him.
When they got back to the tent

---

1. Alan was a maternal ancestor of Temujin. She urged her sons to unite rather than fight against one another. By uniting in battle, all five sons became leaders of clans.

Mother Ujin could see on their faces what they'd done.
She looked at her two sons,
then pointing first at Temujin said to them:
"Killers, both of you!
When he came out screaming from the heat of my womb
this one was born holding a clot of black blood in his hand.
And now you've both destroyed without thinking,
like the Khasar dog who eats its own afterbirth,
like the panther that heedlessly leaps from a cliff,
like the lion who can't control its own fury,
like the python that thinks: 'I'll swallow my prey alive,'
like the falcon that foolishly dives at its own shadow,
like the river pike who silently swallows the smaller fish,
like the he-camel who snaps at the heels of his colt,
like the wolf who hides himself in the blizzard to hunt down his prey,
like the mandarin duck who eats his own chicks when they fall behind,
like the jackal who fights with anyone who's touched him,
like the tiger who doesn't think before seizing his prey,
you've killed your own brother!
When we have no one to fight beside us but our own shadows,
when there's nothing to whip our horses with but their own tails,
when our mouths are filled
with the bitterness of what the Tayichigud have done to us,
and we ask ourselves:
'How can we get our revenge on them?'
you come complaining to me, saying:
'How can we live with these brothers?'
and now you do this!"
This is how she spoke to her sons,
reciting ancient phrases and quoting old sayings to them in her anger.

Chapter 6

The
Americas

PREFACE

In the desert regions of the Americas, ancient people looked up at the sky and prayed for rain. Rain filled the rivers, replenished the springs, and fed the crops that the Indians lived on. When rainfall was ample, food and water were plentiful, and the Indians could spend time building cliff dwellings, crafting and painting pottery, and raising families. When the rains did not come, the desert heat killed crops and starved children. Many anthropologists believe that occasionally, scant rain came for years on end, and the Indians were forced to leave their cities and pueblos to look for more hospitable land, a better life. When archaeologists try to trace what happened to the ancient desert people of the twelfth century, they find many clues; luckily, arid climates preserve human artifacts well. Yet in the end, archaeologists must guess about the disappearance of many of these people. The Indians, many say, prayed for rain, but it did not come.

The Chimú Indians of coastal Peru, the Toltec Indians of central Mexico, and the Anasazi Indians of the southwestern United States eked out a living during the twelfth century in the Americas. They have left behind ancient ruins that show that they were sophisticated people. They built homes and roads, made beautiful pottery, spoke languages, grew crops and designed irrigation methods to water them. They also waged war, and some offered human sacrifices to the gods. Their ancestors and their benefactors inherited many of their customs and much of their knowledge. Modern people marvel at their example of the human spirit, for they not only endured but prospered in the face of incredible odds.

The Chimú Indians in what is now Peru succeeded the Mochican Indians, but the two people are often referred to together as the Mochican-Chimú civilization because of the similarities of their geographical range and their customs. The Mochican-Chimú civilization was the longest-lasting civilization in Peru except for the Mayan civilization which succeeded it. Accounts from the Spanish conquistadors, Mayan records, and the ruins of their civilization have provided a fairly complete record of their history. The arid climate of coastal Peru preserved their pottery, which has been called the Chimú language because it depicts scenes of their daily lives that communicate across the centuries.

Ancient ruins still stand outside Mexico City as a testament to the great civilization of the Toltec Indians. The ruins are what is left of the great Toltec city, Tula, a metropolis of some thirty thousand people of various ethnic and linguistic backgrounds. The Toltecs began to decline in the 1100s, but the archaeological record provides no concrete evidence that explains their demise. Many archaeologists believe that the expanding population of Tula could not be sustained in the arid environment of central Mexico. Nonetheless, the Toltec legacy endured in the minds and bodies of the Aztecs—fierce warriors whose cities contained the riches that were the envy of the Spanish conquistadors—who claimed them as ancestors.

The disappearance of the Anasazi Indians from North America has been a mystery that has occupied archaeologists for many years. The ruins of their great civilization are extensive, covering most of the four-corners region of the southwestern United States, but the ruins do not explain the disappearance of the Anasazi. The rediscovery in the 1800s of these ancient pueblos—community dwellings built of stone or adobe by Indian tribes in the American southwest—inspired what has proven to be an enduring fascination with the ancient ones. Many who study Anasazi ruins believe that the Anasazi home range was affected by a persistent drought that forced the people to flee their pueblos.

The Chimú, Toltec, and Anasazi Indians produced remarkable civilizations in the face of physical hardship. Although they did not possess the technology that allows modern people to mitigate the harshness of desert environments, the Indians endured long enough to leave to their successors a legacy of art, architecture, and proof of the human spirit that continues to inspire people in modern times.

Talking Pottery: The Chimú Indians of Peru

Victor W. von Hagen

The Chimú Indians—also called the Kingdom of Chimor—occupied the central coast of Peru from around 1000 to 1400 A.D., and began a large imperial expansion toward the end of the twelfth century. According to Victor W. von Hagen, the Chimús succeeded the Mochica Indians, and together, their civilization endured longer than any other in Middle America except for the Mayan civilization. Much is known about the Mochicas and Chimús because the desert climate in which they lived preserved many of their artifacts. Hagen argues that among the artifacts the pottery is exceptional in its graphic and lifelike depiction of Mochica-Chimú life. From this sculptural pottery it is known that the Mochica-Chimú were of Mongolian descent, that the men painted their faces to show their social standing, and that they were involved in continuous warfare with neighboring tribes. The pottery also shows that women planted and harvested crops, wove fabrics, and had many children. According to Hagen, both men and women enjoyed sex to an astonishing degree—Mochica-Chimú pottery graphically depicts men and women engaged in sexual acts—which amazed their successors, the Incas, and later, the Spanish Conquistadors. Victor W. von Hagen is the author of several books on ancient Indians including *The Ancient Sun Kingdoms of the Americas: Aztec, Maya, Inca* and *Highway of the Sun.*

Excerpted from *The Desert Kingdoms of Peru* (Greenwich: New York Graphic Society Publishers, 1964). Copyright © 1964 by George Weidenfeld & Nicolson. Reprinted with permission from Laurence Pollinger, Ltd.

Of all of the many and varied tribes that preceded the Incas, none have left a greater impression upon the history of Peru than the desert kingdoms of the Mochicas and the Chimús. The physical remains of their past—cities, temples, pyramids—even though destroyed and half-covered with sand, are still impressive. Graves have yielded and continue to yield their golden hoard, and with it, feather ornaments, superb weavings and carvings, and above all, the fine, realistically moulded pottery, a pottery so graphic that it is interpreted as their language. Despite the pathos of distance and the destruction brought on by man and time, there are remains of roads, fortresses, defence walls, vast irrigation projects and step-terraces—an eloquent monument to a people who have left their imprint on the road of time.

The Chimús (who succeeded the Mochicas and were called the Kingdom of Chimor) were the last of the tribes to be conquered by the Incas, before the latter were themselves overwhelmed by the Spaniards within the next fifty years. However, before the Incas could effectively stamp out the cultural memory of the Chimús, through their technique of selective manipulation of remembered history, they were themselves involved in a civil war, the struggle between Atahualpa and Huascar for the Inca Empire. This was quickly followed, in turn, by the Spanish intrusion. Here, then, is the reason that much of the Chimú and the Mochica remains are known to us today.

The Mochicas and the Chimús have had a continuous archaeological history, which began roughly in the third century BC and went on (with a hiatus between the years AD 1000–1250) until the year 1461, when they were overwhelmed by a full-scale Inca invasion. This was followed by the final quietus by the Spanish, and so the rest became silence. These 1400 years of continued existence, on a high cultural plane and within the same geographical area, an area of titanic desolation marked only by river-oases paradises, is one of the most prolonged in America's cultural history; only the Maya civilization of Middle America has had a longer duration.

Pottery as Language

The impression that the Mochicas, and later the Chimús, have left on Peru is timeless, since the ceramics recovered from their graves are so exact that their tribal customs, their lives, loves and deaths, can be read as a pictorial history. The desiccating quality of the Peruvian coastal desert has preserved this culture. Their dead were buried along with their possessions, and their very corpses were preserved in so fine a state that one can often observe such subtleties as the effects of arthritis, the wear of teeth and the pruning of nails.

Where all else has perished, there are the ceramics. These are unequalled anywhere in the Americas. With a penchant for realism, their potters have left lifelike portraits of warriors, priests and courtiers, the possessed and the unpossessed, the halt and the blind. Diseases which afflicted them are exhibited in this pottery with clinical exactness. Most of the facial features—the piercing of the ears and the nose septum, the squint of the eye, the hook of the nose—are depicted in this sculptural pottery. All food cultivated or obtained is effectively and realistically presented. The landscapes which are often found painted on the pottery are as detailed as Persian miniatures: one sees the sun glare down upon the wasteland; the desert flora and the dry mountains loom up beside; the plants grow in the cultivated greenness of a river oasis; maize fields bend tasselled heads which sway in the off-shore winds. There are also figures in the landscape, running and dancing, while war is presented with all its rapine and slaughter. Animal and birds, which formed so intimate a part of their lives, are moulded or painted on these ceramics with a warmth of feeling rarely found in other American cultures. Woman, when she appears in the pottery, is handled tenderly, a rather unusual feature in early American art, for her lot was that of an unequal concubinage and a weary servitude. There is also here in this iconographic parade a realistic and engagingly candid picture of their love life—at times so shockingly sexual that it disturbed even the Incas, their latter-day conquerors. No culture in the Americas and few others in the world have left so graphic a picture of the intimate and libidinous details of sensuous love.

This pottery record naturally has its limitations: the Mochica-Chimú gods are nameless, since their vases do not bear, like those of the Greeks, the name of the represented god. Nor do their paintings have the rows of talking glyphs that the Maya often inserted to give us a date. There are no subtleties here, no nuances; beyond the graphic, one must surmise and deduce. It was only after the 'study of the antique' gave way to scientific archaeology that scholars were able to link the creators of this vivid pottery with the widely scattered remains of pyramids, roads, fortresses and vast irrigation works, and thus gauge the impressiveness of the Mochica civilization. This Mochica culture had developed before the Christian era—the earliest Carbon 14 date is 267 BC—and endured despite a massive onslaught from without to emerge later as the Chimú Empire. . . .

Mochica and Chimú Man

Mochica [and Chimú] man, as he pictures himself in his own iconography, was short, thickset, and graced with a longish, dolichocephalic head—a normal head unless distorted by artificial flattening. Their skulls—and there are many extant—which the desert has preserved for thousands of years because of the preservant qualities of the desiccating sands, show that their teeth, like those of most grain-eating peoples, were excellent and usually devoid of cavities. We have an exact and precise knowledge of their faces and general appearance because of the thousands of portraits left to us in their effigy pottery. These portraits have a high level of realism, in which every facial characteristic is shown. The face is round, with high cheekbones, and dominated by a hook nose with wide-flaring nostrils. The mouth is wide and full-lipped, and the dark eyes are almond-shaped and set into the face suggesting a slant, because of the epicanthic fold about the eye, which is, of course, one of the signs of the proto-mongoloid descent. There are a wide range of faces, old and young. Most faces are painted, and one might, from a superficial glance, believe that these are portraits of other peoples than the Mochicas. However, it is not true, as is suggested by the German archaeologist Ubbelohde-Doering (who ought to know better) that these variegated portraits show that it is most 'likely that the [Mochicas'] portraits are representative of the whole of Ancient Peru rather than of a particular tribe only'.

Mochica hair-styles are not clear, since almost all are portrayed—unless they are shown captured—wearing headgear of one form or another. Mostly, it seems, the hair was cropped close to neck length, and cut in bangs over the forehead. All men pierced their ears. A wooden plug was inserted, which was removed for war or festival and replaced by ornamental ear-spools: painted wooden ones for those of the baser sort, or beautifully hammered gold sets with gold, pearl or turquoise inlay if one belonged to the directing classes, for the size and sumptuousness of the ear-spool was doubtlessly a status-symbol. In addition to the ears, the nose-septum, the cartilage tissues between the nostrils, was also pierced, into which many inserted a crescent-shaped, golden ornament which hung down to the lips.

Presumably, the Mochica skin-colour was, as it is now in their descendants, a light bronze, varying in colour, dark or light, depending on the place and the individual. However, the true skin colour was never quite discernable, since they invariably painted their face, arms, body and legs. Face-painting was general. No one has ever attempted to explain the pattern of the Mochica face-painting or the reasons for it—magical or indicative of social status—yet individual facial designs must run into hundreds of different patterns. The most common pattern, used by warriors, was the painting in either red or black of both sides of the face, leaving part of the centre of the face unadorned. In some, the eyes were encircled, and long black streams suggested the tear-stains of the 'Weeping-god'. Others made what the early Spaniards thought to be a cross, a cross-bar extending from the top of the head to the chin, and many painted their faces so that the curving lines about the lips and chin resembled beards. A not uncommon design is that of a man, sitting cross-legged, with a 'painted moustache', such as was sported in reality by Chinese mandarins (this has often been grasped at by those who wish to prove a trans-Pacific contact in historical times with Asia).

Face-Painting as Status Symbol

Face-painting indicated caste, the mark of rank; designs may well have been the equivalent of an escutcheon, as is true of many, if not most of the Amazon Indians. Designs were symbols, yet symbols that were not just something figurative, but very real. As with masks (when an Indian wears a mask of a god, he *is* that god) when a red dye is used as a blood surrogate (for smearing the body with blood has as its aim the increasing of the vital principle of life), then that red dye *is* blood. The Mochicas used, as most, the juice of the plant called *genipa,* which turns blue-black; red was obtained from the berry within the husk of the achiote. The brush was usually a spatula made from a river-reed. Women in many American tribes were, and are, the face-painters.

What was the object of Mochica face-painting? It might reflect on the Mochicas, because 'face-painting confers upon the individual his dignity as a human being; it helps him cross the frontier from Nature to culture, and from the mindless animal to the civilized man. Furthermore, it differs in style and composition according to social status and thus has a social function.' Face-painting was, too, a clan index, since, like most Peruvian tribes, the Mochicas were arranged in a sort of social pyramid, in which the common man, who formed the base, belonged to a sort of earth-cell (the Incas called it an *ayllu*). Land was held collectively by a group or clans related by blood ties. Each had a totemic device—circle, square, animal-head, fish—and if the Mochica vases are minutely studied, it can be discerned that the designs of face-painting are often repeated in ear-spools, on lances or clubs, or even on their shields.

Like most American Indians, the Mochicas had little facial hair, and that which appeared was plucked out; the presence of silver and copper hair-pincers in graves provides evidence of this fact. However, older men did have straggling hairs, which, with the indifference to personal appearance usual in old age, they probably made no attempt to remove. There is also in Mochica pottery a mysterious figure of an old man who is bearded and unpainted. This old man is represented with full white moustache and broad 'imperial'. His ear-spool decorations are invariable, a motif which suggests a wave design. If one is to assume that all else represented in their pottery is of their lives and realistically displayed (except in the sententious variations of religious themes)—food, sexual positions, costumes, animals—then what is the reality of the bearded man? What was he?

Mochicas dressed for the climate. This climate, it must be remembered, was not just hot desert; it was also wind-blown, and the cold of the night winds caused a rapier-like refrigeration to set in. 'They all went about', wrote Pedro de Cieza de León, speaking generally about the coastal yuncas,[1] 'attired in shirts of cotton and long blankets.' The Mochicas also left us in their pottery a very detailed idea of how they dressed. The same Pedro de Cieza de León, assembled with many other knights of the royal army arrayed against Gonzalo Pizarro, spent some time at Tumbes in 1548. There he observed that 'their clothing consisted of a shirt [a form of poncho that looked like a foreshortened version of the Victorian nightgown] and a blanket; they also wore a head-dress which was a round affair, made of wool, and sometimes spangled with gold or silver leads . . . known as *chaquira*. The apparel was woven from cotton . . . of which they gather as much as they need in the valley [of Tumbes].'

Clothing

The poncho was a colourfully woven garment, as shown by the designs left on painted ceramics, in which the ponchos are spread out so that the full design can be seen. Underneath, men usually wore a breech clout. As Cieza observed, 'the Indians and their women wear a kind of apron to cover their privities. On their head they wear a kind of crown of small beads which they call chaquira and some use them of silver and others of jaguar or panther skin. The women's dress is a blanket from the waist down and another covering them to the shoulders; they wear their hair long. In some of these villages the caciques [indian chiefs] stud or fill their teeth with gold . . . when the chieftains died, they built a round tomb with a vaulted roof, the entrance facing the sun, and buried them together with living women in their arms and other things.'

The Mochicas picture themselves as going barefooted. The impression that they wore stockings comes from the fact that the men, particularly the warriors, painted their feet up to their knees in black. However, sandals made of cabuya-fibre or leather of llama or sealion have been found in graves. The focus of attention was the turban. It marked caste and social status. The ordinary man wore an unadorned turban, which was wrapped around the head and tied under the chin. The other piece was a long stole, which when wind or cold demanded, was wrapped about them to bundle up their heads. They breathed through a cloth drawn over the nose that gave them a forbidding appearance, with nothing more to be seen than their dark, robber-like eyes.

Man, amongst the Mochicas, was made for war. Youths grew up in the ceaseless wars between the valley oases or in the limited ones

---

1. Indians who lived in the hotlands of Peru.

with the mountain-dwellers. The Mochica and the Chimú, therefore, were farmer-warriors, part of an agrarian militia. Each was a member of an earth-cell, a clan to which he belonged by blood-ties, and he wore the totem symbol of his clan on his shield, lance or helmet when he went into battle. He married young; he built his mud house by communal effort; he developed the fields allotted to him by the clan-holdings, communally; and he fought and died in the same manner.

Mochica and Chimú Women

Mochica women, naturally, were of a more delicate structure, although they are often portrayed as heavy-set. Yet the skeletal remains show them to have been very short and delicate, veritable 'Lolitas'[2] in stature and not much more than five feet tall. They were, as the conquistadores found, comely, hard-working and, as their pottery reveals, libidinous. Their hair was long, cut in bangs over the forehead and braided with colourful woollen strands. Mummies have been found with the coiffure so described intact. They used cosmetics (which were often buried with them), combs, and silver ear-spoons to take out earwax; they also used silver depilatory tweezers and mirrors of obsidian or polished turquoise. They did not perforate their ears, but all wore necklaces. Unlike Mochica men they did not wear an elaborate headdress, but like them they went about barefoot.

They covered their brown bodies with a poncho, more delicately woven than the man's, except, said Cieza, that the coverpiece 'was full and wide like a cape with openings on the sides for the arms'. They married young, between fourteen and eighteen years of age. They had, one gathers from the evidence of graves and the pottery, many children, and apparently did not wean them until they were over three years of age. Among the Mayas, Bishop Diego de Landa found the women 'marvellously chaste', but a padre who was in Peru on a similar mission as Landa in Yucatán and was well acquainted with their Muchic language, told Cieza some things about the Chimús' (who were the Mochicas' descendants) sexual behaviour which made him gasp in astonishment: 'The women committed sodomy (i.e., anal copulation) with their husbands or other men even while nursing their own children.'

Women helped in the fields with planting crops and later harvesting them. They educated their children. They also spun cotton and wool fibres and wove most of the wonderful fabrics found in graves and tombs. Doubtless, they made the ceramics cast from moulds. They also made the intoxicating *chicha* liquor by masticating boiled corn, by which process the enzymes of starch were transformed into sugar, and then fermented into a beverage ('it is amazing', says Cieza

2. Lolita—a young girl who attracts the attention of an adult man—is a character in the novel by the same name written by Vladimir Nabakav, a Russian-born American novelist.

in an aside, 'how much beverage or *chicha* these Indians can drink, for the glass is never out of their hand').

Monogamy was general among the lower man in both the Mochica and Chimú communities. Polygamy was reserved for the higher man of the directing class, of whom Cieza observed that 'they had many wives, selecting them among the most beautiful', which of course gave these members of the Mochica-Chimú harem a dubious ending, for the chieftains, when buried, were by custom certain that 'their most beautiful and best loved women' went with them.

Mochica-Chimú Sex-Lives

There were monogamists in fact, but none of necessity. Even so, it remained the custom of the lesser man. With him, as with the middle classes now, a woman, since she consumed, was regarded as a persistent debit. It really depended on an Indian's wealth whether he had one woman or many. Among all peoples, even the primitive, poverty makes the sexes equal; polygamy is too expensive for one of modest means. Whatever the primitive reason, based either on tribal *mores* or economic status, monogamy was the rule; severe punishments were meted out for those who disregarded it.

Children were born with the aid of a midwife. Their 'speaking' pottery shows a woman being delivered of her child; the midwife stands behind her and presses on her stomach, while another is on hand to sieze the child's head. Various unguents and other primitive *materia medica* are shown in boxes. Woman is treated tenderly in much of the pottery; she is shown nursing her children, washing her hair, making bowls of the intoxicating beverage, *chicha*. A woman had nearly equal rights with man and did not follow the traditional idea that she was mere chattel. Women, in fact, in the coastal yuncas often became leaders of tribes; Pizarro, in his first visit to Peru, in 1527, when near Santa, was visited by an 'Indian woman of rank, followed by a numerous train of attendants of such power that she gave him several men of her tribe as hostages in order to exhibit her sensitive apprehension of her guests'. Divorce was possible, usually by repudiation, but when death ended marriage, the widow had either to wait for a considerable length of time or enter into a levirate marriage with her husband's brother.

The sexual life of primitive peoples is closely tied up with the social life of the community, far more than in most civilized communities. So it is that the Mochica-Chimú pottery is in considerable part preoccupied with sex-life. Certainly the Frenchman who wrote that 'l'animal ignore la diversité l'accumulation des aptitudes; l'homme seul est luxurieux,'[3] may well have had the Mochica-Chimú in mind,

---

3. The Frenchman means that animals mate in order to procreate, whereas humans often have sex just for pleasure.

for little else disturbed both Inca and Spanish conqueror than the prevalence of sodomy among the coastal yuncas. The Incas, when they finally conquered them in 1460–1470, found most of them addicted to anal copulation, practising it with both men and women. Aghast at such 'waste of seed', for loss of children was loss of people, they regarded this practice as abominable, and tried to stamp it out by destroying families, even whole tribes. It persisted, nevertheless.

The Demise
of the Toltecs

Richard A. Diehl

The Toltecs—ancestors of the Aztecs—lived in central Mexico from around 900 to 1200 A.D. in the city of Tula. Around 30,000 people of different ethnicities lived in Tula, and they engaged in ancient customs such as ritual sacrifice, cranial deformation, and cannibalism. The Toltecs were also a skilled and cosmopolitan people who, like modern humans, raised children and planted crops. During the 1100s, according to Richard A. Diehl, Toltec civilization began to decline. Mythical accounts attribute the fall of the Toltecs to a feud between a good god, Quetzalcoatl, and a bad god, Tezcatlipoca. Diehl argues that there were many real causes for the decline of the Toltecs, however. One explanation is that the climate changed, causing drought and famine. An increasing population of both native-born Toltecs and immigrants from other regions likely exacerbated the food shortage. The immigrants would also have increased the ethnic tensions that already existed in Tula, resulting in further internal instability. In addition, external conflicts with people in the surrounding cities might have made trade more difficult, making food even scarcer and hastening the Toltec's decline. Richard A. Diehl is a professor in the college of arts and sciences at the University of Alabama.

Toltec power and culture came to a catastrophic end in the latter part of the twelfth century when famine, rebellion, and chaos replaced the growth and prosperity of the previous two centuries. By

Excerpted from *Tula: The Toltec Capital of Ancient Mexico*, by Richard A. Diehl. Copyright © 1983 by Thames & Hudson. Reprinted with permission from Thames & Hudson.

AD 1200 Tula [Toltec capital] was a ruined shell of its former self and the Toltecs had dispersed all over central Mexico. This chapter is concerned with the Toltec collapse and the factors behind it. First we will look at a native account recorded by Sahagun, then the scanty archaeological information will be reviewed. Next we will examine two syntheses of all the available information; one was proposed by Nigel Davies in his recent book T*he Toltecs Until the Fall of Tula,* the other is my own reconstruction. . . .

The Toltec collapse is described in several historical sources. The stories vary and frequently contradict each other because the accounts are based on different historical traditions and all probably contain later modifications and embellishments. Furthermore the Mesoamerican penchant for cloaking mundane history in myth was never given a freer rein than in the telling of the Toltec disaster; in fact, some of the accounts are comparable to the *Odyssey*[1] in their narrative power as well as their credibility.

Sahagun's Version

The account we find in Sahagun is one of the most mythical to have been preserved. His informants attributed the Toltec collapse to an epic conflict between cosmic forces personified by the gods Tezcatlipoca and Quetzalcoatl. The Mesoamerican cosmos was often portrayed as a duality symbolized by Quetzalcoatl (good, day, light, and established élite religion) in opposition to Tezcatlipoca (evil, night, darkness, and sorcery). In the Toltec drama, Tezcatlipoca was played by himself, and a priest or ruler named Ce Acatl Topiltzin Quetzalcoatl represented the divine Feathered Serpent. Huemac, a Toltec ruler who may have shared sovereignty with him, also appears.

The fable's basic theme is that Tezcatlipoca created so much misfortune among the Toltecs that they all perished or fled Tula. In the words of Sahagun's informants, 'A great mockery was made of the Toltecs, since the devil had slain very many of them. It is said in sooth he made sport of the Toltecs.'

The living Quetzalcoatl was famous for his life of virtue, chastity, sobriety, and ritual penance. In the opening scene Tezcatlipoca disguised himself as an elderly healer who tricked Quetzalcoatl into drinking pulque[2] to cure an ailment. One drink led to another and soon our paragon of virtue was drunk as the proverbial lord. At that point many of his disgusted followers deserted him. Tezcatlipoca then turned his malevolent attentions towards Huemac. First he ap-

1. The second epic of Homer—Greek poet who also wrote the *Iliad*—which recounts the wanderings of Odysseus after the fall of Troy and his eventual return home. 2. A fermented, milky beverage made in Mexico from various species of agave.

peared naked in the Tula marketplace disguised as a Huastec chili vendor. Huemac's virtuous daughter fell in love with the stranger and implored her father to allow them to marry. He reluctantly agreed, but his followers were so angered by the scandalous affair that he decided to send his son-in-law into a battle from which he would not return. According to Huemac's plan, the Toltec warriors were to abandon Tezcatlipoca to the enemy with only a cadre of dwarves and hunchbacks for support. When the plan was put into operation Tezcatlipoca defeated the enemy and the Toltecs had to accept him as a hero. During the victory celebration he sang magic chants which caused many Toltecs to lose their wits, fall into canyons, and turn to stone. Next he took the form of a valiant warrior and slew more Toltecs in hand-to-hand combat. Then he sat in the marketplace holding a dancing miniature figurine in his hand. Many onlookers were trampled to death as they tried to get close enough to view this marvel. Next he persuaded the Toltecs to stone him to death as a sorcerer; they were only too happy to oblige him, but the odor from his decomposing body caused additional deaths throughout the land. The Toltecs tried to remove the body but it became extremely heavy and many people were crushed to death when the ropes they were using to pull it broke. After this Tezcatlipoca cast a series of spells which made people uneasy and led some to offer themselves as sacrificial victims. His final deed was to turn the foodstores sour and have an old woman toast maize, filling the land with its aroma. The hungry Toltecs came from far away to get the maize but she killed them when they approached her.

Quetzalcoatl and Huemac realized that all was lost and each decided to flee. Quetzalcoatl destroyed his temples constructed of gold, coral, feathers, and other precious substances; changed the cacao trees into mesquite bushes; and drove away the birds with precious plumage which had inhabited the land. Then he left Tula accompanied by his remaining followers and wandered through foreign lands, including Cholula, until reaching Tlapallan on the Gulf coast. There he fashioned a raft of serpents and according to Sahagun, set off across the sea. Other accounts say that he burned himself in Tlapallan and rose from the ashes to become Venus, the Morning Star. Huemac fled to Cincalco, a cave in Chapultepec hill in the Basin of Mexico, where he lived out his days.

The Archaeological Record

Archaeological findings at Tula verify the fact that the city met a violent end; they do not tell us much about what actually took place or why. Acosta uncovered evidence of fire and destruction in every building he excavated at Tula Grande. Unfortunately he paid only scant attention to the detailed stratigraphy in the soil levels above the

Tollan phase structures and failed to recognize the complex sequence of events reflected in these upper levels. Although some of the destruction he noted undoubtedly occurred at the time of Tula's collapse, much of it took place in later times. The evidence for this is clear in Acosta's reports but its significance is not brought out.

Acosta accepted Jimenez Moreno's date of AD 1170 for Tula's collapse. This date is based on information contained in the historical sources and although the correlation of the native dates with our own calendar is still not completely resolved to everyone's satisfaction, most authorities accept Jimenez Moreno's interpretation. Hopes that our excavations would provide additional information on the subject of Tula's collapse were not fulfilled. Our radiocarbon dates indicate that the Canal Locality houses were abandoned as much as a century before this occurred. It would appear therefore that the urban peripheries were abandoned before the central core of the city and that Tula's decline was a long process rather than a sudden cataclysmic event.

Much remains to be learned about the process of Tula's decline. How rapidly did it occur? What factors caused it? Why couldn't the Toltecs reverse the trends which must have been evident to them? Davies has attempted to outline the events which led to the collapse and to answer some of the questions posed above, so let us now examine his reconstruction of the situation.

Explanations of the Toltec Collapse

The scenario Davies proposes is based on documentary accounts and archaeological facts. His sequence of events is as follows:

1 The northern Mesoamerican frontier gradually shifted southward through time, opening Tula to attack in the twelfth century. The initial attack occurred in about AD 1120 and caused some Toltecs to migrate southeastward into lands claimed by Cholula[3].

2 Immigrants from the northern frontier zone who had settled within the borders of the Toltec state turned on their hosts and answered Cholula's call for help against the Toltec intruders. One group, led by Mixcoatl, 'Cloud Serpent', eventually settled in the Basin of Mexico after helping the Cholulans.

3 In AD 1166 Mixcoatl's son Ce Acatl Topiltzin gained control of Tula and the Toltec throne. He assumed the title Quetzalcoatl and became the Ce Acatl Topiltzin Quetzalcoatl of Toltec history and legend. Tula enjoyed a brief renaissance under his rule but his success bred conflicts between his followers and the traditional Tula-born faction led by Huemac. Increased pressures from the Huastecs and northern Chichimecs (who were farmers rather than true nomadic

---

3. City in southeastern Mexico and Tula's rival.

Teochichimecs) triggered the downfall of both men and each fled to a different part of the Basin of Mexico.

4 Toltec power and civilization ended by AD 1179 and most of Tula's inhabitants moved to various parts of central Mexico.

Additional Explanations

If this reconstruction is correct, as I believe it to be, what basic cultural processes led to these events? Davies, Pedro Armillas, and others have dealt with this issue, and all seem to agree on certain points which I will take into account in my reconstruction.

I believe the Toltecs were faced with internal problems and external threats which they could neither control nor resolve. The major internal problems were subsistence difficulties and a poorly integrated social system, the external threats came from enemies in several directions. We will consider each of these factors in turn.

Subsistence agriculture has always been a precarious enterprise in the arid Tula area. Low rainfall and broken topography limit the amount of arable land and normal fluctuations in annual precipitation cause more bad years than good ones. Irrigation was as essential in the past as it is today but the technology involved was very different. These days water is stored behind large dams and raised to the level of the fields with mechanical pumps and long canal systems. In addition, the never-ending flow of water from the Mexico City waste disposal system supplements the limited amount of local water. None of these features was available to the Toltecs. For them dry years meant total crop losses on unirrigated fields and river levels which were so low that water could not be drawn off into the canal systems. A single bad year caused hunger; several in a row could easily create famine. The Toltecs faced this problem all along, but it became more critical as the population grew. Although the government undoubtedly sponsored construction of irrigation systems, the size of the irrigated area was constrained by the available moisture and hilly terrain. The productivity of the Tula area in poor years must have placed rather a low ceiling on the carrying capacity, i.e., the number of people who could be supported by the area on a long-term basis. I suspect that the Tula area became overpopulated in this sense by AD 1100, although I cannot prove it.

At this point the skeptic may reasonably ask several questions. Why did the Toltecs not construct dams and reservoirs for water storage or import food from surrounding areas in bad years? The answer is that they did not do so because they lacked the technology to dam up the large fast-flowing rivers of the region. Even the small arroyos could not have been successfully controlled because flash floods which follow the torrential summer storms would have destroyed the dams in a few minutes. Furthermore, the absence of waterwheels and other devices for lifting water out of its natural courses made its storage for irrigation of elevated fields impossible.

The Toltecs certainly depended on imported food for some of their supplies. Some of the imports were in the form of tribute from conquered provinces, the rest were purchased with urban craft products. Nevertheless they faced two grave problems in this regard. Their transportation system was rudimentary and expensive, and the areas they controlled were not particularly productive. The absence of wheeled vehicles and draft animals meant that all transportation had to be accomplished with human bearers or canoes. Aztec human bearers called *tanemes* normally carried loads of about 23 kilos (50 lbs) a distance of 19 miles (30 km) a day, and the same was probably true of the Toltecs. In addition to the relatively small load, the bearers had to be fed cultivated foods while on the road. According to William Sanders and Robert Santley, bearers consumed too much food to make the journey worthwhile if they were on the road more than five days or travelled more than 94 miles (150 km). The Toltecs had very few really good agricultural zones within a five-day walking distance from Tula. Whilst the Basin of Mexico was the most productive area within this radius, Cholula may have controlled the most fertile southern section of it throughout much of Tula's history.

Famine and Discord

The historical accounts contain many references to food shortages and famines, references which are often coupled with allusions to conflicts and battles over farm land and food stores. For example, several battles are said to have occurred at Xochitlan, a village near Tula with permanent springs close by. Mastache has shown that these springs were used for irrigation in Aztec times and perhaps earlier. Hence conflict over irrigation water and the produce from critical areas in difficult times was to be expected.

In addition to the normal problems of agriculture in this area, the Toltecs may have been exposed to relatively small but very significant climate changes. Pedro Armillas has suggested that northern and central Mexico experienced a phase of decreased summer precipitation at this time. The reduced rainfall would have created serious problems in marginal arid areas such as the Tula river valley and surrounding zones by making rainfall agriculture much more tenuous than before and lowering river levels. Unfortunately we do not have good studies of the ancient climate with which to prove or disprove this attractive hypothesis. Armillas based his argument on the premise that climatic changes documented elsewhere in the world indicated similar changes in northern and central Mexico. This proposition was reasonable at that time but paleoclimatology is a complex subject and we now know that climate changes in one area do not necessarily imply changes elsewhere. Thus we need studies of the climatic history of the Tula area before we can accept drought as a factor in the Toltec collapse.

The second major internal problem the Toltecs faced was a breakdown in social integration. The Tula population was a heterogeneous mixture of people from different areas perhaps speaking several languages. Multi-ethnicity of this sort was common in ancient Mesoamerican cities; urban centers attracted people with many backgrounds and skills and formed them into a cohesive social unit. The Toltec population included people from the Basin of Mexico, the Gulf coast, and various parts of northern Mexico. The Toltecs seem to have successfully integrated these diverse elements early in their history, though the documentary sources suggest severe ethnic conflict near the end of the Tollan phase. The Tezcatlipoca-Quetzalcoatl saga discussed above can be interpreted as a power struggle between a northern faction identified with Tezcatlipoca and an older established Nahuatl-speaking group under Quetzalcoatl's banner. There is also evidence for a group of Huastec speakers associated with Quetzalcoatl as Ehecatl, whose sympathies seem to have lain with the northerners.

What caused this disintegration? I suspect that whatever cohesiveness the Toltecs achieved initially was later strained by economic difficulties including subsistence problems and the loss of markets for manufactured goods. When these problems arose, people took sides based on ethnic affiliations and their leaders were unable or unwilling to share power, wealth, and opportunity with others. The continual flow of migrants into the city further hampered effective social and economic integration. In order to understand how and why this happened, we must first examine the external problems facing the Toltecs.

The Toltecs were confronted by two major external difficulties; the southward retraction of the Mesoamerican frontier, and competition from neighboring states. The changes in the location of the northern frontier were part of a long and poorly understood process which began during the Middle Horizon and was still continuing at the time of the Toltec collapse. The factors which caused it are unclear and probably varied as time went on; it seems likely, however, that climate change, local northern political events, and repercussions from the rise and fall of central Mexican states all played a role.

The climate change theory is attractive even though it remains unproven. If precipitation did decrease in northern Mexico, the effects on agriculture and settled village life could have been disastrous. Consecutive years of poor harvests would have forced farmers either to emigrate or to adopt a nomadic hunting and gathering lifestyle.

The wealthy and relatively well-watered lands to the south would have attracted people even if those areas were experiencing the same kinds of difficulties. In addition the later migrants would have been joining predecessors with whom they shared cultural, linguistic, and economic ties. If climatic deterioration peaked after AD 1000, the Toltecs may have faced the prospect of hosting the largest number of migrants in their history when they were least able to do so because of their own subsistence problems.

Immigrants and Rivals

Agricultural difficulties were only one of the factors prompting southward treks by frontierspeople; shifts in mining and trade patterns suggest other economic difficulties as well. The causes of these changes are likewise unclear, though exhaustion of raw materials was obviously not a factor. Rebellions of the type which devastated La Quemada and Casas Grandes may have been common occurrences if the northern rulers were as oppressive as Weigand and DiPeso suggest. Perhaps the rebels achieved freedom at the price of economic chaos which forced at least some of the people to emigrate.

The unsettled conditions in the north created two problems for the Toltecs. First, the migrations introduced unwanted groups of foreigners into the Toltec heartland. Immigration was not a new phenomenon at Tula but the Toltecs' ability to absorb outsiders diminished as their difficulties grew. Although the immigrants probably arrived in small groups and their total numbers may not have exceeded a few thousands, their wanderings must have turned them into battle-hardened veterans. Whatever their original occupations, they soon learned that wielding a sword or bow was easier and more profitable than farming. These refugees-turned-mercenaries probably offered their services to the highest bidder and often turned against the Toltecs just as Mixcoatl had.

In addition to the problem created by the immigrants, the northern chaos cut off the Toltecs from exotic raw materials and markets for their manufactured goods. Although northern societies accounted for only a small percentage of Tula's trade volume, the loss of access to the exotic raw materials found there had a substantial impact on Toltec politics and alliances. Mesoamerican alliances were fragile arrangements often maintained only as long as both parties benefited. Junior allies expected gifts of exotic jewelry, costumes, and other élite goods in addition to military support from their patrons in exchange for their loyalty. The fact that the Toltecs could no longer provide any of these must have made their allies ponder the wisdom of the arrangements and served as a stark indication of growing Toltec weaknesses. The absence of garrisons and large standing armies made defections easy, particularly since other potential patrons such as the Cholulans were always available. The loss of allies had both military and economic repercussions. Former friends became enemies, former markets for obsidian and other craft products were closed to Toltec merchants, and each loss created favorable conditions for new disasters. Within a few generations the Toltecs will have found themselves surrounded by hostile neighbors on all sides.

Cholula may have been Tula's primary rival in central Mexico. Mixcoatl allied himself with the Cholulans and according to one tradition his son went to Cholula after fleeing the Toltec capital. Cholula had much to gain from the Toltec collapse; access to the rich Morelos cotton lands, uncontested control of the Basin of Mexico, and freedom from Toltec competition for its own obsidian industry were only a few of the potential benefits.

Huastecs and other Gulf coast inhabitants may also have contributed to Toltec difficulties. Some of the groups were Toltec allies at one time but the tenor of the relationship seems to have changed near the end. Control of the Pachuca obsidian mines was one obvious bone of contention between the two groups. There is no evidence that the Huastecs wrested control of the Pachuca mines from Tula, though this may in fact have happened. Such a takeover would have had a devastating effect on the Toltec economy. Unemployed craftsmen would have posed a threat to internal stability and created a further drain on the limited stores of foodstuffs. Also, the imported foods purchased with obsidian tools would no longer have been available. The only real option open to the craftsmen was emigration to Cholula and other cities where they could be sure of obtaining employment and a steady supply of raw materials.

The Tarascans west of Tula may have posed an additional threat to the Toltecs. The Late Horizon Tarascan state based at Tzintzuntzan did not emerge until post-Toltec times but it may have had predecessors we do not know about. Even though very little archaeology has been done in the Tarascan homeland, there are several hints of strong interaction with the Toltecs and we have reason to believe that part of the area was under Toltec control at one time. The loss of control over this area would have cut off the Toltecs from the Zinapecuaro obsidian source, access to the Pacific coast lowlands, and markets for Toltec products.

No single factor was sufficient in itself to cause the Toltec collapse but their simultaneous occurrence after AD 1100 initiated a chain reaction in which each new problem compounded the effects of the others until even a Toltec Solomon[4] could not stop the process of decline. Wise leadership in the early phases might have reversed

4. King of Israel in the tenth century.

the process but even if this had happened, the success would only have been temporary. I do not view history as a predetermined, mechanical chain of events, but I do believe that all complex human societies contain structural features and patterns of behavior which eventually become the seeds of their destruction. They also contain the building blocks for future societies and civilizations. The Toltecs were a segment of the culture history of the Mexican people. In a metaphorical sense they accepted the cultural heritage of their predecessors, modified it into a new way of life and passed it on to the Aztecs, who repeated the process. Netzalhualcoyotl, 'Fasting Coyote', an Aztec philosopher-king who ruled Texcoco, is credited with a poem which speaks about men but applies equally well to civilizations. Eric Wolf chose it as an introduction to *Sons of the Shaking Earth,* his classic book on Mesoamerican civilization. I find it a fitting epitaph for the proud and resourceful people who created Toltec culture.

> All the earth is a grave and nothing escapes it;
> nothing is so perfect that it does not descend to its tomb.
> Rivers, rivulets, fountains, and water flow,
> but never return to their joyful beginnings;
> anxiously they hasten to the vast realms of the rain god.
> As they widen their banks, they also fashion
> the sad urn of their burial.
> Filled are the bowels of the earth with pestilential dust
> once flesh and bone, once animate bodies of men
> who sat upon thrones, decided cases, presided in council,
> commanded armies, conquered provinces, possessed treasure,
> destroyed temples,
> exulted in their pride, majesty, fortune, praise, and power.
> Vanished are these glories, just as the fearful smoke vanishes
> that belches forth from the infernal fires of Popocatepetl.
> Nothing recalls them but the written page.

The Rise and Fall of the Anasazi Indians

Linda S. Cordell

The Anasazi Indians were ancient people who occupied the plateau country in the southwestern United States from around 200 to 1300 A.D. The majority of Anasazi territory was arid and inhospitable, and life for the Pueblos—Indians who live in community dwellings—was hard. Linda S. Cordell maintains that as the availability of natural resources—particularly water—fluctuated, so did the pattern of pueblo settlements. When there was abundant rainfall, the people lived together in large settlements; during droughts—such as those that occurred in the twelfth century—the people dispersed and settled into smaller pueblos. During these times of dispersal there was less cultural exchange between settlements, and the people made fewer innovations to their pottery and architecture. During the twelfth century, however, potters and builders refined their skills in making crafts and building pueblos. Surviving pottery and, particularly, architecture—some of which consists of cliff dwellings built high in the walls of canyons—have inspired an enduring fascination with these ancient people. Perhaps most intriguing to modern people is the "mysterious" disappearance of the Anasazi around 1300, which, according to Cordell, could have been the result of a severe drought. Linda S. Cordell is an anthropology professor at the University of Colorado at Boulder.

Excerpted from *Ancient Pueblo Peoples*, by Linda S. Cordell. Copyright © 1994 by St. Remy Press and Smithsonian Institution. Reprinted with permission.

The first time many Americans heard the name Anasazi or learned anything at all about the ancient ruins of the Southwest was at the Chicago World's Columbian Exposition, which ran from May to October of 1893. There, a gigantic Anthropological Building housed more than 150 exhibits devoted to archaeology and ethnology. Included were collections from Mesa Verde, Colorado, and Grand Gulch, Utah. The Mesa Verde collections had been amassed in 1891–1892 by Richard Wetherill. The Wetherill family were ranchers in Mancos, Colorado. Richard had learned about the ruins by exploring and digging in them. His interest in, and respect for, the people who had built the cliff dwellings were greatly enhanced when he guided Baron Gustaf Eric Adolf Nordenskjöld, a young Swedish archaeologist, to Mesa Verde in 1891. Nordenskjöld was trained in the techniques of excavation and recording proper for his day, and Wetherill learned much from him. Nordenskjöld's later (1901) publication was the first scholarly description of the ruins of Mesa Verde, and it made his professional reputation.

The Ancient Ones

To the visitors at the Chicago fair, Wetherill described the Anasazi as ancient inhabitants of North America, among the very few about whom there was, at the time, any information at all. The name Anasazi, he explained, was a Navajo word used to refer to the ancient people, then long gone, whose ruined houses were found by the Navajo when they first entered the plateau country of southern Colorado. In a vague way, Wetherill knew that the name referred to ancient enemies, but whether or not this meant that the Navajo had actually encountered and fought with these people he did not know.

The name Anasazi was officially sanctioned by Alfred V. Kidder in 1936 as a less cumbersome alternative to Basketmaker-Pueblo. Neil M. Judd, another of the great first fathers of Southwest archaeology and the excavator of Pueblo Bonito, noted that although the word Anasazi was not included in the 1912 vocabulary of the Navajo language published by the Franciscan Friars, it was well known to all who had worked in Navajo country where ruins of the ancient ones abound.

Among early anthropologists, such as William Henry Holmes, Jesse Walter Fewkes, and Frank Hamilton Cushing, who had worked among the Pueblos,[1] there was never any doubt that the Anasazi were ancestral Pueblo. But the vast land along the San Juan River that sheltered ancient Pueblo homes was occupied by Navajo, a people completely different in culture and language from the Pueblos.

1. Members of tribes who live in community dwellings built of stone or adobe in the Southwestern United States.

From the perspective of the ranchers and explorers of southern Colorado and Utah, the ancient ones had vanished. The Navajo knew little about them. It is also likely that most visitors to the Chicago fair, and many among the more than 16 million tourists who have since visited Mesa Verde National Park, did not understand that Navajo and Pueblo peoples are very different, have mistrusted one another, and often have been enemies.

Anasazi Country

The vast landscape that was once the homeland of the Anasazi centers on the Colorado Plateau, but extends from central New Mexico, on the east, to southern Nevada, on the west. The northern boundary loops through southern Nevada, Utah, and Colorado, while the southern boundary follows the Colorado and Little Colorado rivers in Arizona, and the Rio Puerco to the Rio Grande in New Mexico with extensions eastward toward the Great Plains on the Cimarron and Pecos rivers and the Galisteo Basin. The plateau portion of this region is generally high, with elevations ranging from about 4500 to 8500 feet (1370 to 2600 meters). The mesas are capped by extensive, nearly horizontal sedimentary formations and support pinyon-juniper woodland except at the higher elevations where there

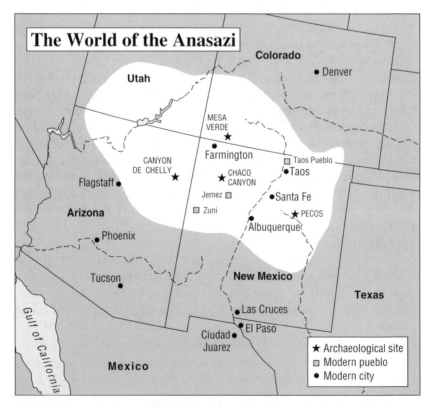

The World of the Anasazi

are forests of ponderosa and yellow pine. Steep-walled canyons and escarpments are common features. Wind erosion has sculpted windows, bridges, and spires out of the sandstone. Where softer sandstone overlies harder sandstone, shales, or limestones, the wind has hollowed out rock overhangs, creating the shelters and caves used by the Anasazi over the centuries. Moisture from the winter snows percolates through the sandstone and accumulates at junctures of sandstone overlying shales, forming seeps and springs that were key sources of household water for the Anasazi.

Other parts of the Anasazi homeland are basin-and-range country similar to that occupied by the Mogollon [ancient pueblo peoples]. The San Juan, Gallup-Zuni, Galisteo, and Albuquerque basins are low, arid, and somewhat featureless landforms supporting desert grasses and shrubs, except along stream-beds where there are willows, reeds, grasses, and dense shrubs. Also within the Anasazi domain are mountains that reach elevations of 12,000 feet (3650 meters). The highest are capped by meadows and draped in great evergreen pine forests. The mountains are the origins of the rivers and streams fed by winter snows. For the Anasazi, the mountains were sources of timber for building, game animals, obsidians and cherts used for flaked tools, and mineral ores used as pigment in paints.

The major rivers of Anasazi country—the San Juan, Little Colorado, Chama, Rio Grande, and Pecos—are relatively great rivers for the arid landscape. They carry heavy silt loads and are deeply entrenched for miles or are subject to flooding. Difficult to tame with the technology available to the Anasazi, they were less important for agriculture than their smaller tributaries, such as the Chinle, Animas, La Plata, Jemez, Santa Fe, and Taos. As with other parts of the Southwest, the accumulation of winter snows provides moisture crucial for germination of seeds in the spring. The amount of snowfall and the duration and intensity of summer thunderstorms vary from year to year and area to area. Anasazi agricultural and social strategies buffered these variations remarkably well. At times, though, there was nothing the Anasazi could do but leave their fields and homes, just as 19th– and 20th–century homesteaders of this region have also had to do when all else failed.

Although not quite as large as the Mogollon region, the Anasazi area is large enough so that developments did not proceed at a uniform pace across its entirety, and there were stylistic and other differences from one location to another. As with the Mogollon, archaeologists divide the Anasazi area into named subregions. From west to east, these are the Virgin, Kayenta, Tusayan, De Chelly, and Winslow (or Middle Little Colorado), Northern San Juan, Cibola (or Chaco), and Rio Grande. The names do not imply a single political structure, language, or ethnic derivation, however. Rather, they refer to geographically circumscribed subregions within which ceramic technology, ceramic design styles, and architectural forms are distinctive and relatively homogeneous. The rate of change is also internally consistent.

The Emergence of Anasazi Culture

The most general framework used for the entire Anasazi region is the Pecos Classification, originally proposed in 1927 as one outcome of the first Pecos Conference and published later that year by A.V. Kidder in *Science* magazine. Although the classifications were not initially tied to calendar dates, the development of tree-ring dating overcame that particular difficulty. Nevertheless, as the dendrochronology dates began to accumulate from excavations throughout the region, it became obvious that change had not occurred at a uniform rate. In a summary written in 1940 for the Smithsonian Institution, Neil Judd remarked that the most illuminating fact to have emerged from what he termed an avalanche of fieldwork was the discovery that Pueblo culture had advanced rapidly but without uniformity, so that there was no smooth and regular progress as had been proposed by the Pecos scheme.

The Anasazi sequence began, as had the Mogollon, when pottery was added to a way of life based on a mixed economy of maize agriculture and gathering and hunting, which had developed as a continuation of the local San Jose Archaic. Over much of the Anasazi area, pottery occurs at about A.D. 200 to 300, but is not abundant until about A.D. 500, or the Basketmaker III period according to the Pecos Classification. The pottery of the later date is gray in color. Cooking ware was undecorated, but serving vessels were decorated with black painted designs on an unslipped, gray background. By the 6th century, the Anasazi were living in shallow pithouses in communities of variable size. Small, basally notched projectile points replaced the larger, side-notched Archaic points, indicating a change from the spear-thrower to the bow and arrow. Beans were added to the list of crops at this time. Basketmaker III burials reveal longheaded (when measured from front to back) individuals of medium stature. Skulls were not artificially deformed. By contrast, from about A.D. 700 to historic times, the Anasazi flattened the backs of their skulls by using hard cradleboards for infants. Cradleboards, like swaddling, are used to keep babies safe and out of trouble. Since it matters little for the child's safety whether or not the back of the board is padded, the hard board was presumably used to achieve what must have been considered an aesthetically pleasing result.

Between A.D. 700 and 900, Pueblo I in the Pecos scheme, there was a major change in Anasazi housing. In the early part of the period, sites consist of long arcs of *jacal* (pole-and-mud) surface storage rooms placed behind a squarish pithouse. Somewhat later, hearths and domestic debris indicate that the surface rooms were used as living rooms. Pithouses were retained, however, and were used either as kivas[2] or, during the coldest months, as dwellings. The pithouses may have served both functions. Culinary pottery has un-obliterated coils at the vessel neck, a treatment called neck banding. In addition to black-on-white painted pottery, red-on-orange and black-on-red types were produced. This also is the first period during which cranial flattening was practiced.

Pueblo II, dated between 900 and 1150, was a time of marked dispersal and regional differentiation among the Anasazi. During this period, the events in Chaco Canyon changed course abruptly and eventually had tremendous influence on the entire San Juan River and adjacent mountains. . . . It is certain, however, that Chaco influenced the Anasazi of neighboring areas.

The Anasazi in the Twelfth Century

Outside Chaco Canyon and the San Juan Basin, Pueblo II was a time when sites were somewhat smaller and more dispersed than before. Pueblo II cooking pottery has exterior corrugations, and painted wares are predominantly black-on-white with designs in a variety of regional styles. During this time, surface architecture was constructed more regularly of masonry and became primarily residential. The pithouse with elaborated features was retained as a communal structure, or kiva.

Pueblo III dates from 1150 to 1300. In the Pecos Classification, Pueblo III is traditionally described in developmental terms as Great Pueblo. It was a time of little innovation but great refinement in Pueblo skills and crafts. Domestic architecture consisted of multistory pueblos constructed with well-shaped masonry. Kiva architecture was also elaborated in some areas, with tower kivas and great kivas incorporating specialized floor features. Also noticeably refined and executed were the designs on black-on-white pottery. Then, in A.D. 1130, a severe drought affected the region. Some Anasazi areas were abandoned, and the population pulled in to a shrinking core area. The system that had been developing and operating in Chaco Canyon from A.D. 900 ceased to function as it had. Chaco was not actually abandoned at this time, but the character of its occupation changed and its influence greatly diminished.

After 1150, the population of areas around Chaco Canyon, such as Mesa Verde, Canyon de Chelly, and Zuni, grew rapidly, and large, aggregated settlements were constructed. By 1300, the entire northern tier of the Anasazi world had been abandoned. There were no

2. An underground or partly underground room used primarily by men for ceremonies or councils.

longer Anasazi living in what is now southern Nevada, Utah, or Colorado. Attempts to explain an event of this magnitude have occupied archaeologists for nearly a century. With the abandonment of so much of the Anasazi region, Pueblo IV witnessed a population increase in the Chama and Rio Grande regions, at Zuni, and in the Little Colorado region and the Hopi mesas. At this time, too, the Mogollon region was dominated by events at Casas Grandes in Chihuahua. Nevertheless, while communities in much of the Anasazi world vanished, the people themselves, together with their skills, ideas, and beliefs, moved into the then thinly occupied territories where their descendants continue to live successfully to the present day.

Anasazi Society

In 1927, when the Pecos Classification was codified, the Four Corners region and the Northern San Juan drainage—the country explored so diligently by Richard Wetherill, his patrons, and friends—was known in more detail than any other part of the Southwest. The classification works far better within the Four Corners region than it does elsewhere, as is to be expected. In the last 65 years, a great deal has been learned about the Anasazi of the Four Corners and the Anasazi of other settings. The avalanche of data to which Neil Judd referred in 1940 must seem like an anthill beside the information that has been accumulating ever since. The development of the Anasazi regional tradition will be explored in more detail for two areas: the Northern San Juan Basin and immediately adjacent localities, on which the original classification focused, and the Kayenta area to the west, which provides unique details and perspectives on the variety in Anasazi society.

The Northern San Juan has long been considered the wellspring of Anasazi culture. In excavations carried out between 1956 and 1968 in conjunction with construction of the Navajo Reservoir, archaeologists A. E. Dittert and Frank Eddy surprised their fellow southwesternists by discovering Basketmaker sites that dated from about A.D. 200 to 700 (equivalent to Basketmaker II and III in other parts of the San Juan). They found a brown pottery ware and both surface dwellings and shallow pithouses. Brown ware has long been thought to be a hallmark of Mogollon culture. The received wisdom was that the difference between Mogollon brown ware and Anasazi gray ware was a question of the technique used in firing. Brown wares were fired in an oxidizing atmosphere, where the air is allowed to circulate openly, whereas gray wares were fired in a reducing atmosphere, from which air is blocked. Since the late 1960s, brown ware has been reported from Basketmaker sites in the Northern San Juan region, but its occurrence is rare. The pottery itself is very friable, and the sites where it exists are often obscured by later occupations.

Two discoveries, reported in the early 1990s, have shed some light on the appearance and nature of this early northern brown ware. Studies by Dean C. Wilson, a ceramic specialist at the Museum of New Mexico, have demonstrated that the brown ware comes from the use of iron-rich alluvial clays. The earliest Mogollon and the earliest Anasazi pottery were brown wares made of this kind of clay. The clay seems to have been used when people were farming the alluvial clay bottomlands, possibly when neither their social network nor the annual patterns of movement included areas where there were better-quality geologic clays. The second recent finding is that in the northern San Juan area, if not elsewhere as well, the sites with this earliest occurrence of pottery-making among the Anasazi are virtually invisible from the surface. They are either buried under later occupations or beneath quantities of alluvium. Both conditions led to their having been overlooked in the field and markedly underrepresented in the literature.

Basketmaker Settlements

By A.D. 550 to 650, Basketmaker III communities were well established across most of the Colorado Plateau. The typical Basketmaker III house was a shallow pithouse, round—or square with rounded corners—with an antechamber and fairly consistent floor features. These include a central hearth, ash pits, often mud dividers or wing walls that separate activity space inside the dwelling, and some interior storage cists. Within this general pattern, there are a number of regional variations. In the Kayenta area, and the San Juan Basin, pithouse walls are often lined with upright slabs. In the Kayenta region, storage pits are consistently located behind the pithouses. In the Mesa Verde region, one excavation—the Gilliland Site—consisted of four pithouses and numerous outside work areas with *ramadas* (shade structures), completely encircled by a stockade. In the Mesa Verde region, pithouse entryways are oriented to the south. In Chaco, the entryways point to the southeast, and there are many other minor differences as well.

Basketmaker communities vary considerably in size, but it is not always clear how many people lived in them at the same time, nor how sedentary the Basketmaker way of life really was. For example, Shabik'eschee Village, situated on one of several small mesas that protrude above the south side of Chaco Canyon, has long been considered typical of Basketmaker III settlements. Frank H.H. Roberts, Jr., originally and meticulously excavated Shabik'eschee in 1926 and 1927. He found 18 pithouses, more than 48 exterior storage pits, and one oversize structure regarded as a great kiva. Shabik'eschee is most often discussed by archaeologists because it has been excavated and carefully studied, not because it is unique.

Sites of similar size and age cover the tops of the small mesas fingering into the canyon above Chaco Wash. Recent surveys have recorded at least 163 such settlements at Chaco Canyon alone. If all these sites and all their pithouses were occupied at one time, then 16,000 people—an absurdly high figure—would have lived there. Roberts, in fact, recognized two distinct periods of occupation at Shabik'eschee based on the stratigraphy of the structures.

Archaeologists Wirt H. Wills and Thomas C. Windes have recently reevaluated Shabik'eschee, based on a review of the original field notes and subsequent work. They argue that Shabik'eschee represents one kind of Basketmaker III settlement strategy. The strategy involved a small resident core population—perhaps one or two families—and periodic use by a larger group. Wills and Windes maintain that the larger group would have been attracted to the site at times when there was an unusual abundance of resources. The basic Basketmaker strategy, they conclude, would be one of small, seasonally occupied camps.

What seems to be another, highly unusual, example of Basketmaker response to local abundance has been reported for the Upper San Juan by archaeologist Nancy Hammack. A site known as L.A. 4169 consisted of two compact clusters of burned pits that had been excavated from a clay ridge above the present shore of the Navajo Reservoir. Part of the site had been excavated by Dittert and Eddy in 1962–63, the rest in 1987. The pits themselves were quite well preserved, because they had been dug out of massive silty clay and then burned. Thus, they became what Hammack calls in-place terra-cotta storage jars.

Times of Abundance

Fired clay features such as these are amenable to archaeomagnetic dating, and samples were taken from five pits. The results indicated not only that the pits belonged to Basketmaker III times (A.D. 600), but that, in all likelihood, the five had been fired at roughly the same time. Given their size—a volume of 5.0 cubic meters—and the admittedly extreme assumption that all the pits had been used at the same time, Hammack estimates a total of 110.5 cubic meters of stored food. Using commonly applied figures based on maize, she finds that the storage capacity of the site would have fed at least 138 persons, or 27 families, for a period of one year! As was suggested for Shabik'eschee, there appear to have been times when a great abundance of a particular food resource encouraged large population aggregates, at least temporarily. We do not know how frequently these local abundances occurred; probably they were unusual, and the overall poverty of southwestern environments certainly supports this view. Still, the estimated storage capacity at L.A. 4169 gives one pause when we remember that the early Anasazi led difficult and impoverished lives.

Painted Basketmaker III ceramics mark the beginning of two different conventions in the manufacture of black paint. One was preparing black paint by using a mineral—usually iron oxide—as pigment, in some kind of flux. The use of mineral-based paints centered in northwestern New Mexico, especially in the San Juan Basin, and extended east to the Rio Grande and south to Mogollon country. West of this, in the Kayenta area and farther west, a carbon-based black pigment was produced from vegetal materials—most commonly, the Rocky Mountain bee plant. The two traditions coexisted until potters in the central Anasazi area, the San Juan Basin, Mesa Verde, and the Chuska drainage switched to carbon pigments. This occurred gradually between about 1050 and 1200. South of these areas, from the Rio Puerco east to the edge of the Great Plains, mineral paints were retained until nearly historic times. Initially, the painted pottery of both traditions was much the same: a pattern of simple lines, apparently derived from basketry patterns decorating the interior of bowls.

Basketmaker III seems to have been a time in which much of what we see as Anasazi for the next 700 years crystallizes over the Colorado Plateau. This pattern includes the cultivation of corn, beans, and squash; the use of plain gray cooking ware and black-on-white serving and storage vessels; and the use of the bow and arrow. Although surface pueblos replaced pithouses as dwellings, the use of semisubterranean rooms continues in the pueblo pattern as communal rooms and kivas. Even in rock art there is a Pueblo style that is first seen in Basketmaker III. It consists of strongly pecked elements that include stick figures with rectangular bodies and small heads, and the depiction of a flute player who is represented in a variety of human, animal, and insect forms, both with and without a humpback. Other elements in this style are human hand- and footprints and animal tracks. The rock art is produced on cliff and rock faces, often in panel groupings.

In traditional Hopi legend, there is a hump-backed flute player, named Kokopelli. As part of traditional Pueblo religious ritual, altars are set up displaying panels which depict images of great symbolic importance. Some figures in Basketmaker III rock art appear to be masked, and masking is another significant element in Pueblo rituals. The combination of economic, organizational, and ideological elements that are so obviously essentially Pueblo led scholars to view Basketmaker III as an emergent Pueblo culture. It is also worth acknowledging that we do not know what these symbols meant in Basketmaker society or whether or not the elements that we regard as interrelated correspond to Basketmaker behavior and beliefs. Further, in part because many Basketmaker III pithouse set-tlements were apparently occupied on a seasonal basis, the mobility that was part of the Basketmaker III economic strategy implies a set of community and regional relationships that were quite different from those of later, sedentary Pueblos.

The configuration of settlements in the Anasazi area changes be-tween about A.D. 750 and 850. The Pueblo I villages of this period consist of long, arced rows of contiguous surface rooms with a deep, squarish pithouse placed to the south, or in front of the surface rooms. The surface rooms are generally of jacal construction, rather than masonry, but serve as both storage and residential areas. Back rooms that lack floor features, especially hearths, most likely were used for storage. Openings connect these to front rooms with hearths. These, in turn, may open on a portico or outside work area, often also with hearths.

Large Settlements

Some Pueblo I settlements are very large by any standard. The quin-tessential grandfather of all Pueblo I sites was excavated in 1932 at Alkali Ridge, in southern Utah, by J. O. Brew of Harvard's Peabody Museum. Alkali Ridge Site 13 consisted of 130 surface rooms, 16 pithouses, and 2 kivas. Site 13 is not unique. Sites that are similar in size have been recorded in several locations in southwestern Col-orado and southeastern Utah. In general, these sites are located in the relatively well-watered, northern tier of Anasazi settlement.

Recent excavations and reevaluation of older work have shown that most Pueblo I sites were occupied a mere 30 years or less. The rather brief duration of these settlements has permitted archaeolo-gists to estimate their population more easily than those of other sites. These estimates indicate larger populations than one might sup-pose. Using conservative techniques, the estimates indicate that some of these sites housed up to 600 individuals in three separate but closely spaced settlement clusters. The sheer size of the settlement suggests that social mechanisms were already in place, capable of reducing potential conflicts between individuals and families. The large number of people, even if they were only together for 30 years, suggests that Pueblo I settlements had the ability to integrate indi-viduals from several different households in a social context and to maintain that integration for longer than a human generation.

Archaeologist Timothy A. Kohler has worked extensively with Pueblo I sites in the course of a multiyear excavation project near Dolores, Colorado. Kohler observed that the large Pueblo I sites near Dolores were founded when rainfall conditions were particularly good for crops grown without benefit of irrigation. At the same time, areas both to the west and in general at lower elevations, were not experiencing moisture patterns favorable for dry farming. As a result, some of those areas of low elevation were abandoned at this time, possibly as people moved to higher settings. In the more arid western portion of the Colorado Plateau, settlements remained small.

Questions about why and how populations congregate are central ones in archaeology, just as they are in anthropology, geography, and certain fields of biology. Kohler argues that the centralization of population into large settlements creates difficulties for farmers. Some, if not most, fields will be farther away from living areas, obliging farmers to spend time walking to and from their fields and to carry harvested crops greater distances than would be the case if households were located next to their own fields. There must then have been some perceived advantage in forming large settlements. Kohler suggests that one advantage of Pueblo I aggregation was that it facilitated the sharing of agricultural food among community members. At the same time, because only members of the same community were tightly integrated socially, limits could be placed on the extent of the food-sharing network. In those low elevation subregions where dry farming was more tenuous, individual households may have been able to move to new locations in the face of an agricultural failure.

Boom and Bust

Within localities such as Mesa Verde, some archaeologists argue that the clusters of Pueblo I villages represent the largest population reached prehistorically. Others suggest that although Pueblo I villages do tend to occur in clusters, not all clusters of villages were occupied at the same time. Nevertheless, Pueblo I seems to represent one aspect of a longer-term Anasazi pattern. Simply stated, there were times when larger populations could be supported, but they were not long-lasting. There was an oscillation between coming together and dispersal that, when seen at a different scale, becomes an oscillation between occupation and abandonment. If dispersed populations gather in one place, then most of the land they once occupied is abandoned unless someone else moves in. From the perspective of one area, the cycles become what archaeologists William Lipe and R. G. Matson refer to as boom and bust. The instability of congregated populations derives from one of two factors: either the inability of the southwestern environment to support them over a substantial period or the failure of mechanisms of social integration to keep people together.

We do not know how the Pueblo I aggregates were organized socially. Throughout the plateaus where populations were somewhat dispersed, there are great kivas that may have integrated several settlements. At the big, aggregated Pueblo I settlements, very large pit structures with unusual floor features may have served a similar function.

Certain general features and symbols seem to have integrated much of the Anasazi area during Pueblo I. Black-on-white ceramics share a design style, called Kana-a or Red Mesa, that is strikingly similar throughout the region, even though the pottery was made locally and might differ in technological details, such as type of pigment. Items of trade included marine shells, shell artifacts, and pottery. The trade pottery is generally San Juan red ware. This includes types made in southern Utah and traded out to the Mesa Verde, Chaco, and Kayenta areas. These red wares do not make up substantial percentages of decorated ceramics in the regions into which they were traded, but they do demonstrate information flow throughout very large parts of Pueblo territory.

Between about A.D. 900 and 1150, the Anasazi reached their greatest territorial extent. At the same time, places like Mesa Verde experienced a slight population decline. Pueblo communities were smaller than they had been in Pueblo I, but they were greatly dispersed over the landscape. In the western Anasazi region, peoples of the Kayenta Anasazi tradition expanded north of the San Juan and west to the Grand Canyon and the Virgin River area of southern Nevada. As archaeologists George Gumerman and Jeffrey Dean have noted for the main Kayenta area, Pueblo II habitation sites occupied "virtually every conceivable spot," avoiding only floodplains during times when they were buried by streams which deposited quantities of sediment on them.

Agriculture and Animal Husbandry

At Mesa Verde, Pueblo II settlements were dispersed on all the locally available topographic situations (mesa tops, talus slopes, canyon bottoms, and side canyons). This dispersal is associated with the first indications of methods used to enhance agricultural production. These are soil and water-control features such as check dams, terraces, and linear borders.

For the Kayenta area, Gumerman and Dean note that the only real change in material culture at this time is a decrease in the quantity, and particularly the quality, of stone projectile points. This reflects, they suggest, the diminished importance of the larger game animals since population expansion probably depleted the game supply. At Mesa Verde, excavated rooms containing turkey dung and egg shell indicate that turkeys were either domesticated or tamed and kept at about this time, potentially confirming an important solution to declining game supplies.

During the same period, sites become very standardized in appearance. Domestic sites consist of a block of masonry habitation and storage rooms generally arranged in an east-west line, L-shape, or short arc. In front of these rooms, in a north-south line, are a midden[3] and a kiva. This pattern was described as a "unit pueblo" by T. Mitchell Prudden in 1903. Today archaeologists often refer to these sites as Prudden Unit Pueblos. Gumerman and Dean note that these sites rarely contain more than 12 rooms. Such sites could hardly have accommodated more than a moderately large extended family. Nevertheless, they appear quite self-contained and economically independent. On the other hand, archaeologist Arthur Rohn has commented that for the Mesa Verde and Northern San Juan in general, such unit pueblos could not have been functioning communities in any real sense. Although they are treated as separate sites by archaeologists, Rohn comments that they do form some spatial clustering on the landscape. The larger spatial clusters are more likely communities of day-to-day interaction.

Architecture and Ruins

For the western Anasazi area, Gumerman and Dean observe that although the early years of Pueblo II saw a considerable exchange in raw materials for stone tools and finished products, an increasing use of local resources becomes dominant by A.D. 1000. By that date, there are highly specific local traditions in ceramics and architectural forms. Some of the architectural specialization extends to the Northern San Juan region, where it is reflected particularly in kiva architecture. For example, Mesa Verde kivas are known for their stone pilasters and for assuming, eventually, a keyhole shape. In the San Juan Basin, kivas are generally round with an interior encircling bench. Common kiva floor features include a hearth or firebox, a deflector, and a ventilator. A small hole in the floor is referred to as a *sipapu* by archaeologists because this is the term used for them in modern pueblos, where they represent the *shipap,* the place where humans emerged from the underworld.

As people began to inhabit surface rooms and use the pit structure more for communal and, probably, ritual functions, and as the form of pit structures was modified and standardized, it is appropriate to use the term "kiva" and to consider that these structures likely did serve functions similar to those in modern Pueblo villages. The forms of kivas and their various floor features demonstrate continuity over centuries in this aspect of architecture. We cannot, however, be certain that various forms of ritual or even the use of kivas by specific groups of people, such as adult males, is of similar antiquity.

At the same time that much of the Anasazi area was looking inward and becoming provincial in terms of decreased exchange and

3. A dunghill or refuse heap.

interaction, the communities in Chaco Canyon and the San Juan Basin were expanding and becoming the first regionally organized system in the Pueblo homeland. As we have seen, the Chaco system developed during a period when rainfall was quite good, or at least adequate for corn, and farmers should have prospered. Perhaps it was the relatively benign climate, as a background, that enabled the rest of the Pueblo II world to remain self-contained and self-sufficient. If so, this climatic background was so forgiving as to allow virtually any settlement and economic strategies to work. Success, however, may well have been the seed of eventual decline. As Anasazi farmers extended their communities and fields to increasingly peripheral areas, they depleted the available supplies of game, firewood, and probably some wild plant foods as well. Poor soil and inadequate growing conditions made many of the peripheral areas marginal for the cultivation of corn. When conditions reverted to their difficult "normal" state of aridity, or with the onset of the drought of 1130, those communities on the most distant edges of the Anasazi realm, and those closer in but inhabiting poor farmland, were the first to be abandoned and left in ruins.

CHRONOLOGY

900
Chaco Canyon (to 1300): The hub of 125 Anasazi villages linked by 250 miles of road

1079
Peter Abelard: theologian and philosopher (to 1142)

1096
First Crusade begins following an appeal by Pope Urban II to free the Holy Land

1098
St. Robert founds the first Cistercian monastery at Citeaux, France

1099
Crusaders capture Jerusalem; Godfrey of Bouillon is elected King of Jerusalem

1104
Crusaders capture Acre

1113
Founding of Order of the Hospital of St. John in Jerusalem (Knights Hospitalers)

1115
St. Bernard founds the Abbey of Clairvaux, France; John of Salisbury (to 1180)

1119
Hugues de Payens founds the Order of Knights Templars

1122
Concordat of Worms: conference of German princes ends the dispute between pope and emperor over appointing bishops; Eleanor of Aquitaine (to 1204)

1127
The Sung dynasty loses control of northern China to the Jin

1135
Moses Maimonides (to 1204)

1136
Geoffrey of Monmouth's history of Kings of Britain popularizes Arthurian romances

1139
The Second Lateran Council ends a schism in the Church following the illegal election of Anacletus II as rival to Innocent II

1140
Abbey church of St. Denis near Paris; regarded as first building in Gothic style

1147
The Second Crusade, following an appeal by St. Bernard of Clairvaux

1148
The Crusaders fail to capture Damascus

1150
Begin Anasazi Pueblo III Period—The Great Pueblo

1152
Marriage of Louis VII of France and Eleanor of Aquitaine; Eleanor of Aquitaine marries Henry of Anjou; Frederick I Barbarossa, Holy Roman Emperor (to 1190)

1154
Henry II, King of England (to 1189)

1155
Civil wars ravage Japan (until 1185)

1156
Hogen and Heiji insurrections in Japan; Taira samurai clan is dominant at court

1161
Explosives are used in China at the battle of Ts'ai-shih

1162
Thomas Becket is appointed Archbishop of Canterbury and quarrels with Henry II over Church rights

1164
Becket is forced to flee to France

1167
Birth of Temujin (Genghis Khan)

1168
The Toltec state in Mesoamerica falls after its capital Tula is sacked

1169
Saladin, vizier of Egypt (to 1193); sultan from 1174

1170
Becket returns to Canterbury and is murdered

1173
Thomas Becket is canonized

1174
Saladin conquers Syria

1177
Baldwin IV of Jerusalem defeats Saladin at Montgisard

1179
Saladin beseiges Tyre

1180
Truce between Baldwin IV and Saladin; Philip II, king of France (to 1223); Alexius II Comnenus, Byzantine Emperor (to 1183)

1183
Andronicus I, Byzantine Emperor (to 1185)

1184
Kamakura period in Japan (until 1333)

1187
Saladin captures Jerusalem and defeats the Crusaders at the Horns of Hattin

1189
Third Crusade (ended 1192); leaders: Frederick Barbarossa, Philip of France, and Richard of England

1190
Mongol leader Temujin begins to create an empire in eastern Asia; Frederick Barbarossa is drowned on his way to Palestine

1191
Richard I conquers Cyprus and captures Acre; Zen Buddhism is introduced to Japan

1192
Richard I captures Jaffa, makes peace with Saladin; Minamoto Yoritomo, Shogun of Japan

1200
Beginning of Chimú imperial expansion

1202
Fourth Crusade (ends 1204)

1204
Crusaders capture Constantinople and sack it, installing a Latin ruler

1206
Temujin is proclaimed Genghis Khan, "Emperor Within the Seas"

1212
Children's Crusade: 30,000 children set out from Germany and France to Palestine; thousands are sold into slavery

FOR FURTHER READING

Europe: The Rise of the Papacy and the Crusades

Walter Capps, *The Monastic Impulse.* New York: Crossroad, 1983.

Giles Constable, *The Reformation of the Twelfth Century.* New York: Cambridge University Press, 1996.

Sharon K. Elkins, *Holy Women of Twelfth-Century England.* Chapel Hill: University of North Carolina Press, 1988.

H.A.R. Gibb, *The Life of Saladin.* Oxford: Clarendon, 1973.

Bennett D. Hill, *English Cistercian Monasteries and Their Patrons in the Twelfth Century.* Urbana: University of Illinois Press, 1968.

David Knowles, *Archbishop Thomas Becket: A Character Study.* London: Raleigh Lectures on History, 1952.

Thomas F. Madden, *A Concise History of the Crusades.* Lanham, MD: Rowman & Littlefield, 1999.

Colin Morris, *The Papal Monarchy: The Western Church from 1050 to 1250.* Oxford: Oxford University Press, 1989.

Geoffrey Regan, *Lionhearts: Saladin, Richard I, and the Era of the Third Crusade.* New York: Walker, 1999.

Beryl Smalley, *The Becket Conflict and the Schools: A Study of Intellectuals in Politics.* Totowa, NJ: Rowman & Littlefield, 1973.

Europe: Chivalry and Courtly Love

Richard Barber, *The Knight and Chivalry.* Ipswich: Boydel, 1974.

W.R.J. Barron, *The Arthur of the English: The Arthurian Legend in Medieval English Life and Literature.* Cardiff: University of Wales Press, 1999.

J.S. Critchley, *Feudalism.* Boston: G. Allen & Unwin, 1978.

Raymond Thompson Hill, *Anthology of the Provencal Troubadours.* New Haven, CT: Yale University Press, 1973.

Maurice Keen, *Chivalry.* New Haven, CT: Yale University Press, 1984.

Melrich Vonelm Rosenberg, *Eleanor of Aquitaine: Queen of the Troubadours and the Courts of Love.* Boston: Houghton Mifflin, 1937.

Aldo D. Scaglione, *Knights at Court: Courtliness, Chivalry, and Courtesy from Ottonian Germany to the Italian Renaissance.* Berkeley and Los Angeles: University of California Press, 1991.

Europe: The Twelfth-Century Renaissance

J.H. Burns, ed., *The Cambridge History of Medieval Political Thought.* Cambridge, England: Cambridge University Press, 1987.

Georges Duby, *The Europe of the Cathedrals, 1140–1280.* Trans. Stuart Gilbert. Geneva: Skira, 1966.

Georges Duby, *Women of the Twelfth Century.* Trans. Jean Birrell. Chicago: University of Chicago Press, 1997.

Stephen C. Ferruolo, *The Origins of the University: The Schools of Paris and Their Critics, 1100–1215.* Stanford, CA: Stanford University Press, 1985.

C. Warren Hollister, *The Twelfth-Century Renaissance.* New York: Wiley, 1969.

Urban Tigner Holmes, *Daily Living in the Twelfth Century.* Madison: University of Wisconsin Press, 1966.

John of Salisbury, *The Letters of John of Salisbury.* Ed. W.J. Miller and H.E. Butler. New York: T. Nelson, 1978.

Victor A. Murray, *Abelard and St. Bernard: A Study in Twelfth-Century "Modernism."* New York: Barnes and Noble, 1967.

Helen Huss Parkhurst, *Cathedral: A Gothic Pilgrimage.* Boston: Houghton Mifflin, 1936.

D.W. Robertson, *Abelard and Heloise.* New York: Dial, 1972.

Asia

Woodbridge Bingham, Hilary Conroy, and Frank W. Iklé, *A History of Asia. Vol. 1, Formation of Civilizations, from Antiquity to 1600.* Boston: Allyn and Bacon, 1964.

Daniel Cohen, *Conquerors on Horseback.* Garden City, NY: Doubleday, 1970.

René Grousset, *The Rise and Splendour of the Chinese Empire.* Berkeley and Los Angeles: University of California Press, 1965.

Michel Hong and Ingrid Cranfield, trans., *Genghis Khan.* London: Saqi, 1990.

Eiko Ikegami, *The Taming of the Samurai: Honorific Individualism and the Making of Modern Japan.* Cambridge, MA: Harvard University Press, 1995.

Marius B. Jansen, ed., *Warrior Rule in Japan.* Cambridge, England: Cambridge University Press, 1995.

James T.C. Liu, *China Turning Inward: Intellectual-Political Changes in the Early Twelfth Century.* Cambridge, MA: Harvard University Press, 1998.

Jeffrey P. Mass, *Antiquity and Anachronism in Japanese History.* Stanford, CA: Stanford University Press, 1992.

Jeffrey P. Mass, *The Kamakura Bakufu: A Study in Documents.* Stanford, CA: Stanford University Press, 1976.

Edwin O. Reischauer, *Japan: Past and Present.* New York: Knopf, 1967.

Makoto Sugawara, *The Ancient Samurai.* Tokyo: East Publications, 1986.

Jing-shen Tao, *The Jurchen in Twelfth-Century China: A Study of Sinicization.* Seattle: University of Washington Press, 1976.

The Americas

Helen Sloan Daniels, *Adventures with the Anasazi of Falls Creek.* Durango, CO: Center for Southwest Studies, Fort Lewis College, 1976.

Nigel Davies, *The Toltecs, Until the Fall of Tula.* Norman: University of Oklahoma Press, 1977.

William E. Davies, *Anasazi: Subsistence and Settlement on White Mesa, San Juan County, Utah.* Lanham, MD: University Press of America, 1985.

Hermann Leicht, *Pre-Inca Art and Culture.* Trans. Mervyn Savill. New York: Orion, 1960.

Martha Moliter, *The Hohokam-Toltec Connection: A Study in Culture Diffusion.* Greeley: University of Northern Colorado, 1981.

Jorge C. Muelle, *Concerning the Middle Chimú Style.* New York: Kraus Reprint, 1965.

Ruth Murray Underhill, *First Penthouse Dwellers of America.* New York: J.J. Augustin, 1938.

INDEX

Abelard, Peter, 139, 150, 151, 156, 172
 castration of, 169
 devotion to figures of the past, 159
 as first professor, 165
 importance of personal emotions to, 159–60
 intellectual battles of, 165–66
 letter from Heloise, 173–79
 letter to Heloise, 179–84
 literary knowledge, 158, 161
 on marriage, 167–69
 quarrels
  with monks, 169
  with St. Bernard, 34, 170–71
 in refuge, 169–70
agriculture
 Anasazi Indians, 22
 improvements in European, 15–16
 Toltec Indians, 22, 268–69
Ailred of Rievaulx, 159, 161
Americas. *See* Anasazi Indians; Mochican–Chimú Indians; Toltec Indians
Amida Halls, 20
Anacletus II (pope), 34
Anasazi Indians, 21, 254
 agriculture by, 22, 286
 animal husbandry by, 286
 archaeological expeditions on, 275
 architecture of, 287
 Basketmaker communities of, 281–82
 data on, 280
 dwellings, 22–23, 281, 283–84, 286–87
 emergence of, 278–79
 food abundance among, 282
 geographic landscape of, 276–78
 name of, 275
 population instabilities of, 279–80, 285–86
 pottery of, 278, 279, 286
  black-painted, 283
  brown ware, 280–81

 poverty among, 282–83
 rock art by, 283
 self-sufficiency and containment of, 287–88
 settlements of, 284–85
Anselm, 139, 156, 158
Aphrodisius, Alexander, 196
Aquinas, Thomas (saint), 145–46, 146
architecture, 18–19, 140
 Anasazi Indian, 22–23, 279, 281, 283–284, 286–87
 Chimú Indians, 21
 Chinese, 20–21
 classification system for, 202–203
 Gothic, 140, 147
  arrival of, 202
  cathedrals, 204–205
  use of pointed arch, 19, 204–205
 Japanese, 20
 Norman, 204
 Romanesque, 201–202
 symbolism of church, 200–201
Aristotle, 139, 142, 145–46, 149–50, 163
Armillas, Pedro, 268, 269
Armstrong, Karen, 61
Arnold of Brescia, 170
art
 Chimú Indian, 21
 rock, of Anasazi Indians, 283
 stained glass windows, 19, 140, 147
 Sung dynasty, 207
 Toltec Indian, 22
Asia. *See* China; Japan

Barnes, Harry Elmer, 215
Becket, Thomas
 ascetic life in exile, 47–48
 concessions with King Henry II, 45–46
 criticism of, 54–55
 and John of Salisbury, 187
 martyrdom of, 48–49, 55–56
 miracles of, 49